JEWISH THINKERS

General Editor: Arthur Hertzberg

Ibn Gabirol

GW00702790

Ibn Gabirol

Raphael Loewe

PETER HALBAN

WEIDENFELD & NICOLSON

LONDON

FIRST PUBLISHED IN GREAT BRITAIN BY
PETER HALBAN PUBLISHERS LTD
42 South Molton Street
London W I Y I HB
1989

British Library Cataloguing in Publication Data

Loewe, Raphael
Ibn Gabirol——(Jewish thinkers).
1. Jewish philosophy, ibn
Gabirol ca 1022–ca 1076
I. Title. II. Series
186'.6'0924

ISBN 1-870015-24-X

Typeset at Oxford University Computing Service
Printed in Great Britain by
Butler & Tanner Ltd, Frome, Somerset

CONTENTS

NOTE ON TRANSLITERATION

Transliteration of Hebrew and Arabic words has been kept as simple as possible and the use of diacritical signs restricted to essentials. Initial *aleph* is normally not indicated; medially it is represented by '. *gim(el)* = *g* in Hebrew, *j* in Arabic. *ḥeth* = *ḥ*, *ṭeth* = *ṭ*. *kaph* without *dagesh* = *kh*. *'ayin* = '. *ṣade* = *ṣ*. *qoph* = *q*. Vowels are not differentiated except in the Appendix on Hebrew Metrics, where half-vowels (vocal *shewas*) are rendered by a raised inverted e (ᵊ) or an a.

PREFACE

To write a short book about Solomon ibn Gabirol is almost an insult, but we live at a time when tabloid information, like fast food, is the order of the day: and there is the further extenuation that no book, exclusively devoted to him, has appeared in English since Zangwill's translation of *Selected Religious Poems* in 1923, except for Bernard Lewis' prose version of *The Kingly Crown* (1961). It was because I found Zangwill's verse renderings unsatisfactory that I began, many years ago, to try my own hand at translating Ibn Gabirol, choosing for the most part poems that Zangwill had not attempted. Some results are included here.

If this little book merely attracts a dilettante interest, it will have failed in its purpose. Ibn Gabirol was, many would claim, the greatest of the Spanish-Jewish poets, even though popular enthusiasm for Judah Halevi has tended to overshadow him. I intend it to be an appetizer, which is why all the verse translations are accompanied by the Hebrew original. Ibn Gabirol's philosophy can be studied in depth with the help of Jacques Schlanger's two books in French (see bibliography, p. 189), and his poetry in the magisterial edition, in Hebrew, by Dov Jarden, and in F. Bargebuhr's monumental if somewhat daunting German volume. If I succeed in encouraging perhaps half a dozen readers to address themselves seriously to these works, and can assist perhaps a further twenty towards attaining a more mature appreciation of the nature and genius of Hebrew, the work may perhaps have served its purpose. For Ibn Gabirol understood, as did the Kabbalists after him, that language—and in particular the Hebrew language—is something rather more than a hit-or-miss means of human communication, liable to misconstruction and misrepresentation. Those who would learn to identify, at each reading, ever greater depth in his poetry in the way that, say, Beethoven's *Emperor Concerto* can yield up more of its profundity each time that it is heard, must train themselves to share something of his own austerity as a metaphysical poet. In an age when popular enthusiasm has created a kind of neo-orthodoxy, that identifies the significance of Hebrew in the circumstance that it has been tailored to suit a vernacular revival, that is a discipline to which not many are prepared to submit themselves; and I can hardly myself expect the seven thousand in Israel who, Elijah was assured, would not bow the knee to Baal.

The only verse renderings printed here that have been previously published are that of the elegy on Yekúthiél (pp. 65–71) (*Judaism* 18, 1969), the wedding-song (p. 85) and the introduction to *Nishmath* (pp. 87f.) (*Interpreting the Hebrew Bible, Essays in honour of E. I. J. Rosenthal*, ed. J. A. Emerton and S. C. Reif, 1982, pp. 142, 155), as well as the garden poem (pp. 58f.). This last—the only version here that is not my own—is by Nicholas de Lange, and appeared in the *Tel Aviv Review* 1, 1988. I am grateful to him for permission to use it. I am likewise most grateful to Professor M. Jarden and his family for allowing me to reproduce the Hebrew text of the poems here translated from the late Dov Jarden's magisterial edition of Ibn Gabirol's poetical works.

I

THE HISTORICAL
BACKGROUND

IT is probable that Jews did not settle in Spain until well into the Roman period, perhaps the earliest record of their presence being a tombstone of the third century CE from Adra; another, from Tarragona, may ascend to the first-second century and that from Tortosa is probably of a similar date. But no later than the fifteenth century—and probably long before—Spanish Jewry was referring its origins to biblical times, maintaining that a certain Pyrrhus, who had allegedly been one of Nebuchadnezzar's lieutenants at the capture of Jerusalem and was son-in-law to Hispanus, Hercules' vice-regent in Spain, had settled his captives from the house of David in Toledo, Seville and Granada.[1] The classical allusions will not ante-date the renaissance, and the tradition overlaps one current in non-Jewish circles regarding Hispanus, supposedly associated with Hercules, whose conquest of Spain after the Trojan War gave Spanish national sentiment a claim to links with remote antiquity analogously to legends regarding Brut and Francus, eponymous ancestors of Britain and France respectively.[2]

The cultivation of a myth by the Jews of Spain regarding their primeval origins reflects the long-standing continuity of their settlement; through much of the first Christian millennium there had been numerically significant communities in the eastern part of the Iberian peninsula. The tradition probably also enjoyed some spurious corroboration from folk-memory regarding pre-Roman colonization by the Phoenicians, both from Tyre itself and especially from

3

Carthage, the daughter-city of Sidon, whose language—closely akin to Hebrew—had left its imprint in Spanish place-names: Seville (Latin Hispalis) is cognate with *shephelah*, lowland, the name of the coastal strip of Palestine/Israel since biblical times. Although this is no more evidence for remote Spanish-Jewish antiquity than the alleged Zion-compound of Marazion in Cornwall (likewise visited by Phoenician traders) it supports the fantasies produced by British-Israelite assumptions, the intensity of Punic colonization of Spain, and its demographic legacy, no doubt made Spanish-Jewish claims to an early arrival seem the more plausible, at least to the unsophisticated elements in the community.

Roman rule in Spain disintegrated under the impact of the irruption of the Vandals and others in the fifth century; and in the absence of any strong central authority the power exercised by the Church became correspondingly more significant. Church councils held in Spain, from that of Elvira at the beginning of the fourth century, had taken account of the presence of Jews, and were concerned to distance Christians from too close contact with them; but the early enactments cannot be regarded as severely repressive. The coming of the Visigoths in the fifth century at first made little difference, since the form of Christianity they professed was Arianism, and there was consequently little sympathy between them and the Catholic bishops. But the conversion of King Reccared to Catholicism in 587 set in train an anti-Jewish policy that was to become progressively more harsh, and in 613 Sisebut's decree enjoining forced baptism on the Jews initiated a century of martyrdoms. Egica (687–702), in an attempt to sap the still substantial economic power exercised by the Jews through land-cultivation based on slave-labour, demanded the surrender to his treasury of all Jewish property, including slaves, that had ever been acquired from Christians. During the seventh century Islam and Arab rule advanced westwards along the southern shore of the Mediterranean and it is not to be wondered at that Spanish

Jewry looked on the Arabs as liberators; after Tariq's capture of Gibraltar (named after him Jebel al-Tariq) in 711 they proved co-operative, being utilized by him as garrison troops in the wake of his victorious advances through the peninsula.

In the following centuries, Spain beckoned to adventurous Muslims in the eastern Mediterranean and its hinterland, rather as in the sixteenth century North America would attract, alongside such protestants as felt alienated by the Anglican compromise, those merely seeking their fortune in the Virginian plantations, or in the way that, in the eleventh century, the emptiness of Asia Minor proved a magnet for landless younger sons in Europe as the background of what became, at the end of that century, the crusading movement. Lack of evidence makes it impossible to say whether Jews in the near east shared in the colonizing enterprise of their Muslim neighbours who settled in Spain, although the presence in the eastern parts of the peninsula of strong Jewish communities might well have encouraged them to seek their fortunes in the west. But it was political vicissitudes of Muslim imperialism in the east that were pregnant with consequences of major significance regarding the history of the Jews in Spain through the last quarter of the first Christian millennium and beyond.

From 661 CE to 750 the lands of Islam had been subject to the Omayyad caliphs, whose capital was Damascus. They were then displaced by the Abbasids, ruling from Baghdad, who, being determined to eliminate the line of their rivals, tricked them by the promise of amnesty, only to slaughter more than 70 members of the family near Jaffa. However, a one-eyed grandson of Hisham, one of the last caliphs in Syria (died 743), named 'Abderraḥman ibn Mu'awiya, was saved by his cynicism, his astuteness, and his own sense of destiny. Keeping on the move, he evaded Abbasid pursuit and, with two freed slaves, he made his way to Egypt and thence to Kairouan, the capital of Muslim North Africa, where the governor was another 'Abderraḥman (ibn Ḥabib al-Fiḥri).

The latter had been told by a Jew that one of his name would establish a dynasty, but was disabused as to his own imperial aspirations since, as his informant pointed out, he was not himself of royal blood. When his namesake appeared, with physical features matching the soothsayer's prophecy, he would have had him executed but for the Jew's intervention: such an act would be homicide, and if the young 'Abderrahman was indeed destined to found a royal line, also futile. The prince continued westwards dogged by agents of the governor for four years, eventually finding himself in Morocco amongst the very Berber tribe of which his own mother had been a member.

Here he began to entertain notions of establishing himself in Spain, where a substantial number of former subjects of the Omayyads, mindful of loyalties towards their erstwhile masters, had taken refuge. He made contact with them and, in 755, he was invited to Spain. The Muslim governor, Yusuf al-Fihri, was deserted by most of his troops and forced into unsuccessful parley. During the winter 'Abderrahman gained support in southern Spain, and in the spring of 756 he entered Seville, defeated Yusuf outside Cordoba and entered the capital, to be proclaimed, in his twenty-sixth year, ruler (*Amir*, i.e. commander) of all Muslim Spain. The new Omayyad dynasty which he founded endured for over 250 years, passing through ten descendants of 'Abderrahman to Muhammad II (1009); after which the line was disrupted by rival claims, finally petering out in 1031.

Because of the antipathy of the Arabs to strong central government and the demography of Muslim Spain, where a sizeable section of the population was of native Spanish, Christian (or nominally Christian) descent and but superficially islamicized, 'Abderrahman I (756–88) and most of his successors constantly had to take the field in order to assert their authority; and this they achieved but intermittently. In addition to his political aim of the cultural integration of all ethnic elements, 'Abderrahman preferred to choose as his

6

personal aides Jews and Christians rather than Arabs. Heavy taxation was required in order to finance his autocratic, indeed despotic, rule but neither Christians nor Jews were involved in the frequent revolts that marked his reign; and through eight generations of Omayyad rule, Jews suffered neither from governmental repression nor violence. Indeed, Jewish solidarity with the regime contrasts with the resentment of the Christian minority through the reigns of 'Abderraḥman's successors; and later, under 'Abderraḥman II (822–52), Christians in Merida would even solicit armed intervention from the Carolingian emperor Louis the Pious. The relatively firm government that 'Abderraḥman I himself maintained attracted some Jewish immigration into Spain, especially from North Africa, but also from Syria and Egypt, although the substantial flow did not begin until the reigns of Hisham I (788–96) and Ḥakam I (796–822).

A reflection of the degree of Jewish integration in the Omayyad establishment is afforded by the celebrated controversy of Bodo and Paul Alvaro. Bodo, a Christian priest at the court of Louis the Pious, made his way to Spain, where, in 838, having adopted Judaism and the name Eliezer, he began to write polemically against Christianity. Alvaro, a leading member of the Christian community in Cordoba under 'Abderraḥman II, engaged in apologetic correspondence with him. The incident not only attracted attention in the Church outside the peninsula but, within Spain itself, the Jewish leadership made capital out of the situation in its rivalry with the Christians. In 847 the latter approached Charles the Bald and the Carolingian bishops with a view to bringing pressure to bear on 'Abderraḥman II to hand over Bodo to the Franks—with what result is not known. The affair contributed to the growth of a clerical fanaticism that for a while encouraged Christians to court martyrdom by publicly reviling Islam: a provocation in the face of which the government had (albeit with reluctance) to enforce the death penalty on the 'martyrs of Cordoba'. What is here significant is the absence of any anti-Jewish repercussions. The same holds good for the troubled reign of Muḥammad I (852–86), whose energies were largely absorbed by the suppression of attempts to assert local or regional independence by both Muslims and Christians. Jewish loyalty was never in doubt; and the circumstance that the Muslim assault on Barcelona, in the Carolingian Spanish march, may have been aided by Jewish collaborators within the city, underscores the preferability for Jews of a life under a Muslim regime as contrasted with conditions under Christian rule, whether Frankish or in the independent Asturia. At the same time, pragmatism secured Jewish co-operation with the independent rule locally established by Arabs, whether Muslim, as in Toledo, or Christian, under the Banu Qasi, in Aragon. 'Umar ibn Hafsun, the doughtiest of all rebels against Muḥammad I and 'Abdullah (888–912), eventually himself turned Christian, and in 891 most cities in Andalusia were in his hands; Lucena, the only city faithful to the Amir, was largely Jewish, and it successfully withstood the attempts of 'Umar's forces to take it by storm. The disturbed conditions of the time precipitated considerable emigration of Arab Christians northwards into Asturia, old Castile, and Leon; and some Jews—particularly those possessed of skills in demand in the north—were tempted to join them. Consequently when the Christian reconquest of Spain began, there were already Jewish communities of long standing in the Spanish-speaking areas.

It was 'Abdullah's son 'Abderraḥman III (912–61) who re-established Omayyad authority throughout the Muslim area of the peninsula, an achievement which he marked by assuming the title of Caliph (i.e. successor [sc. of Muḥammad]). His reign began the golden age which, in cultural terms, would outlive his own dynasty—an age symbolized by his building the magnificent palace of Az-zahra outside Cordoba. Cordoba itself, with a population of a quarter of a million, was at this period the largest city in Europe. The integration of all ethnic groups, including recently arrived

Berbers, which was one of 'Abderraḥman's main political objectives, was reflected in the composition of his staff of officials; a policy of which the pre eminence in his entourage of a Jewish minister, Ḥasdai ibn Shaprut, is the outstanding example.

Ḥasdai, who was born in Jaen about 910, was one of those who, like Roger Bacon in thirteenth-century England, prefigure the European renaissance. He received in Cordoba a liberal education combining Hebrew and rabbinic studies with Arabic and Latin, but his vocation was for medicine, skill in which earned him an appointment at court when he was in his early thirties, some time after 940. Known there as Abu Yusuf, he was assigned charge of the excise department, and was also established by the Caliph as supreme authority over Jewish matters. Because of Ḥasdai's knowledge of Latin, 'Abderraḥman relied on him heavily in his dealings with Christian states. When, in 948, the Byzantine emperor Constantinus VII Porphyrogenitus sent a delegation to Spain in order to renew diplomatic ties, they brought amongst other gifts a magnificent Greek manuscript of Dioscorides' *materia medica*. This work was already available in Arabic, but 'Abderraḥman requested the emperor to send a Greek teacher and, when in 951/2 a monk named Nicholas arrived, Ḥasdai collaborated with him in accurately translating the botanical terms into their local Arabic equivalents. He also fulfilled an important role in the protracted negotiations regarding the avoidance of giving offence to Islam by the emissary of Otto I of Germany, and again in diplomatic dealings with the King of Leon in 955. In 958 he even achieved the diplomatic coup of prevailing upon the deposed Sancho I to come to Cordoba in order to be cured of his obesity.

Ḥasdai ibn Shaprut maintained a wide correspondence with Jews both in Palestine and in the Diaspora. He made representations to the Byzantine court on behalf of persecuted communities in southern Italy; and, most spectacularly, in 954 he despatched for forwarding by two Jews who came to

Cordoba with the emissary of Otto I a letter addressed to the King of the Khazars—a war-like people based on the Crimea, the conversion of whose king and nobles to Judaism would later be made by Judah Halevi the occasion of a fictional apologetic dialogue. In the tenth century, unsettled political conditions in Iraq, Syria and Egypt were impelling large numbers—Muslims and Jews—to emigrate, and many settled in Spain. For the Jews, the standing enjoyed by Ḥasdai with the Caliph, and his opportunities for promoting Jewish advancement were an extra encouragement to make their way there. On the death of ʿAbderraḥman III, Ḥakam II (961–76) succeeded and an account of his accession ceremonial survives (though late, it is clearly dependent on eye-witnesses). It may be presumed that although no officials' names are mentioned, Ḥasdai will have participated, along with the other great officers of state; and this circumstance might have impressed the occasion the more firmly upon Jewish folk-memory because of their vicarious pride in it. That would perhaps account for the possibility that a Hebrew poem which describes the celestial protocol, composed by Solomon ibn Gabirol some seventy-five years later, reflects popular reminiscence of a great Muslim state occasion.[3]

The cultural efflorescence of the Cordovan caliphate reached its zenith under ʿAbderraḥman III and Ḥakam II, whose infant son Hisham II (976–1009) was but a puppet in the hands of Ibn Abi Amir—nominally his minister—who styled himself Al-manṣur ('the Victorious [through Allah]'). Although Al-manṣur's dictatorship in effect brought the caliphate to an end, his government maintained the by now traditional Omayyad policy of tolerance towards non-Muslim subjects of the Muslim rule, whilst he himself campaigned unremittingly against the Christian kingdoms in the north of the peninsula: in 997 he destroyed the shrine of Santiago de Compostela, the most venerated Christian sanctuary in Spain.

Al-manṣur died in 1002; and when the childless Hisham

complacently bequeathed the caliphate to Sanjul, one of Al-manṣur's sons, his action soon led to an uprising in which both the Az-zahra palace built by 'Abderraḥman III and Al-manṣur's own palace were sacked. Hisham abdicated (1009) in favour of Muḥammad II, to be briefly restored, and die in 1013. A series of Omayyads then disputed the succession with 'Ali ibn Ḥammud (1016–18), from North Africa and his family. When the last Omayyad, Hisham III (1027–31), was deposed by the Cordovan aristocracy, the caliphate came to an end, and Muslim Spain lapsed into a multitude of splinter-kingdoms (ṭaifas, i.e. parts). All that it is necessary to note here is that Cordoba itself was governed at first by an aristocratic council and then, until 1070, when it was annexed by Seville, by the Banu Janwar; Saragossa was governed by the Banu Hud and Granada by the Banu Ziri; Malaga, Solomon ibn Gabirol's birthplace, was ruled by the Hammudid line, late of Cordoba, until it was annexed to Granada. Ḥabbus ibn Maqsam and his son Badis, under whom Granada achieved its cultural apogee, were both served by Samuel Ha-nagid (Isma'il ibn Nagrela, 993–1055/6) as vizier; and Samuel Ha-nagid counted amongst the recipients of his patronage Solomon ibn Gabirol.

In the tenth and eleventh centuries, Al-andalus, as that part of Spain under Muslim rule was called in Arabic, evinced a prosperity that afforded the necessary substratum for cultural advance. An economy based on agriculture, and re-inforced by an efficient fiscal system and the constant flow of captives and sequestrated property from the Christian north, made Muslim Spain an important entrepôt of the slave-trade, whilst her artisans produced high-quality work both for the foreign and the domestic markets, including gold and silver-ware, textiles, and silk: leather goods from Cordoba (whence 'cordwain'), and steel weapons from Toledo won a reputation for excellence which they retained into and beyond the European renaissance.

In matters of the mind and spirit Muslim Spain had

been arid until the reign of 'Abderraḥman III (912–61), not least owing to the dominant influence of the Malikite school of jurists, who tolerated the cultivation of the arts insofar only as mathematics and astronomy were relevant to the management of the Islamic religious calendar. But under 'Abderraḥman and his successor Ḥakam II (961–76) there was established an age of brilliant culture that would outlive the Omayyad caliphate into the period of the Ṭaifite petty-kingdoms, to be recognized in retrospect not only as a golden age in the annals of Islam, but as having contributed powerfully to the intellectual history of the Christian west. It suffices to mention, by way of example, the cusped arch which, invented in the east, was profusely used in the great Cordoba mosque, and passed into the repertoire of Christian ecclesiastical architecture; Maslama of Madrid (died 1008), a mathematician, astronomer, and alchemist, who wrote *inter alia* a commentary on Ptolemy's *Planisphaerium*; and Abu-'l-qasim ('Abulcasis', 'Abecasis') (died 1013), one of the court physicians of Ḥakam, whose medical encyclopaedia was later translated into Latin, Hebrew, and Provençal. Both 'Abderraḥman III and Ḥakam II were themselves men of learning and liberal views who attracted round themselves scholars and poets from Asia, Africa, and Europe; and the architecture and furnishings of their Az-zahra palace combined with the dignity of its court protocol to convey an aura of authoritarianism fused with enlightenment. Ḥakam established an educational foundation for the children of the poor. Not the least significant feature in the culture of the age was the degree of bilingualism prevalent across the population. Because of the high demographic proportion of the so-called *muwalladun*, i.e. aboriginal stock originally of Christian or nominally Christian belief who had been (in some cases but superficially) islamicized, Romance as well as Arabic was spoken or understood by many (at least as regards the male population; the women are likely to have remained unilingual). Among the Arabic-speaking, so-called Mozarabic Christians the clergy also knew the Latin that they used in their liturgy. The Jewish sector commanded, in varying degrees, a knowledge of biblical and liturgical Hebrew, whilst the capacity to read talmudic and midrashic texts was a skill attained in the rabbinical schools that (as will be explained below) spread what may be called a secondary Jewish education beyond the ranks of those concerned to make a career in the juridical structure of their own community.

Muslim linguistic studies in Spain therefore enjoyed an especial attention. The discipline concerned itself with the language of the Qur'an, the speech of the Qoreish (Muḥammad's own tribe) being considered *ex hypothesi* the most perfect form of Arabic; and also with the study of pre-Islamic Arabic poetry, which was regarded as evincing a classical quality in its prosody and literary devices. Following the example of the Caliph, prominent figures would play the Maecenas to their own *coterie* of scholars and poets, utilizing the latter to fulfil the role of public-relations officers. The circulation across the country of panegyrics extolling their patrons' exploits served the purpose for which, today, politicians and publicists look to the media. The direct impact of all suchlike activities on the inner cultural life of the Jews in Spain will be noted below (p. 56).

In Visigothic Spain the Jewish communities had been largely isolated from contact with Jews elsewhere but, with the coming of the Arabs, links were forged with the 'Babylonian' Jewry of Iraq the rabbinical schools of which constituted the intellectual capital of Jewry. Spanish Jews set about acquiring talmudic texts and increasing their mastery of the Aramaic in which most of the Talmud is written. Educational standards were improved when, after 773, defeated in his attempt to secure the Exilarchate in Baghdad, Natronai b. Ḥabibai came to Spain, where (according to tradition) he prepared from memory a copy of the Babylonian Talmud; but the relative strength of Jewish expertise in

North Africa still made Kairouan a kind of collection-point and clearing-house for financial contributions and queries regarding *halakhah* (jurisprudence and procedure) referred to Sura and later Pumpeditha in Iraq. None the less, the *yeshiboth* (talmudic academies) of Lucena and Barcelona were noteworthy institutions. From the end of the ninth century Spanish Jewry, perhaps by now feeling surer of itself, loosened its ties with Babylonian Jewry: and the position of Ḥasdai ibn Shaprut (see p. 9) as a minister at the court of 'Abderraḥman III—who appointed him head of the Jewish communities in the caliphate—enabled him to exercise both substantial influence and charitable concern in Spain and elsewhere, including Palestine and the Byzantine empire. Ḥasdai also attracted Jewish scholars from Palestine and Iraq to enjoy his patronage in Spain. Although contact was renewed for a time with the major Babylonian academy, now transferred to Baghdad, it suited 'Abderraḥman's policy that the Jews in his domain should strive for self-sufficiency in matters of their own religious law. The fact that the Babylonian academies had entered a period of rapidly progressive decline would have been conducive of such emancipation in any case, but it was made possible by the coming of Moses b. Enoch to Spain around 950.

Moses b. Enoch was a product of south Italian Jewry, whose traditions (including an interest in liturgical poetry) looked towards Palestine rather than to Babylonia. At that time the Omayyad fleet was patrolling the western Mediterranean, in order to disrupt the shipping of the rival Fatimid kingdom based on Kairouan and, in one of its operations, Moses b. Enoch was captured and brought to Spain, where he was ransomed by Jews. According to a legend—now generally regarded as fictitious—the ship, whose home port was Bari, was carrying four rabbis on a fund-raising mission, who were redeemed by Jews in Alexandria, Tunis, and Cordoba, where each became a leading rabbinical figure.[4] What is certain is that Moses b. Enoch found his way to Cordoba, where his erudition made so great an impression that the local rabbi resigned his position in his favour. Moses b. Enoch's appointment was enthusiastically endorsed by Ḥasdai ibn Shaprut, and the rabbinical school in Cordoba began to attract students from all parts of Muslim Spain.

Although Jewish devotion to textual study of the Hebrew Bible was of long standing, it would have been surprising if the Islamic linguistic scholarship that was cultivated so assiduously in Spain had not given Jewish intellectualism an extra fillip, and—quite apart from poetic innovation in Hebrew—it did in fact stimulate the development of the study of the grammar and vocabulary of biblical Hebrew as disciplines in their own right. Ḥasdai himself, like the Muslim notables of his time, gathered round him a distinguished circle of Jewish scholar-poets. These included the lexicographer Menaḥem ibn Saruq, whose Jewish education had been financially assisted by Ḥasdai's brother Isaac. Menaḥem acted as Ḥasdai's secretary, but the relationship went sour, in part due to intrigue, and it has to be recognized that Ḥasdai persecuted his former protégé mercilessly. Another member of his circle was Dunash ibn Labraṭ, who had been born in Fez c. 920 and had studied in Iraq under Saʿadiah Gaʾon. Primarily a poet to whom belongs the achievement of introducing Arabic metrical schemes (with the necessary adaptation) into Hebrew poetics, Dunash was led by his art to study linguistic purism and, together with a school of disciples writing, like Ibn Saruq, in Hebrew, he launched into bitter criticism of the latter's dictionary. These followers of Dunash included Judah ibn Ḥayyuj (c. 945–c. 1000), who chose to write his own studies of Hebrew grammar in Arabic.

Dunash's poetry reflects the interpenetration, within the pluralistic society of contemporary Andalusia, of spiritual and secular values despite their occasional incompatibility in regard to ethical behaviour, etc. It was thus a rich cultural tradition, within which (as far as the Jews were concerned) the Arabic stream fructified and enriched the Hebrew one that constituted the social background of the birth, about a century after that of Dunash, of Solomon ibn Gabirol.

2

SOLOMON IBN GABIROL

THE known biographical facts are sparse, and it is not the
business of a serious student to elaborate the known facts
romantically, even though he must take note where tradition
has done so. His full name was, in Arabic, Abu Ayyub
Sulaiman ibn Yahya ibn Jebirul or, in Hebrew, Shelomoh ben
Yehudah ibn Gabirol. From the occasional appendage of
ha-malaqi to the acrostic signature of his poems it is certain
that he was born in Malaga, but the circumstance that the
surname *ha-qortobi* (of Cordoba) is sometimes attributed to
him indicates the immediate provenance of his family. It may
be surmised that his parents fled from Cordoba at the time of
the massacre that marked the end of the siege of the city by
the Berbers in 1013. Regarding the date of Solomon's birth
the evidence is equivocal. The earliest source, which is
contemporary, comes from a short literary history entitled
Tabaqat al-umum (Categories of the Peoples) by the Muslim
writer and Toledo judge [Abu-'l-qasim] Sa'id [ibn Ahmad]
al-andalusi (1029–70), the fourth chapter of which contains a
section on Jewish scientific writers. It includes the following:[1]

> And of the number of those who were interested in
> some philosophical sciences was also Sulaiman ibn
> Yahya, called Ibn Jabrival, a citizen of Saragossa. He
> was very fond of the subject of logic. He had a subtle
> mind and chaste austerity [the textual emendation
> meaning 'cut off in his prime' is probably gratuitous, as
> tautological], passing away at an age over thirty, shortly
> before the year 450 [sc. of the *Hijra* = 1058].

From references in Ibn Gabirol's poems to his own age that

17

can be correlated with a known date—that of the execution of Yequthiel ibn al-mutawakkil in 1039—Bargebuhr has shown[2] that he must have been born in 1021/2, in which case if Sa'id al-andalusi's date is correct, he will have died at the age of thirty-six (see, however, p. 23). His parents took him to Saragossa while he was still young and both died there, his mother in 1045 and his father before then. Saragossa also harboured among its refugees from Cordoba the grammarian Ibn Jannaḥ, with whom the young Ibn Gabirol was in contact, as one of a circle of distinguished Jewish intellectuals; and it was at Saragossa that he acquired a thorough Jewish education and training in the use of philosophical sources in Arabic. A phenomenal capacity to compose poetry in Hebrew manifested itself from a very early age, inviting comparison with the precocious musical talent of Mozart. However, he suffered from a painful and disfiguring disease —perhaps tuberculosis of the skin, or furunculosis (boils)— the symptoms of which he describes in one of his poems.[3] Conceivably the social embarrassment caused by this affliction explains why there is no hint anywhere of Ibn Gabirol's having ever married or being at all familiar with female company. There is, indeed, a marked streak of sublimated eroticism in his poetry, which might be taken to point to physical impotence.

A constant awareness of his complaint is likely to have been a factor in the stormy temperament revealed in Ibn Gabirol's relationship with his patrons, a trait of character noted by the poet and critic Moses ibn Ezra (c. 1055–after 1135) in his Arabic Kitab al-muḥaḍarah w'al-mudhakharah (Conclave and Reminiscence).[4] With the omission of literary allusions to Plato etc. what he has to say about Ibn Gabirol is as follows:

Abu Yaḥya Sulaiman ibn Gabirol of Cordoba was born in Malaga and educated in Saragossa. He exercised great self-control, curbing himself for the cultivation of higher things. He purged his soul of all taint of desire and gained a familiarity with some of the best philosophical writing, as well as studying the [mathematical] sciences. Although he was younger than all contemporary poets (and philosophers), many of them —in differing degrees—masters of a fair turn of language and of great poetic power that made their style and capacity for felicitous allusion the hall-mark of a school, he excelled them all in the quality of his own creative writing. He was, indeed, a craftsman who attained perfection in the use of language—one who had achieved a mastery of what constitutes the object of all poetry, and could direct his aim unerringly upon his target. His method of handling metaphysical themes places him alongside the later Muslim poets and earned him a reputation as lord of language and prince of poetry, thanks to his torrent of mellifluous speech and the fairness of the concepts therein expressed. He was the cynosure of all eyes: not a finger but would be crooked to beckon towards him. He was the first to introduce the 'art of poetry' (? Arabic *qariḍ* is of obscure reference: *taqriḍ* means the art or criticism of poetry; perhaps 'flowery metrical schemes' is here meant) into Hebrew, therein setting a pattern for his successors, as anyone can see who makes a deep study of his poetry and learns to appreciate the power of its allusiveness to the institutions of the Torah and the corpus of rabbinical tradition. This youthful poet composed panegyrics (albeit allowing himself to exaggerate), dirges (yet indulging in hyperbole), and love-poems (in which he abased himself overmuch). In his personal asceticism he went too far; his poems of exculpation and apology embody flattery, and his satire can exceed the bounds of propriety. Despite his vocation for philosophy and the learning that he had acquired, his irascible temperament dominated his intellect, nor could he rein the demon that was within himself. It came easily to him to lampoon the great with salvo upon salvo of mockery and sarcasm. He was carried off by death whilst still young, at the beginning of the 'eighth' [understand the ninth] century [of the Jewish era, which began in 1040 CE] in Valencia, where he is buried, being somewhat over thirty years old. Although critics have faulted details in his poems and have drawn attention to some insignificant errors, the perceptive reader will readily account for their occurrence as being due to the author's youth, or even the ingenuousness—occasionally purblind—of a writer who was still almost a child.[5]

Moses ibn Ezra will certainly have known some of Ibn Gabirol's contemporaries. Of the other medieval writers who refer to him the only one to include biographical matter lived a century later. Judah b. Solomon Al-ḥarizi (1170–1235), writing after 1216, was understandably less sure regarding chronology. In his *Taḥkemoni*, written in exalted rhymed prose, he makes several references to Ibn Gabirol, on whom he lavishes unqualified praise;[6] the only one which concerns us is the following:[7]

At the end [*sic*] of [Samuel Ha-nagid's] life (993–1055/6) there was born Rabbi Solomon 'the less' (*Ha-qaṭan*, Ibn Gabirol's self-chosen soubriquet in his acrostic signatures), whose poetry wafts a fragrance that has never since been matched . . . Had he lived longer he would have produced stupendous wonders in the mystery of the muse, but his garland was plucked away while his greenness was yet tender, with the sap of youth still about him: his lamp extinguished in his twenty-ninth year, nor ever saw he thirty. During the ninth century (1040→) the aforementioned poets all died . . .

In Saragossa Ibn Gabirol enjoyed the patronage of Yequthiel ibn Ḥasan al-mutawakkil ibn Kabrun (Qapron),[8] a

Jew who clearly occupied a position of considerable importance at the Muslim court even though there is no mention of
him in historical sources and he is, indeed, unknown except
for Ibn Gabirol's references to him. In 1039, when he was in
his hundredth year, he was put to death by 'Abdullah ibn
Ḥakam when he deposed and murdered his uncle Mundhir II
of Saragossa; a year later those who had compassed his death
were themselves executed, and Ibn Gabirol subsequently
commemorated the passing of his patron—apparently far-
famed for his general philanthropy—in a moving elegy (see
pp. 65–71). He had already written poems to Samuel
Ha-nagid, the vizier of King Ḥabbus of Granada and, from
1037, the latter's son Badis: a statesman-soldier-poet whose
combination of talents puts one in mind of such renaissance
figures as Sir Philip Sydney. One must presume that Ibn
Gabirol could count on Samuel's material support on deciding
to leave Saragossa (possibly as late as 1045). With the death of
Yequthiel his relations with the local Jewish community had
reached breaking-point. As a liturgical poet, he probably
officiated also as a synagogal precentor (rather than salaried
'cantor' in the modern western Jewish sense), but this did not
prevent them from actually denouncing him to the Islamic
authorities as entertaining heretical views. The case came to
nothing, but Ibn Gabirol shook the dust of Saragossa off his
feet, as he recalls in a defiant poem of farewell:[9]

. . A crowd whose very sires I would not use
As sheepdogs; shame's blush never could suffuse
Their face, though cheeks were rouged to simulate.
Giants they deem themselves—for me to rate
No more than grasshoppers. Should I dare speak
They remonstrate—it might as well be Greek.
They bleat, 'talk so that folk hear what you say,
Not foreign languages'. I am away,
Beneath my feet like mire I stamp them hard,
My tongue I brandish—'tis my sole poignard . . .

The foregoing extract is paralleled by other passages in the poems that evince an arrogance which cannot be evaluated without also taking into account the transparent sincerity of the expressions of self-abasement in some of Ibn Gabirol's devotional poems. Self-vaunting was a conventional feature of Arabic poetry, and a group of poems by Ibn Gabirol falls within this *genre* (see p. 56). But one may surmise that an additional factor behind such passages as that quoted lay in his sense of intellectual isolation, compounded perhaps by the social restrictions which his illness involved—in one of his poems he laments his inability to participate in congregational worship which, in Judaism, is an idiom for the reaffirming of social and ethnical solidarity no less than of the expression of religious devotion. And in fairness to those whose philistinism Ibn Gabirol castigates it should be remembered that it was this same Jewish bourgeoisie that we have to thank for having preserved his poems, not merely by having them copied but—more significantly—by incorporating many of his hymns into their liturgical rite even though (if Ibn Gabirol's objurgations are in part justified) the content will occasionally have been above their heads.

Despite Ibn Gabirol's sentiments it was in Saragossa that he had produced much—perhaps all—of his philosophical work as well as writing many of his best-loved poems. No information of substance is forthcoming regarding his subsequent movements. In a poem 'on leaving Al-andalus' that concludes with four lines of Arabic (following a convention by which Arabic poets would lapse into the popular dialect, or even the romance vernacular, as a so-called *muwasshah* or refrain),[10] he talks of leaving Spain and of travelling to Palestine and the near east, but there is no evidence that Ibn Gabirol ever went overseas. It may be assumed that since Samuel Ha-nagid retained his services as a poet-press-officer (see p. 56), he will have kept him at Granada or within easy reach of it. That he was at some time in Granada is surely proved by his well-known description of the lion-fountain in

the Alhambra, completed in 1060–65.[11] We have merely
Moses ibn Ezra's statement—followed by others—that his
death took place in Valencia.

Joseph ibn Ṣaddiq (died 1149) declared that Ibn Gabirol
died in 5430, i.e. 1070,[12] as did Abraham Zacuto, writing in
the sixteenth century.[13] A legend recorded in a late source has
it that Ibn Gabirol was murdered by a non-Jewish scholar
envious of his learning, who proceeded to bury his body
beneath a fig-tree which then produced so magnificent a crop
as to cause general amazement and lead to investigation.[14]
Under torture the accused confessed to his crime and was
executed. The story is paralleled by that of the alleged murder
of the poet Judah Halevi on reaching Jerusalem; both lack any
significant evidence, and are the product of introspective
Jewish brooding on allegedly ceaseless victimization by a
gentile environment.

As already noted, Ibn Gabirol must have been born in 1021/2.
If he really died as late as 1070 the reports—the earliest of
which, emanating from Moses ibn Ezra, is that of a younger
contemporary—that he died aged about thirty are clearly
exaggerated. Perhaps, rather, Ibn Ezra retrospectively con-
fused the thirties of the century that began in 1040 with Ibn
Gabirol's own second or third decade. But in addition to the
poem describing the Alhambra (see pp. 58f.), which shows that
Ibn Gabirol was alive in 1060 + , there are several references in
his *oeuvre* to the thousandth anniversary of the destruction of
the second temple at Jerusalem, a catastrophe which, although
it in fact took place in 70 CE, is dated in Jewish tradition as
68.[15] One of these equates the millennium explicitly with the
year 461 of the Islamic era (the *Hijra*) which began on 31
October 1068. Unless, therefore, all the poems involved are
to be denied to his authorship—an arbitrary position to
adopt, and a most implausible one in regard to the poem
describing the Alhambra—it must be allowed that Ibn
Gabirol died, aged about fifty, *c.* 1070. Even for that life-span,

his literary output was remarkable. He reserved Hebrew exclusively for poetry, whether liturgical or social (rather than 'secular': see pp. 54f.), choosing to write his prose works in Arabic; the creation of a Hebrew philosophical vocabulary was a process that began in the century following his death (see p. 28). As regards his poems, the latest edition admits 538 items to the canon. He himself claims to have written twenty books.[16] His extant works do not amount to that number, but a catalogue of seventeen tracts, ascribed to 'the Jew, King Solomon' has been preserved. This curious form of words has arisen out of the confusion of the less familiar *malaqi* (of Malaga) with *melekh* (king). The list was taken over by the fifteenth-century Italian-Jewish philosopher Yoḥanan Allemano,[17] who quotes as his authority the Muslim Abu Afla'h of Saragossa, who was writing before 1110.[18] The items enumerated are:

1. *Sepher Nisyonoth* (Experiments)
2. *Sepher ha-ziqnah* (On Old Age)
3. *Sepher meshalim* (Apothegms: ? identical with Ibn Gabirol's *Choice of Pearls*, see p. 26)
4. *Sepher ha-shelemuth* ([Moral] Perfection)
5. *Sepher ha-meʿallelim* (Causes)
6. *Sepher ha-yiḥud* ([Divine] Unity)
7. *Sepher ha-derishah* ([Methods of] Enquiry)
8. *Sepher qeri'ath ha-shemirah* (The Occasioning of Permanence(?))
9. *Sepher ha-raṣon* (The Will)
10. *Sepher gillui ha-shiqriyyuth* (Exposure of Falsity)
11. *Sepher ha-yashar* (*-yosher*) (Rectitude)
12. *Sepher ha-rephu'oth* (Medical Remedies)
13. *Sepher ha-'emunah* (Belief)
14. *Sepher ha-beḥiruth* (Concept of Election)
15. *Sepher shemirath ha-zeruz* (Sustained Application)
16. *Sepher kittoth ha-ḥakhamim* (Schools of Philosophy)
17. *Sepher ha-takhliyyuth* (Teleology)

To this list taken from Abu Afla'h, Allemano adds four more, making a total of twenty-one, which he states are mentioned by Apollonius:[19] viz.

(a) *Sepher ha-mar'oth ha-'elyonoth* (Celestial Visions)
(b) *Sepher niqra' yamli'ush* (Iamblichus (?)[20])
(c) *Sepher niqra' mela'khah 'elohith* (The Work of the Deity)
(d) *Sepher qera'o beḥirath ha-middoth* (Choice of [Moral] Qualities; presumably identical with the *Improvement of Moral Qualities*, see pp. 31f.)

The question has been raised as to whether Ibn Gabirol wrote commentaries on the Hebrew Bible, since references to his views are occasionally adduced by later commentators, notably by Abraham ibn Ezra.[21] Since, however, these tend to be speculative observations or philosophical identifications, e.g. that of Jacob's ladder (Genesis 28.12) with the superior (i.e. rational) soul, it seems improbable that he would have set himself to comment on any biblical book throughout. The quotations, if not traceable in his existing *opus*, could be to lost works or even—as late as the twelfth to thirteenth centuries—to oral tradition current in Spain. At the same time, his poetry is so replete with biblical reminiscence and allusion (even to so unfamiliar a text as Chronicles) that one might argue a case for classifying the whole corpus as 'creative exegesis' in a general sense, comparable to the exegetical treatment of the Homeric stories by the Greek dramatists or of history by Shakespeare.

Some of Ibn Gabirol's longer verse pieces have occasionally been considered as individual works—with some justification, in view of their comprehensiveness: such is the grammatical treatise entitled *'anaq* (Giant), written when he was nineteen, of which only a hundred lines survive.[22] A similar claim could be made for his *'azharoth*, or catalogue of the 613 precepts that constitute the framework of the Jewish law, still sung in the Sephardic liturgy on *Shabu'oth* (Pentecost),[23] composed when he was sixteen years old, and perhaps, pre-eminently for his *kether malkhuth* (*Royal Crown*, see pp. 103f.). But organizational constraints mean that such items should be left aside here, and we mention only his prose works. Fuller details of these, and a glimpse of his poetry, will be found in later chapters.

The Choice of Pearls, to give it the conventional English title (Arabic *muhtar al-jawahir*[24] (selection of jewels); the medieval Hebrew version is styled *mibhar ha-peninim*), is, as the name implies, an anthology of homespun adages derived from Arabic (sometimes ultimately Greek) sources as well as from rabbinic tradition, the assemblage of which has been denied to Ibn Gabirol although it is now generally accepted. It is to be assigned to a date around 1045. The following are specimens:

I find humility a greater help than all my fellow men.[25]

Were it not for three faults, men's affairs would be successfully accomplished: the aged are not listened to, desire is not restrained, and man's self-pride.[26]

Separation from the world brings leisure to the heart and rest to the body; but love of the world causes disquietness of heart and weariness of the body. Who acknowledges God will not grieve over want, and will not be worried about sustenance or his fellow-men.[27]

The two other works written in Arabic, viz. *Improvement of Moral Qualities*, dated 1045, and *Fountain of Life*, will be considered in the next chapters.

3

ETHICS

It may be helpful to begin with a thumb-nail sketch showing how ancient Greek philosophy survived through what are generally regarded as the dark ages of Europe, to make its renewed impact on the west in the high middle ages, and into the renaissance and beyond. The original texts were, of course, still current in the Greek-speaking eastern Roman empire ruled from Constantinople, where, however, the Church was concerned with them only in so far as they lent themselves to being fitted into a Christian theological scheme. From Syria eastwards the vernacular spoken, and the Bible version used by most Christians, was Aramaic; and their desire to have access to the works of the Fathers of the Greek Church stimulated the translation of the most important of these into Syriac, i.e. that form of Aramaic rendered specifically Christian by the use of a particular script, but in other respects close to the language of the Jewish Targums and the Talmud. In the wake of this literary process, during the middle centuries of the first millennium CE, philosophical and scientific texts by pagan authors, including much of Aristotle and some of the major dialogues of Plato, were likewise finding Syriac translators. When, from the seventh century onwards, Arabic became a progressively wider lingua franca and Islamic culture absorbed the intelligentsia of those lands upon which Islam had imposed itself, the need began to be felt for Arabic versions of scientific and non-Christianized philosophy, and the work of translation was begun in the ninth century by the physician Ḥunain ibn Isḥaq of Baghdad and his successors. During the following centuries some of the classical

27

texts became the subject of commentaries by Islamic scholars. The next stage was the translation, in response to Jewish demand, from Arabic into Hebrew; and as the intellectual élite of the Christian west gradually became aware of what was available in Arabic, into Latin—either direct from the Arabic, or via a Hebrew intermediary version or viva voce collaboration with a Jewish translator. The function of the Jewish factor was sometimes crucial here. To take an example, even though it lies beyond the age of Ibn Gabirol, the commentary on Plato's *Republic* by Ibn Rushd ('Averroes') (1126–98), the Arabic original of which is lost, was preserved in a Hebrew translation that was published by E. Rosenthal in 1956.

The Greek originals became known once again in Europe with the fifteenth-century renaissance, in part due to migrations following the fall of Constantinople to the Turks in 1453. Ibn Gabirol, in the eleventh century, had access in Saragossa through his Arabic vernacular to recent scientific works. Thus, to cite two examples, he can be shown to have used the *Elements of Astronomy* by Al-fargani ('Alfraganus'), and the encyclopaedic work entitled the *Epistles of the Brethren of Purity* (see p. 111).

Plato and Aristotle had been the dominating figures of systematic thought in fifth–fourth-century Athens. Despite the development in late antiquity of other schools—Stoicism, Epicureanism etc.—it was first the ghost of platonism embodied in Neoplatonism, and later Aristotelianism, that powerfully influenced the philosophical endeavours of Muslims and Jews described above, these two approaches impinging upon each other according to individual emphasis or reservation. At the risk of over-simplification, we may summarize the contrasting approaches of the original masters as follows. Plato and his school postulated ideal prototypes of which every existent entity, be it concrete or an abstract concept, is a necessarily imperfect example. Aristotelianism starts from particular instances, regarding generalizations as merely provisional statements. It is therefore easy to see the initial attractiveness of platonism (in some form) to the proponents of the three monotheistic faiths based on revelation; but experience of the Aristotelian approach would lead Jewish and other thinkers of intellectual rigour to reject the synthesis of revelation and idealism, and to insist that although the scientific method (of which Aristotle is the begetter) must be prosecuted as a self-substantive discipline and its proven findings respected, faith and reason have to be correlated—in theory, at any rate—without prejudice to either. Thus it was that within Judaism, Neoplatonism progressively gave ground, becoming less significant to those concerned to essay a philosophical account of their faith.

Neoplatonism,[1] while looking towards Plato with whose thought it claimed an integral continuity, in point of fact drew freely on all the philosophical systems of antiquity except Epicureanism. It came into being in the third–fourth centuries CE in Alexandria; starting with Ammonius Sacas, its effective founders were a series of pupil-teacher relationships —Plotinus, Porphyry, and Iamblichus (died *c.* 330). The poles around which Neoplatonism revolves are the ideal world, wherein exists the primeval Being and whence the soul originates, and the world of phenomena subject to human experience. All existence is derivative from primeval being, which projects itself as *nous* (mind) to become its archetype: the mechanism being a chain of 'emanations', i.e. a transmissional process in which each stage is necessarily less pure—as being remoter from the ideal—than its predecessor. The soul, striving to transcend the limitations of sense-perception, possesses the faculty of traversing these levels as it strives, through ever less coarse stages, to reach the supra-rationality of the supreme Being. The world-soul, embracing all individual souls, having exercised the option (rejected by supra-mundane intelligences) of uniting with the corporeal and thus subjecting itself to disintegration, itself generates the physical world. Matter, its *substratum*, is morally neutral, as being potentially the host of form; if it remains without the impress of form, it is evil. The programme by which the individual soul can retrace its course is through the practice of virtue and ascetic discipline, its acme being the attainment of a perfect passivity in which it may lose itself in the contemplation of the supreme Being. With Iamblichus, the archetypal *nous* of Plotinus becomes the *Demiurge*, or world-fashioner, and the system is complicated by an elaborate mathematical scheme to find room for popular religion and its objects of worship. As regards psychology, noteworthy is Iamblichus' repudiation of Plotinus' theory of the divine origin of the soul, and his insistence that the source of evil is the will.

As a system which, while postulating the one, yet recognized the function of a multiplicity of derivative agencies that are styled 'gods', Neoplatonism was scholastically systematized by Proclus (411–85); but it was St. Augustine (354–430) who was the channel through which the heritage of ancient pagan philosophy was passed to western Christianity until, thanks to the process described above (p. 28), the original authors became accessible again in Latin translation. While Neoplatonism as a self-substantive, non-'religious' system could not admit the concepts of creation within time or of revelation which, with differences of dogmatic formulation, are cardinal to each of the three monotheistic religions, Christian systematic theology came to ingest much of the complex of Neoplatonic thought in competition with which it had itself evolved during its own formative centuries. To a lesser degree the same may be said, from the ninth century onwards, of Islam and Judaism.

Within Judaism there are some points of contact in the philosophical scheme of Sa'adiah Ga'on (882–942), but the first Jewish writer in whose works Neoplatonic impress is clearly reflected is the physician Isaac Israeli (or Isaac

Judaeus) (850–932, or even 955).[2] His Arabic books On Definitions and *The Elements* were translated into Latin as well as Hebrew, and his medical works were well known in the west into the age of print. Far more influential, however, as a metaphysical thinker was Solomon Ibn Gabirol, whose *magnum opus*, *The Fountain of Life*, was well known in its Latin translation even though within Jewry it was ultimately consigned to oblivion (see pp. 39f.). But it is convenient first to deal with his short ethical treatise, entitled *The Improvement of Moral Qualities*.

This tract was probably written in 1045. Its Arabic title, *kitab islah al-ahlaq*,[3] means 'book for the correction of faults': the Hebrew translation of 1167 rendered this by *tiqqun middoth ha-nephesh* (adjustment of the qualities of the soul), whence the common English title. The modesty which Ibn Gabirol uses in it when speaking of his own awareness of his limitations as a moralist may serve to confirm the view that when, in his social poems, he sometimes vaunts his intellectual prowess and literary achievements (see pp. 22, 56), he is merely conforming to the conventions of contemporary Arabic poetry.

It is clear from the frequency of biblical references that are intended to illustrate (rather than to pre-determine[4]) his argument that the work was aimed at a Jewish readership, not a general one as was the case with the *Fountain of Life* (see p. 39). It is, in fact, a tacit criticism of Sa'adiah's treatment of ethics in the tenth chapter of his *Beliefs and Convictions*.[5] The fact that Ibn Gabirol's approach evinces similarities to that of Bahya ibn Paquda's *Duties of the Heart* (Saragossa, second half of the tenth century) has given rise to discussion as to their relative priority.[6] However, if Bahya's *floreat* was *c.* 1080[7] he would have been Ibn Gabirol's junior.

An immediately striking feature is the fact that only passing note is made of the ethical function of the 'rational' soul[8] which is deemed to be peculiar to man and the celestial beings, as distinct from the 'animal' and 'vegetative' (or nourishing) soul also, according to Aristotelian psychology, present in man. That is not to say that Ibn Gabirol was concerned to elaborate an ethical system independent of metaphysical theory and religious sanction, or to ignore the element of free will; his treatment of sin and penitence in the *Royal Crown* (pp. 108–10, 143–61) at once disposes of any such suggestion. What dictated his concentration on the 'animal' soul (which he never labels as such here) was his decision to formulate an approach that would correlate the five senses with the four elements and four humours (see diagram, p. 35) as having a bearing upon the cardinal virtues and vices which he identifies. The linking of the four elements to the humours (air/blood, water/white gall, earth/black gall, fire/yellow gall)[10] is found also in the description of man as a microcosm by Shabbethai Donnolo (Italy, 913–*c*. 982) and was also followed by Isaac Israeli[11] (see pp. 30f.). In starting from the premise that it is the senses that make possible the identification of these entities, while being themselves susceptible to their influences, Ibn Gabirol proceeds to construct a complex connecting man's physical make-up and his spiritual potential, which ethical behaviour can realize. The biblical citations which he produces as 'evidence' of the dominant role of each sense in regard to various ethical departments[12] indicate his appreciation of a feature of Hebrew psychology which the modern scholar recognizes as being of crucial importance for the understanding of the Bible, i.e. that its language refers to emotions in terms of their physical manifestations: anger 'waxes hot', passion (*qin'ah*)— whatever its cause—is thought of as a 'flush' (Arabic *qana'a* means to *become* intensely *red* or *black*), and so on.

In his own introduction Ibn Gabirol proceeds from the proposition that man is the crown of the creation *qua* possessing, like the angels, the 'rational' soul;[13] but *qua* microcosm, he is composed of the same four elements as the macrocosm,[14] and is equipped with organs that operate through his five senses. With some exegetical licence,

reference to all five of them can be discovered in Ecclesiastes
9.11. Use of the various faculties ought to be mutually
proportioned so as to achieve ethical improvement, in the
same way that pharmaceutical prescriptions have to be finely
balanced to avoid malign effects.[15] He then proceeds to
survey each of the senses in turn, beginning with that of sight
as primary—'like the sun to the universe'.[16] Unlike the other
senses, its perception is instantaneous, regardless of distance. A
philosophic adage has it that 'the soul has spiritual tints that
sometimes become apparent in the motion of the eyelid'.[17]
Sight is therefore of paramount importance in regard to
ethical decision, cf. Numbers 15.39 ('whoring after your own
eyes').[18] After following the scheme through for the remaining senses, Ibn Gabirol declares that [the faculty of] each may
be considered a genus, within which various species of virtue
and vice are to be identified—four species in each genus,
yielding a total of twenty qualities.[19] Within the province of
sight fall pride, humility, pudency (i.e. commendable shyness)
and impudence. Pride is revealed in the haughty glance, cf.
Isaiah 2.11; 5.15, and meekness keeps its gaze averted from
evil (Habbakuk 1.13, although the text refers not to *humility*
but to divine *purity*). The brazen stare reveals indifference to
shame (Isaiah 3.9), as does a face set hard as rock (Jeremiah
5.3); and the wicked must find their own eyesight failing
them (Job 11.20). Shyness, on the other hand, receives divine
reward (Proverbs 3.34),[20] lowliness and greatness of reputation being dependent upon an individual's own self-view and
the view taken of him by others, cf. the case of Moses
(Numbers 12.3, Exodus 11.3).[21]

Analogous treatment of all the senses yields the following
table of (largely paired) virtues and vices:[22]

SIGHT	HEARING
Pride	Love
Meekness	Hate
Pudency (commendable shyness)	Mercy
Impudence	Hardheartedness

SMELL	TASTE
Wrath	Joy (cheerfulness)
Goodwill	Grief (apprehensiveness)
Jealousy	Tranquillity
Alertness	Penitence

TOUCH
Generosity
Niggardliness
Valour
Cowardice

Before tabulating them thus, Ibn Gabirol produces a diagram[23] (see p. 35) that purports to show how the four temperaments (or 'humours') affect the four elements in such a manner as to predispose the individual towards developing sundry ethical qualities. Whoever wishes to improve them[24] must practise self-discipline from youth onwards, as human experience proves and scripture states (Proverbs 20.11; 22.6). He then claims to be able to find allusions to all twenty of the qualities that he lists in Psalm 37 ('fret not thyself because of evil-doers, neither be thou envious of the workers of iniquity'),[25] verse 23 of which ('the steps of man are ordered by the Lord') indicates not determinism, but the happiness or misery contingent upon reward or punishment.[26] He states his intention[27] of explaining in the body of the work how the various qualities originate in the senses, but in his conclusion[28] he admits that, in the interest of succinctness, he has not in fact carried the scheme through. In the synopsis provided by Wise in his introduction this omission is made good.[29]

We conclude by citing, with slight abbreviation, Ibn Gabirol's treatment of two virtues.

Of pudency (which falls within the purview of the sense of sight) he writes:[30]

A wise man was asked, 'What is intelligence?' and he answered, 'modesty.' Again he was asked, 'What is modesty?' and he replied 'intelligence.' This quality,

alike in respect of heat

	PRIDE IMPUDENCE	
FIRE YELLOW GALL	HATE ALERTNESS	AIR BLOOD
	COWARDICE	

alike in respect of dryness

alike in respect of moistness

JEALOUSY GRIEF HARDHEARTEDNESS

WRATH NIGGARDLINESS HARDHEARTEDNESS

HEAT—DRY OPPOSED

OPPOSED HEAT—MOIST OPPOSED

COLD—DRY COMBINED

OPPOSED COLD—MOIST

VALOUR LOVE JOY GOOD-WILL GENEROSITY

	TRANQUILLITY PENITENCE	
EARTH BLACK GALL	HUMILITY PUDENCY	WHITE GALL WATER
	MERCY	

alike in respect of cold

Diagram as in the Oxford Arabic manuscript (Huntington 382) of
Solomon ibn Gabirol's *Improvement of Moral Qualities*

35

although like unto humility and agreeing therewith, is of nobler rank than the latter, for it is kindred to intelligence. To every man of understanding the nobility of the intellect is patent, for it is the dividing line between man and beast, in that it masters man's natural impulses and subdues passion. With the help of intelligence . . . he comes to acknowledge the unity of God, to worship his Master, and to bear a striking resemblance to the character of the angels . . . The proof of its being thus related is, that thou wilt never see a modest man lacking in intelligence, or an intelligent man devoid of modesty. This being so, man must direct all his efforts to the attainment of this . . . quality. He must prefer it to all his natural impulses, and regard it as superior to all his other qualities, for by means of it he acquires many virtues, and all vice becomes hidden from him. Thus it is said, 'The faults of him whom modesty clothes with dignity will not be remarked by men.' Thus it is said [Proverbs 15.33] 'before honour is humility' . . . Concerning him who understands its ways it is said [Psalm 25.9] 'the meek He will guide in judgment: and the meek He will teach his way.' Even as it is necessary that the intelligent man be pudent in the presence of others, so must he be pudent when alone. It was said that 'pudency and faith are interdependent, and neither can be complete without the other' . . . He who wishes to acquire pudency should associate with those who are modest with respect to him . . . Al-faḍil[31] says: 'By reason of belief and piety, men dwell together for a time. Afterwards they are kept together by reason of modesty, pudency and blamelessness.' Aristotle said in his discourse, 'As a result of modesty one's helpers are multiplied' . . . He who desires to guard this quality should not trifle away his dignity when asked to serve men, for when thou hast once worn out thy dignity, thou wilt find no one to renew it for thee. To be [over-]pudent in speaking the truth or enjoining good

acts, in spreading religion and devotion, is blame-
worthy. The saint said [Psalm 119.46] 'I will speak of
thy testimonies also before kings, and will not be
ashamed' . . . To sum up, according to the opinion of
the philosophers and the sages, this quality is one of the
virtues of the noble soul, and its relation to these is as
that of the spirit to the body. A philosopher said,
'modesty consists in conducting affairs in the best way
wherein it is possible for them to be conducted, and in
leaving them in their best aspects'. He who is modest
will attain to power.

Of alertness, which belongs with wrath, good-will, and
jealousy, to the sense of smell, Ibn Gabirol writes:[32]

I must preface, in treating of this quality, of what nature
it is derived. I would hold that it is of the yellow gall
species. This quality appears usually when the soul is
free from other blameable qualities and when it is not
mingled with aught of grief, and most frequently it is
found in pure and noble souls. Man ought to make use
of it in whatsoever work of art or science he is
engrossed. Was it not said of him [Proverbs 12.27], 'the
substance of a diligent man is precious', which means
that the most precious virtue of the lofty is wide-
awakeness, both in the present and the future life? . . .
In the world *de generatione et corruptione*, he is wide-
awake in his quest of knowledge as well as goodness of
service and faith, and in the attempt to attain to the
world of the intellect. With reference to the reverse of
this quality, i.e. weakness of purpose in worldly affairs
and in the attempt to save souls, it has been said
[Proverbs 24.10], 'if thou faint in the day of adversity,
thy strength is small.' . . . [Proverbs 12.24] 'the hand of
the diligent shall bear rule, but the slothful shall be
under tribute'. Concerning this the poet spake: 'If the
souls become too greatly ambitious, the bodies will be

wearied thereby' . . . The sage . . . exhorted to wide-awakeness in matters religious and worldly in saying [Proverbs 19.5], 'slothfulness casteth into a deep sleep'. This saying is very evident . . . For when the vapours, which are designed to exude from the pores of the body through forcible movements, are motionless and do not dissolve, they mount to the brain, and bring about constant drowsiness . . . The ethical aspect of this quality is, man must not display it in his lust. He shall not be rash in this through his wrath . . . But one ought to employ wide-awakeness in matters relating to religion and law . . . But that intense wide-awakeness which leads to hastiness is culpable . . . A verse reads: 'a cautious man will realize his desires. But he who hastens unduly is bound to stumble' . . . The beauty of the state of wide-awakeness lies in its being potential in the soul and not appearing quickly in action.

4

METAPHYSICS

WITHIN Jewry, or at any rate that portion of it which uses
the Sephardic rite at prayer, it is Solomon ibn Gabirol's
liturgical poetry that has kept his memory green. So long as
Christian scholasticism remained the intellectual framework
of western Europe—i.e. until the Reformation, and somewhat beyond in countries that remained Catholic—his name
in the form Avicebrol or Avicebron (compare Ibn Rushd
> 'Averroes', etc) was well known as that of the author of
the philosophical work entitled *Fountain of Life* (*Fons Vitæ*).
He was not referred to as 'rabbi', unlike Maimonides who
was known as Rabi Mosse [Aegyptus], nor as Judaeus (cf.
Isaac Israeli = Isaac Judaeus), and will have been assumed to
have been a Muslim. The generally current story is that in
1846 the orientalist Salomon Munk astonished both the
world of learning and the Jewish community internationally
by revealing from a literary discovery (see p. 41) that the
philosopher Avicebron and the poet Ibn Gabirol were one
and the same.[1] As we are about to explain, the knowledge
of their identity had not, in point of fact, entirely vanished
from Jewish consciousness. But the circumstance that the
work contains nothing specifically Jewish (or, for that
matter, Islamic or Christian) has lent a lingering plausibility
to the fallacy, although the very title ought to have given
the show away. Consequently, before we survey the book's
contents, we may plot out its story from the date of its
composition—*c.* 1046—until Munk's article, published eight
hundred years later.

The book is cited as early as the twelfth century under the
Hebrew title *Meqor ḥayyim* ('Fountain of Life'); and it may be

assumed that since the Arabic original was not, apparently, intended for an exclusively Jewish readership, Ibn Gabirol himself will have translated the title into *kitab yanbu' al-ḥayat* (since the surviving Arabic is fragmentary this cannot be checked).[2] The title comes from Psalm 36.10(9), 'for with Thee is the fountain of life: in thy light we see light'. Since quotations from the Hebrew Bible are unknown as book-titles in Islam, and equally in medieval Christianity, the fact that the work is so styled ought to have spoken for itself to scholars of the nineteenth century, who were also in a position to know of the following references to it in medieval and later Jewish sources.

[1. The Latin translation was made by John of Seville (died 1157) and Dominicus Gundissalinus.[3] The Latin title refers to Avicebrol, i.e. there is no mention of the author as a Jew.]

2. In 1144, Abraham ibn Da'ud completed an *apologia* for Judaism written in Arabic which was translated into Hebrew in the late fourteenth century[4] with the title *'Emunah ha-ramah* ('Exalted Faith'). In it he severely criticizes Ibn Gabirol's work, referring to it explicitly as *Meqor ḥayyim*.[5] He may also have translated the *Meqor ḥayyim* into Latin.[6]

3. Shem Ṭob b. Joseph Falaquera (Palquera) in his comment-ary *Moreh ha-moreh*[7] (completed 1280) on Maimonides' *Guide for the Perplexed* frequently cites the *Meqor ḥayyim* without the name but as Ibn Gabirol's work, but in one passage he mentions author and title together.[8] We shall revert to Falaquera below.

4. Enoch b. Solomon Al-consṭanṭini (*c*. 1370) quotes Ibn Gabirol in his unpublished *Mar'oth 'elohim* ('Divine Visions'). Details are not accessible to me.[9]

5. Eli b. Joseph Habillo, a Jew of Castile, commenting after 1470–72 on Thomas Aquinas' reference to the *Fons Vitæ* of Avicebron[10] explicitly identifies 'Avisibron' with Ibn Gabirol.[11]

6. Isaac Abravanel, writing in 1511/12, refers in his

commentary on I Kings 3.12 to Ibn Gabirol as author of the *Meqor ḥayyim*.[12]

7. His son Judah, better known as Leone Ebreo, who had been forcibly baptized but probably reverted to Judaism, refers in his *Dialoghi di amore* (Venice, 1545) to 'il *nostro* Albenzubron nel suo libro de fonte vitæ'.[13]

8. Shabbethai Bass, the first Jewish bibliographer (1680), credits the *Meqor ḥayyim* to Ibn Gabirol.[14]

The obvious lacuna in the foregoing list is mention of a Hebrew translation of the Arabic original. It was, however, translated, at least in part, by Falaquera (see above, 3); and the Hebrew selections of the *Meqor ḥayyim* appended to his *Moreh ha-moreh* were published by S. Munk in 1857.[15] Munk himself naturally made no claim to having shown that Ibn Gabirol had written a work entitled *Meqor ḥayyim*: he had merely proved, from collation of the Hebrew selections with the Latin *Fons Vitæ*, that Ibn Gabirol = Avicebron, and that his *Meqor ḥayyim* could be recovered from the Latin version. The enthusiasm that greeted his supposed literary 'discovery' reflects, first, the age-long Jewish neglect of Ibn Gabirol *qua* philosopher as contrasted with, e.g. Baḥya ibn Paquda's Arabic *Duties of the Heart* which, translated into Hebrew, remained a popular classic. Secondly, there was probably an apologetic factor at work in that, in the nineteenth century, culturally integrating western Jewry—predominantly Ashkenazic, and therefore not even familiar with Ibn Gabirol's liturgical poetry— welcomed the opportunity of demonstrating that a text so significant for European scholasticism as the *Fons Vitæ* had proved, emanated from a Jew who had remained faithful to his own religious confession.

The essential framework of Neoplatonism for an under-standing of the *Meqor ḥayyim* has been adumbrated (pp. 28–30). Attention must also be drawn to the palpable influence on Ibn Gabirol's system of the mystical philosopher

Muḥammad ibn Masarra (883–931) who was born in Cordoba. A synopsis of the work will now be given, but it is necessary to preface it with a caveat regarding the use of the terms *universal form* and *matter*, or *prime matter*, that occur in the synopsis itself and on the diagram illustrating the cosmology of the *Royal Crown* (p. 114). Terms like *primeval* are used here to indicate notional (and not necessarily temporal) priority, and are not to be understood to assert that that to which they refer has existed eternally. Nothing in Ibn Gabirol's thinking compromises the uniquely eternal quality of the Deity. 'Immaterial' matter, and 'universal' form, with which as a *sub-stratum* all phenomena and abstract concepts are diagrammatically connected through a series of intermediary stages, are all conceived by him as having been created within time.

It is worthwhile also taking note of the biblical context from which he chose the title for his book: not least, because it will help to clarify how in the *Royal Crown*—which nowhere ignores or conflicts with, but rather pre-supposes the scheme of the *Meqor ḥayyim* and indeed specifically alludes to it (IX, p. 122)—the author has no difficulty in regarding his two statements as being identical, in the sense of being inter-dependently complementary like the two sides of the same coin. For him there is no contrived synthesis here (see below, p. 104). His Jewish contemporaries, like many (perhaps most) believing Jews today, were unable to appreciate the relevance of a philosophical system within which institutional Judaism and its notion of revelation could be subsumed, rather than being themselves manifestly essential building-blocks. They possibly convinced themselves that it was doctrinal matters (regarding which most of them could not themselves have given an articulate account), rather than an understandable exasperation with Ibn Gabirol's mercurial temperament, that justified their breach with him (see p. 21). Subsequent Jewish generations have saved themselves the intellectual effort of examining the complementarity of the *Meqor ḥayyim* and the

Royal Crown by in effect consigning the former to oblivion, and printing the latter for private reading on the Day of Atonement—and largely leaving it unread.

The title comes from Psalm 36, verses 6–13 (English 5–11):

> Thy mercy, O Lord, is in the heavens; and thy faithfulness reacheth to the clouds. Thy righteousness is like the great mountains; thy judgments are a great deep; O Lord, Thou preservest man and beast. How excellent is thy loving-kindness, O God! Therefore the children of men put their trust under the shadow of thy wings. They shall be abundantly satisfied with the fatness of thy house; and Thou shalt make them drink of the river of thy pleasures. For with Thee is the fountain of life [*meqor hayyim*]; in thy light we see light. O continue thy loving-kindness unto them that know Thee: and thy righteousness to the upright in heart. Let not the foot of pride come against me, and let not the hand of the wicked remove me.

The *Meqor hayyim* has as its subject-matter the consideration of universal matter and universal form, the reciprocal relation of these, and the implications regarding a theory of the soul. It is divided into five parts and begins with the author's own summary:

'*Part i* deals with essential preliminaries for establishing of what universal matter and form are, and what constitutes matter and form in phenomena. *Part ii* deals with [non-material] substance and underlying corporeal form. *Part iii* deals with the reality of simple, i.e. non-composite substances. *Part iv* deals with the cognition of matter and form in simple substances; and *Part v* with the essence of universal form and universal matter.'

I here give a synopsis of the whole treatise,[16] which is cast in the form of a dialogue between master and disciple. This is no more than a pedagogic device, met with also in medieval

43

Latin treatises, for achieving clarification or emphasis, and there is present none of the subtlety that lends the Platonic dialogue a charm which constitutes it an art-form in its own right.

Part i: It is a human obligation to fulfil man's final cause by the prosecution of enquiry; this, and its consequences, bring the soul to the superior world, beginning through self-knowledge, and through the endeavour to acquire knowledge—above all knowledge of the primeval being that underlies all things—and to act rightly. For this the appropriate tools are the senses. Prime being cannot be known except through its products.

Universal [created] being consists of universal matter and universal form, the first being the *locus* of the second. Knowledge is tripartite—knowledge of form and matter, that of the will, and that of prime being; since of all things prime being is the cause, form and matter are the created effect, and will is the intermediary instrument. A necessary preliminary to the understanding of the relationship of matter and form is the understanding of the soul—its substance and faculty of cognition.

Knowledge of matter and form proceeds from the identification of their inseparably inherent properties, those of matter being: existence, unique essence, and capacity to sustain the variety of entities on each of which it confers an individual name and essence, diversity deriving from form. Thus the heavens evince form in their colour, shape, physical reality, substantiality, etc.; identification of these leads to the postulation of the existence of a created entity that is their vehicle, i.e. that almost boundless matter whose limit is God. By reversing the analytical process one can discover the presence of universal matter in all particular entities. The fact that diversity is exclusively due to form may be illustrated from different pieces of golden jewellery, their matter being like that of gold bullion.

The properties of universal form are subsistence in something other than itself, and the realization of the potentiality of its *locus*. Individual forms necessarily rest upon a sustaining agent; otherwise they would themselves have to be considered sustainers of the entities concerned, and this is the function of matter. Without form, the existence of matter is potential only. The diversity of the four elements must rest upon something common to them all, form being an accident. But their mutually antagonistic qualities would prevent their combination; and, generation being the result of the combination of opposites, it could not take place except through the action of something external to the elements themselves.

Part ii: In the same way that a body is a physical entity informed by shape, colour, etc., so matter itself must consist of [underlying universal and indivisible] matter, and form. If a number of objects is arranged serially, at one extreme there will stand universal matter that sustains the remainder, and at the other, visible form. In between, each anterior, more subtle entity is the matter of its coarser successor which is form, alternating right through the series. It follows that visible matter is the form of invisible, universal matter *qua* substance, corresponding to the Aristotelian quintessence. One may therefore construct the series, working backwards, (i) individual natural matter, subsisting in (ii) universal natural matter, which in turn subsists in (iii) universal celestial matter, and (iii) in (iv) universal corporeal matter, and (iv) in (v) universal spiritual matter: the last thus necessarily comprises all the rest. The analogous affiliation regarding form is (a) individual natural form, (b) universal natural form, (c) universal celestial form, (d) universal corporeal form, and (e) universal spiritual form.

The substance of the [rational] soul, being close to that of intelligence, can apprehend form without exposure to doubt. Thanks to its subtlety of substance it apprehends everything inferior, i.e. more coarse than itself: and can also apprehend what is superior to itself, such apprehension, however, being the apprehension by an effect of what causes it. The capacity of the intelligence to apprehend form, as something distinct from its *locus*, indicates that forms do, in fact, exist independently. All forms (colour, shape, and similar accidents) are sustained by quantity, and quantity by substance; prime universal matter is like ruled parchment ready for the scribe. Universal matter, *qua* substance, is the *locus* of all the other nine Aristotelian categories (quantity, quality, etc.); and the understanding of this relationship opens the way to the understanding of what is not subject to sense-perception. Experience of physical accident and substance impresses itself on to the sense-organs, but more subtly on to the imagination, and to an even greater degree upon the soul; and the relation of sensible form to the soul resembles that of the written symbols in a book to a reader. Since the inferior is the product of the superior, the inferior mirrors it, and may therefore be used as a means of attaining knowledge regarding the superior. Comparison may therefore be drawn between substance, to which the conventional categories apply, and prime universal matter.

Material substance is necessarily passive, being limited by its quantity and being itself remote from the source of all movement: its receptivity to the action of intelligible substances being similar to the effect of the sun's penetration of what is exposed to it. (Strictly speaking, substance should be differentiated from matter, in that substance may refer to matter already subjected to form; but since what is here concerned is the *substratum* constituted by [matter+] quantity, the two terms are used interchangeably.) The agent that renders actual the potentiality in substance is the will, which impresses forms on it and maintains their equilibrium within it.

Substance, which itself requires no *locus*, is itself the *locus* of quality. But the 'hierarchy' of *loci*, which begin with God's knowledge and end with the *locus* of one body situated within another, consists of two series—spiritual *loci* and corporeal ones. Quantity is also a form without which substance cannot exist, but it can be understood only as an aspect of prime universal form. Created by the infinite and unchangeable One, it is itself likewise a unity, but a unity both finite and subject to change, being divisible and graduated. The nearer that matter which it informs is to its original source the simpler, and vice versa.

The unity which calls into being the matter of intelligence is in essence simple, indivisible, and non-multipliable: its divisibility in actual fact is accidental. Being emulative of its own cause—the ultimate One—the substance of intelligence can understand all the unities (i.e. forms) which constitute the essence of everything, comprising their diversity within its own (relative) simplicity. On the other hand the 'unity' of the soul is subject to growth and to change. The process of progressive coarsening may be compared to the change in water which, pure as it springs from its source, becomes gradually more murky. Thus quantity subsisting in substance is produced by a combination of multiple unities. Whereas accidental form can be actually separated from its substance, 'substantial' form cannot be so separated other than notionally.

It is matter and form that likewise comprise all intelligible entities, be they universal or particular, i.e. spiritual substances—nature, the tripartite soul, and intelligence. Just as the soul sustains and contains the body whilst remaining always distinct from it, so universal spiritual substance contains the universal body without ever being in direct contact with it; the relationship of light to air is comparable.

Part iii: (1–10). Fifty-six arguments are advanced to demonstrate the necessity of postulating a substance intermediary between the Creator, or first author, and substance as underlying the categories of definition.

(11–16). The emanation of substances, by means of which they communicate their form in imitation of the action of the first author, in so far as they find suitable material on which to work. The finer and more luminous a substance is, the more powerful is its effect in action, which derives from the will.

(17–26). Forms in corporeal substance are the product of simple substances which themselves emanate from sensible forms.

(27–36). Spiritual categories that correspond to the material ones. Form exists in the essence of simple substances. The union, both physical and spiritual, of sensible forms.

(37–42). The soul, which since it possesses the faculty of potential cognition, must also possess actual cognition. It is in their conjunction in the soul that sensible forms have their existence, albeit in a lesser degree than in intelligence, which can apprehend the essence of everything, i.e. both its unifying and its simple form; the apprehension of the soul extends merely to apprehension of non-essence, i.e. accident.

(43–51). Analysis of the impressions of simple substances on complex matter, and the interaction of simple substances; proceeding from the axioms that (a) the natural state of the body is at rest, and (b) that all action presupposes an agent. The composition and maintenance of composite bodies thus implies a compositor. The inter-action of simple substances is evinced in the action of the vegetative soul through the growth, reproduction, etc., of vegetable organisms; similarly, locomotion, the movement of thought-processes, cognition and reason afford evidence of the activity of the animal and rational souls respectively, and of intelligence. Inter-relationship of simple substances is expressed in their mutual actions. The activity of nature— i.e. attraction, retention, transformation, and expulsion— relates to the vegetative soul; sensation and movement in animated organisms correspond to the action of the animal soul; this action in turn being outclassed by that of the rational soul that can perceive intelligible objects, even though this faculty again is inferior to the action of intelligence which (being the most perfect of all simple substances) can actually apprehend them. Although everything contained in the inferior is also the property of the superior, the reverse does not hold good.

(52–57). Simple substances relate to each other in terms of emanation, causality, and substantiality: the lower emanates from the higher as a force, to become in its turn the substance of the next lower emanation. The closer that matter is to the origin of force, the better is it predisposed to respond to the action of that force. The will, which is the force that produced simple substances, is infinite in essence albeit finite in effect. Conversely, the substance of intelligence is, *qua* effect, finite: but inasmuch as it is a non-temporal, simple substance, it is infinite.

(58). Man, as microcosm, mirrors the macrocosm, the order of the individual soul corresponding to that of the universe. The ultimate object of cognition is universal activity and passivity.

Part iv: (1–6). Were simple substances pure matter they would be undifferentiated: were they pure form they would be unsubstantiated. Their combination, as matter and form, is proved by (*inter alia*) the changeability of the soul, which is in motion towards the good.

(7–13). Universal intelligible matter and universal sensible matter constitute, between them, one absolutely universal matter: and similarly in the case of form. Prime matter exists as a unity, and similarly universal form: for it is only in virtue of its being united with form that universal matter can be said to exist. Universal form derives its unity from the impression of the sole Creator; existence being the product not of impression, but of creation.

49

(14–18). Form is unity subjected to creation, and it differentiates itself according to its particular material *substratum*.

(19–20). Since the will, infinite in essence, is finite in action, it is possible to speak of a relative distance (in a spiritual, but not in any spatial sense) from the divine origin. The form of intelligence, since it both owes its existence to a Creator and itself unites with matter, is finite. Universal form, inasmuch as it falls within the essence of the will, is like an effect that is inherent in its own cause.

Part v: (1). Intelligence can apprehend universal form and universal matter, (a) because of its own extreme simplicity and fineness of texture, and (b) because universal form and universal matter constitute its own essence, which it understands. Intelligence can also apprehend what is superior to itself, in virtue of its being bound thereto.

(2–5). Matter is a spiritual force, existing in itself and lacking form. Form in itself exists as light, which infuses into that wherein it occurs the property and motion of particular species.

(6–11). Form unites with matter as intelligence unites with the soul, and the soul with the body; the product of this union of universal form and universal matter being the substance of the intelligence. Except in relationship to each other, substance and matter are not meaningful terms. The circumstance of being a unity is a constituent property of matter, for matter in itself is a non-entity—merely possessing potential existence in the mind of God—until actuality is conferred upon it by form. Nevertheless, even without form it would still possess a material, non-formal 'existence'.

(12–16). The form of intelligence: the most perfect of forms, uniting as it does in its essence all forms, knowing them and conferring on each its essence and existence, whilst itself possessing no form of its own.

(17–19). Matter receives form from the will according

to its own capacity, and not that of the will itself. The union of universal matter and universal form is not a cognitive act, like the union of intelligence with intelligible objects. Indeed, the only true form is intelligence, which is also styled the active intellect.

(20–21). Greater corporeality implies greater visibility, and vice versa. But spiritual forms have to subsist in corporeal ones, since visible existence is the mirror of the invisible.

(22–24). Universal matter and form cannot be defined, but merely described, the traditional categories of description being applicable. The final cause for which a simple substance exists inheres in itself, this applying equally to its form and to its matter.

(25–27). A résumé of earlier arguments, proving the indispensability, as correlatives, of sustaining agent and sustained object. The Creator's perfection and the imperfection of creation. Matter and form both pre-exist their union, this pre-existence obtaining in God's knowledge.

(28–29). Form and will are ideally one, and form is thus ideally infinite; but it is rendered finite by contact with matter.

(30–34). Form, as issuing from the will—pure light—is light; matter is the *locus* of form, but will is the *locus* of both form and matter. The union of matter and form—essentially dissimilar—is proof of God's power. Matter, desiring the good, moves towards the One in order to become informed, form being the impression of the One upon matter. But matter being internally diversified, such movement is of various kinds: each existent seeking that perfection which corresponds to its own level of existence, and thus tending towards unity.

(35–40). Knowledge of prime essence is impossible, since form and matter stand at the frontiers of cognition. The will is simultaneously identical with the prime essence and also other than it: it may be approximately described as a divine force that creates matter and form and binds them. If the will is the scribe, matter is the paper and form is the written message.

(41–45). Creation consists in the impression, by the will, of form on to matter. (A digression here deals with the knowledge of the soul.) Creation may be compared to the formation of words—the articulation of sounds, and the notion of speaking.

Conclusion: Created existing things consist of nothing but universal matter and universal form. Movement proceeds from the will, which is a divine force that pervades everything. Beyond, there lies the world of the Deity, knowledge of which is not attainable save through the knowledge of the will. The prosecution of such investigation leads to bliss: 'in pursuit of it, one must renounce the sensible world, and so attach oneself entirely to God from whom all good proceeds'.

There are a few logical faults in the course of Ibn Gabirol's argument which are pointed out by Schlanger in the notes to his French translation of the *Meqor ḥayyim*. However, these may be due to faulty Latin translation of the original Arabic (the holograph of which, and probably all copies, will have been written in Hebrew characters), or to textual corruption of the Latin itself, which can occasionally be corrected from Falaquera's Hebrew selections. In general, however, Ibn Gabirol's syllogistic reasoning is rigorous. It is understandable that as Aristotelianism waxed as the accepted scientific universe of discourse, Neoplatonism waned. Maimonides, who accepted Aristotle's methodology whilst rejecting (on speculative and not dogmatic grounds) his axiom of the eternity of matter, wrote dismissively of the Neoplatonic school, characterizing Isaac Israeli (see pp. 30f.) as 'merely a doctor';[17] he does not mention Ibn Gabirol by name. The modern student, for whom Neoplatonism is even more remote, needs to make an intellectual effort to come to terms with the magnitude of his metaphysical scheme and to appreciate that, had Ibn Gabirol omitted to construct it, he would surely have felt his own vocation as a Jewish thinker to be as unfulfilled as would Maimonides, had he failed to find opportunity to write his *Guide for the Perplexed*. In the present century Isaac Husik pronounced the *Meqor ḥayyim* to be 'a peculiar combination of logical formalism with mystic obscurity, or profundity, according to one's view'.[18] More to the point is the recognition that the *Meqor ḥayyim*, which is presupposed and occasionally alluded to in the *Royal Crown*, was for its author a preliminary study, without which he would probably have felt himself unequipped to write what is surely his *chef d'œuvre*.

5

SOCIAL POETRY

THE conventional division of medieval Hebrew poetry into classes labelled 'sacred' and 'secular' misrepresents one of the major categories of Jewish thought by misconstruing the significance of the Hebrew terms *qodesh* and *ḥol*. The relationship between the two spheres is a complementary and not an antipathetic one. The fundamental notion underlying the root *q-d-sh* is *reserve*: it is significant that the post-biblical Hebrew term for *to betroth* is *le-qaddesh*. God is *qadosh*, holy, as being utterly self-reserved, although those whom He particularly marks out, as well as produce (such as first-fruits) on which He has a claim, and activities overtly associated with his worship or carried out in accordance with prescriptions which He is deemed to have revealed, become, by association with Him, in some sense reserved, i.e. consecrated. *ḥ-l-l*, the root of *ḥol*, includes amongst its meanings (in Arabic, though not in Hebrew) that of *untie*; and *ḥol* is the corollary of *qodesh* in that it is (metaphorically) 'untied', i.e. de-restricted and fit for common use, or unrestricted; although it is of the essence of the Jewish understanding of the numinous quality indispensable to spirituality that the sphere of *qodesh*, the naturally holy together with what has been consecrated, evinces a constant tendency to encroach on what is common (*ḥol*), whilst implicitly acknowledging that to annexe it completely would vitiate the divine economy.

In regard to medieval Hebrew poetry it is important to appreciate that the idiom of these two spheres is one and the same. The Jewish daily round, with its ideal of finding a hundred opportunities each day on which to acknowledge one's God-awareness by reciting a benedictional formula, can never become unconscious of its framework of a theologically aware spirituality, which the institutions of Judaism are designed, by their rhythm, to enunciate and to foster. Whilst the language of these institutions is basically ceremonial rather than verbal, their validating source is either explicit, or at least discoverable, within the Hebrew Bible. Thus it is the content of the Bible, and the register of Hebrew in which it is written, which above all else has informed the Jewish poet's mind until, in recent times, it has come to be regarded as a stranglehold by modern Hebrew writers. The way in which the poet uses biblical reminiscence and quotation—whether assertively, pathetically, ironically, or paradoxically—is not noticeably different according to whether he is inditing a hymn or penning a letter to his friend. The poem in which Samuel Ha-nagid reported to his son his successful relief of the siege of Lorca contains, in its thirty-one lines, at least seventeen immediately recognizable biblical allusions.

The distinction, then, between the two classes of poetic writing is essentially one of *occasion*, which may sometimes dictate the style as well as determining the pattern: and in place of the misleading labels 'sacred' and 'secular' poetry we ought rather to speak of 'liturgical' and 'social' poetry. The liturgical occasion will determine, in broad terms, the theme. For example, an introduction to the *qedushah* ('holy, holy, holy,' etc.) will have to include some description of the angels, and/or draw the parallel between their celestial litany and Israel's worship, and a *ge'ullah* (introduction to the blessing of God 'who hast redeemed Israel') will take redemption as its theme—rather like the key in which a musical composition is to be written—even though the burden of its message may be the apparent failure of redemption from exile to materialize. Social poetry has no such markers integral to its Jewish background; but the circumstance of its adoption of conventions of this genre of

Arabic poetry—even, in the case of highly erotic poems concerning friendship between men, to the point of straining the terms of reference of Jewish ethics which the very fact of writing in Hebrew must be assumed to assert—is eloquent of the degree of Spanish-Jewish acculturation, not least if, as has been maintained (not quite convincingly) by some, the homosexual element here alluded to is but a literary conceit.[1]

Jarden's edition of Ibn Gabirol's social poems includes 294 items, which he groups[2] under the following headings: *Friendship and Praise; Separation; Self-vaunting; Self-pity; Ironical Mockery; Elegy; Asceticism; Nature; Wine; Love,* and a further thirteen poems on miscellaneous topics. Space precludes quoting more than a few, and it cannot even be claimed that those few are fully representative. It must also be recognized that, not surprisingly in so large an *oeuvre,* some poems have survived that might have been better forgotten.

Whilst the economic dependence of a poet on a patron can sometimes engender tensions which—at least in the case of Ibn Gabirol—might find expression in expostulatory verse, it ought not to be assumed that because the patron looked to his protégé for service in regard to his public relations (see pp. 13, 22), the poet's attitude towards him was always an essentially obsequious one. Their situation did not preclude the growth of a mutually appreciative friendship stemming from shared intellectual interests and a universe of discourse, implicit in which was a religious system and a political philosophy held in common. Such is the background to the easy relationship that made Virgil and Horace welcome in the house of the emperor Augustus and that of his minister Maecenas, and it applies equally to the case of Ibn Gabirol and his patron Samuel Ha-nagid, vizier of King Ḥabbus of Granada and his son Badis (see p. 21). The following poem[3] addressed to Samuel falls into place neatly alongside Horace's ode *iam satis terris*[4] addressed to Augustus:

Faith! Thine is understanding wide
As Ocean, and thy learning's art
With answers leaves all satisfied
In mind, thy law makes wise their heart.

Thy visage from an angel's face
Was surely filched: words thou dost find
To guide, might come from that same place
Whence ten commandments were once mined.

How strange! An age when God decreed
Thou shouldst be born, doth not repent
Each day! Thy parents' only[5] seed,
Ten thousand sons' joy has thou meant.

Thou buildest on thy wisdom's site
The world, its fruits to multiply:
In thee the Master's pupils might
His rival Samuel[6] descry.

Dear friend, thy friendship—as God lives—
Is close to my heart as my soul;
If, then, my conversation gives
Thee pleasure, whilst the honeyed bowl

Of words thy lips distil please me,
Then I, though exiled, yet may know
That joy which Israel's few did see
When ewers in God's shrine did flow.[7]

$- - \cup$ $- - \cup$ $- - \cup$	$- - \cup$ $- - \cup$ $- - \cup$
וְתוֹרָתְךָ לְכָל נֶפֶשׁ מְשִׁיבָה	תְּבוּנָתְךָ, אֱמֶת, מַיִם רְחָבָה,
וְצוּרָתְךָ, אֱמֶת, מֵהֶם גְּנוּבָה	וּמַרְאָתְךָ כְּמַרְאוֹת מַלְאֲכֵי אֵל,
כְּאִלּוּ מֵעֲשָׂרָה וְהִיא] חֲצוּבָה	וּמִלָּתְךָ בְּדַבֶּרְךָ נְגִידִים,
וְלֹא עוֹשִׂים מְתָיו כָּל יוֹם תְּשׁוּבָה	וְאֶתְמַהּ כִּי בְרָאֲךָ אֵל בְּדוֹר זֶה

וְאַתְּ לָהֶם כְּמוֹ אַלְפֵי רְבָבָה
וּמִלֵּאת פְּנֵי תֵבֵל תְּנוּבָה
קְרָאוּךָ שְׁמוּאֵל רֹאשׁ יְשִׁיבָה.
אֱלֵי לִבִּי כְּמוֹ נַפְשִׁי קְרוֹבָה
וְאֶרְוָה צוּף שְׂפָתְךָ הָעֲרֵבָה
שְׁאֵרִית עַם לְבִנְיָן הַשְּׁאוּבָה.

יְלָדוּךָ אֲבוֹתֶיךָ לוֹ וֶה,
וּבָנִית בְּחָכְמָתָךְ יְסוֹדוֹת
וְאָמְנָם, לוֹ יְדָעוּךָ בְּנֵי רַב,
יְדִיד נַפְשִׁי, יְדִידוּתָךָ, וְחַי אֵל,
וּמִי יִתֵּן וְשִׂיחוֹתַי עֲרֵבוֹת,
וְאֶשְׂמַח בָּךְ בְּנָלוּתִי, כְּשִׂמְחַת

Samuel Ha-nagid died in December 1056. Around 1060 his
son Joseph (or Yehoseph) commenced the construction of the
Alhambra, vividly described, with its court of the lion-
fountain, in the following poem which is clearly addressed to
Joseph although he is not named in it:[8]

> Ah, come, my radiant friend, along with me,
> Let's lodge us in the villages. For, see,
> The winter's past, and now on every hand
> We hear the voice of turtles in our land.
> We'll linger in the shade and take our ease
> Neath pomegranates, palms and apple trees;
> We'll stroll amid the vines, and peer to see
> The gentle folk who live in luxury
> Within a palace set upon a height,
> Built of the finest stones, a splendid sight,
> On strong foundations firmly fixed, and bound
> With fortress-walls and turrets all around,
> With level galleries above, which show
> The fine display of courtyards far below.
> The chamber-walls are intricately wrought
> With carvings and reliefs of every sort,
> While many-coloured marbles pave the floors,
> And who could count the number of the doors,
> Of reddish hue, as though of algum-wood,
> Like those which in the Halls of Ivory stood,
> And set above the doors are windows bright
> Whose clear transparent panes let in the light.
> The dome is like a royal palanquin
> On which suspended ornaments are seen
> Revolving in a multicoloured whirl

Of onyx and of sapphire and of pearl—
That is by day, but when the sunlight dies
It seems that stars hang in the darkened skies.
It is a sight to sweeten bitter minds,
And here the troubled spirit comfort finds:
I looked at it, and soon forgot my care,
My heart was freed from pangs of deep despair,
My joyful body seemed to float on high
As though an eagle bore me through the sky.
A brimming pool recalls the molten sea[9]
Which oxen bore aloft, but here there be
No oxen tame, but lions in fierce array
Along the margin, roaring for their prey;
The gushing water issues from their maws
And from their mouths in constant streams it pours.
Along the channels there are hollow fawns
Which sprinkle purest water on the lawns
And spray the plants and flowers in the beds
And shower gentle raindrops on the heads
Of myrtle bushes, which release their scents
Upon the air like clouds of frankincense,
And singing birds are glimpsed among the bowers
And in the beds below are fragrant flowers,
As spikenards, roses, henna-plants and balms,
Which vie each with the rest to vaunt their charms,
Though all are passing fair. The hennas claim:
'Our brightness puts the moon and sun to shame,'
While pigeons coo and murmur, and declare:
'Our song is for the doves, that we may snare
Their hearts, for they are precious past compare.'[10]
Then up there rise the pretty boys and maids
Whose glory all the others overshades,
And they too vie their splendours to disclose,
For they resemble young gazelles or roes.
But as the sun began to sing their praise
I answered: 'Silence, sun, deflect your rays,
And praise instead the man who, with his light,

Has darkened you, and hidden you from sight.
Before him kings and ministers give way,
By him kings rule and ministers hold sway:
They have appointed him their overlord,
They are like cattle when the lion has roared;
He guides them like an angel from above,
A shepherd who protects his flocks with love.
And surely no more lavish spirit lives:
Where others merely promise, this man gives;
His undimmed eye is never sought in vain,
His cloud has not withheld its needed rain,
His actions fit his words, it may be said,
As close as golden crown fits royal head.
All rulers flock to him as eagerly
As mighty rivers rush to join the sea.
In truth, he is the lord of all the earth:
He equals the entire creation's worth.'

– – ∪ – – ∪ – – ∪	– – ∪ – – ∪ – – ∪
לְכָה עִמִּי וְנָלִין בַּכְּפָרִים	לְכָה, רֵעִי וְרַע הַמְּאוֹרִים,
בְּאַרְצֵנוּ הֲמוֹן סִיסִים וְתוֹרִים	וְהִנֵּה הַסְּתָו עָבַר, וְנִשְׁמַע
וְתַפּוּחַ וְכָל צִמְחֵי הֲדָרִים	וְנִתְלוֹנֵן בְּצֵל רִמּוֹן וְתָמָר
וְנִשְׁתּוֹקֵק רְאוֹת פָּנִים הֲדוּרִים	וְנִתְהַלֵּךְ בְּצֵלֵי הַגְּפָנִים
וְנִכְנְסָה בָּאֲבָנִים הַיְקָרִים	בְּאַרְמוֹן נַעֲלָה עַל כָּל סְבִיבָיו
וְקִירוֹתָיו כְּמִגְדָּלִים בְּצוּרִים	אֲשֶׁר תָּכַּן עֲלֵי נָכוֹן, שְׁתוֹתָיו
שְׂרוֹנִים פֵּאֲרוּ כָל הַחֲצֵרִים	וְיָצִיעַ מְיֻשָּׁר-מִסְּבִיבָיו
בְּכָפְתּוֹחִים פְּתוּחִים וַעֲטוּרִים	וְהַבָּתִּים בְּנוּיִּים וַעֲרוּיִּים
וְלֹא אוּכַל סְפֹר כַּמָּה שְׁעָרִים	מְרָצָּפִים בְּאַבְנֵי שֵׁשׁ וּבַהַט
מְאֻדָּמִים כְּאַלְגֻּמֵּי דְבִירִים	וְדַלְתוֹתָם כְּדַלְתֵי הֵיכְלֵי שֵׁן
שְׁמָשׁוֹת שֶׁכְּנוּ בָהֶם מְאוֹרִים	וְחַלּוֹנִים שְׁקוּפִים מֵעֲלֵיהֶם,
תְּלוּיָה מִשְׁכִיּוֹת הַחֲדָרִים	וְהַקֻּבָּה כְּאַפִּרְיוֹן שְׁלֹמֹה
בִּדְלָחִים וְסַפִּירִים וְדָרִים	אֲשֶׁר תָּסֹב וְתִתְהַפֵּךְ בְּעֵינֵי
כְּשַׁחַק, כּוֹכָבָיו בַּלֵּיל סְדוּרִים	וְזֶה בַיּוֹם, וּבָעֶרֶב דְּמוּתָהּ
וְיִנְשׁוּ אוֹבְדִים רֵישָׁם, וּמְרִים	וּבָהּ יִיטַב לְבַב כָּל רָשׁ וְעָמֵל
וְהִתְנַחֵם לְבָבִי מִמִּצְרִים	רְאִיתִיהָ וְשָׁכַחְתִּי עֲמָלִי
בְּשִׂמְחָתִי כְּעַל כַּנְפֵי נְשָׁרִים	וְכִמְעַט קָם גְּוִיָּתִי תְעוֹפֵף
אֲבָל לֹא יַעֲמֹד עַל הַבְּקָרִים	וְיָם מָלֵא וְיִדְמֶה יָם שְׁלֹמֹה,

וּמַצַּב הָאֲרָיוֹת עַל שְׂפָתוֹ   כְּאִלּוּ שָׁאֲגוּ טֶרֶף כְּפִירִים
אֲשֶׁר קִרְבָּם כְּמַעְיָנִים יְפוּצוּן   עֲלֵי פִיהֶם זְרָמִים כַּנְּהָרִים
וְאַיָּלוֹת שְׁתוּלוֹת בַּתְּעָלוֹת   נְבוּבוֹת לִהְיוֹת מַיִם מְעָרִים
וְלָרֹס הַצַּמְחִים בָּעֲרוּגוֹת   וּבָאִחִים זֹרֵק מַיִם טְהוֹרִים
וְגִנַּת הַהֲדַס בָּהֶם לְהַשְׁקוֹת   אֲמִירִים, כַּעֲנָנִים הֵם וְזוֹרִים
אֲשֶׁר רֵיחָם כְּרֵיחַ הַבְּשָׂמִים   כְּאִלּוּ הֵם מְקֻטָּרִים בְּמוֹרִים
וְעוֹפוֹת יִתְּנוּ קוֹל בָּעֲפָאִים   וְנִשְׁקָפוֹת עֲלֵי כַפּוֹת תְּמָרִים
וְצִצִּים רַעֲנַנִּים נַעֲמָנִים   כְּשׁוֹשַׁנִּים נְרָדִים עִם כְּפָרִים
אֲשֶׁר מִתְפָּאֲרִים הֵם זֶה עֲלֵי זֶה   וְהֵם כֻּלָּם בְּעֵינֵינוּ בְּרוּרִים
וְאוֹמְרִים הַפְּרָחִים כִּי ״אֲנַחְנוּ   לְבָנִים מוֹשְׁלִים עַל הַמְּאוֹרִים״
וְהַיּוֹנִים מְנַהֲגוֹת בַּהֲגוֹתָן   וְאוֹמְרוֹת: ״נַחְנוּ שָׁרוֹת לַתּוֹרִים
אֲשֶׁר בָּהֶם נָכַשֶׁף הַלְּבָבוֹת,   לְמַעַן מִבְּדֶלְחִים יְקָרִים״
וְקָמוּ הַצְּבָאִים כַּבְּתוּלוֹת   וְכִסּוּ אֶת הֲדָרָן בַּהֲדָרִים
וְגַם הִתְפָּאֲרוּ יַחַד עֲלֵיהֶן,   לְמַעַן הֵם כְּאַיָּלִים צְעִירִים
וְעֵת כִּי נַעֲלָה שֶׁמֶשׁ עֲלֵיהֶן –   עֲנִיתִיו: דֹּם וְאַל תַּעֲבֹר מְצָרִים
וְהוֹדָה לַגְּבִיר כִּי הֶחֱשִׁיכֵךְ   בְּאוֹרָה הַמַּעֲלָה בַּמְּאוֹרִים
אֲשֶׁר שַׁח כָּל הֲדַר מֶלֶךְ לְפָנָיו   וְהָיוּ מַעֲלוֹת כָּל שַׂר חֲסֵרִים
אֲשֶׁר בּוֹ יִמְלְכוּ כָל הַמְּלָכִים   וּבוֹ מִתְיַעֲצִים רוֹזְנִים וְשָׂרִים
הֲקֵימוּהוּ כְּמוֹ מַלְכָּם וְהָיָה   כְּפִיר בָּהֶם וְכֻלָּם הַשְּׁוָרִים
וְהוּא בָהֶם כְּמַלְאַךְ הָאֱלֹהִים   בְּעֵת לֹא מָצְאוּ מֵאֵל דְּבָרִים
מְנַהֵל צֹאן עֲלֵי מִרְעֶה מְנוּחוֹת   וְלֹא נֶעְדַּר מְאוּמָה מֵעֲדָרִים
יְקַר נֶפֶשׁ, עֲדֵי שַׁחַק, נְדִיב לֵב,   בְּלִי יְדֹר יְשֻׁלַּם הַנְּדָרִים
אֲשֶׁר לֹא כָהֲתָה עֵינוֹ בְּמַתָּן   וְלֹא עָצֵר כְּמַכֵּן הַמִּסְתָּרִים
אֲשֶׁר מִלָּיו בְּמִפְעָלָיו קְשׁוּרִים   כְּרָאשִׁים נִקְשְׁרוּ בָהֶם כְּתָרִים
וְכָל הָרוֹזְנִים אֵלָיו יְסוֹרְרוּן   וְכַיָּם נִמְשְׁכוּ אֵלַי נְהָרִים
וְאָמְנָם הוּא כְרֹאשׁ שֶׁל הָאֲדָמָה   וְהוּו וַחָד בְּנֶגֶד חַיָּצוֹן יֵשׁ

Songs in celebration of wine are a feature of Arabic poetry that ascends to pre-Islamic times.[11] The following is a specimen of Ibn Gabirol's ten known poems in this genre:[12]

> Friend, lead me through the vineyards, give me wine,
> And to the very brim shall joy be mine;
> Perchance the love you pledge me with each cup
> May rout the troops around my care's ensign.

And if, in love for me, eight toasts you drink,
Fourscore the toasts in love for you I link;
And should I pre-decease you, friend, select
Some spot where vine-roots twist, my grave to sink.

In grape-juice have my body laved, and take
With divers spices, grape-pips—these shall make
All my embalming. Mourn me not, guitar
And pipe with music's sound shall cheer my wake,

And on the place that shall conceal my mould
Let not the earth be heaped and rocks be rolled
To raise a monument: to mark the spot
Rather a pile of wine-jars, new and old.

– – ∪ – – – ∪ – – – ∪	– – ∪ – – – ∪ – – – ∪
וְהַשְׁקֵנִי וְאֶמָּלֵא שְׂשׂוֹנִים	יְדִידִי נַהֲלֵנִי עַל גְּפָנִים
וְאוּלַי הֵם יְנִיסוּן הַיְגוֹנִים	וְכוֹסוֹת אַהֲבָתָךְ יִדְבְּקוּ בִי
אֲנִי אֶשְׁתֶּה בְּאַהֲבָתָךְ שְׁמוֹנִים	וְאִם תִּשְׁתֶּה בְּאַהֲבָתִי שְׁמוֹנֶה
חֲצֹב קִבְרִי בְּשָׁרְשֵׁי הַגְּפָנִים	וְאִם אָמוּת לְפָנֶיךָ, יְדִידִי,
וְחָנְטֵנִי בְּחַרְצַ־ים וְזַנִּים	וְשִׂים רַחֲצִי בְּמֵימֵי הָעֲנָבִים
עֲשֵׂה כָּנוֹר וְעוּגָבִים וּמִנִּים	וְאַל תִּבְכֶּה וְאַל תָּנוּד לְמוֹתִי
אֲבָל כַּדִּים חֲדָשִׁים עִם יְשָׁנִים.	וְאַל תָּשִׂים עֲלֵי קִבְרִי עֲפָרִים

This is astonishingly similar to a quatrain by Ibn Gabirol's younger contemporary the Persian 'Umar ibn Khayyam (1048–1131), rendered unforgettably (and fairly closely) by Edward Fitzgerald:[13]

Ah, with the Grape my fading Life provide,
And wash my Body whence the Life has died,
And in a Windingsheet of Vine-leaf wrapt
So bury me by some sweet Garden-side.

In point of fact, almost all the motifs that Ibn Gabirol uses here are paralleled in Arabic wine-poems; the wine-jars in place of tombstone which form its climax are borrowed from Ibn al-Mu'tazz (861–908). He thus shows that he knew as well as Horace—*dulce est desipere in loco*[14]—how to enjoy relaxation amongst his intellectual peers. But one can understand his irritation with critics who, no doubt considering themselves to be men of culture and education, were not in his intellectual league yet nevertheless ventured to suggest that he come down to their level. Here is his response:[15]

So—if my heart were set on something slight
It wouldn't toil and moil all day and night?
But where, my friends, should I for joy find cause
Or hope for that which, hoped, the more withdraws?
Spent seeking wisdom, yet I know not rest:
Others their vigour spend in passion's quest.
'For once', you urge, 'give way to low-brow fun'.
But ague worse than foolery there's none.
So I must labour unrelenting on
Though I should overtake King Solomon.[16]
The world's a robe I strip: the mind descries
A light-spun robe to don, azure as skies.
Why not? The world spurns me as hopeless, e'er
Of glory baulked that it would claim as heir,
Eager to open sorrow's gates to me
Whilst in the gates of joy it turns the key.
What makes folk say 'How can your heart so prize
A glory that must wither, poppy-wise?
If strive you must peaks yet unscaled to attain,
Each day's child, fortune-sired, your blade shall stain'.
Pray, bid my critics silence; on my ear
Strike empty echoes of God's mutineer.[17]
If earth cannot on me her crown confer,
Then earth of love divine's no connoisseur.
The heights I tread did she appreciate
Long since before my feet she'd been prostrate.
Wisdom's the gold I treasure, and the Lord
Will treasure those who treasure wisdom's hoard.

God's word set in my mouth, a stone divine
To coal transmuted, sears where it did shine.
Like incense, song blends sweet with sharp: man's nose
Must savour both, the word's sense to disclose;
Had such waft from Lot's house through Sodom blown
His door the townsmen's battering had known.[18]

— — — ∪ — — ∪ — —   — ∪ — — — ∪ — — — ∪ — —

„לוּ הָיְתָה נַפְשִׁי מְעַט שׁוֹאֶלֶת	לֹא הָיְתָה לַיְל וְיוֹם עוֹמֶלֶת"
אֵיךְ אֱעֲלֶה, רֵעִי, וּבַמָּה אֱעֲלֵץ ?	הַאִם אֲיַחֵל ? נִמְשְׁכָה תוֹחֶלֶת!
הֵן מִדְּרֹשׁ חָכְמָה בְּשָׂרִי נֶאֱכָל -	וּבְשַׂר אֲחֵרִים אַהֲבָה אוֹכֶלֶת.
„לוּ אֶמְצְאָה סִכְלוּת מְעַט ?" כִּי אֵין לְךָ	מַכָּה אֲנוּשָׁה תַּעֲרֹךְ אַנְלֶת!
עַל כֵּן מְאֹד אִינַע וְלֹא אֶרֶף מְעַט,	לוּ מָצְאָה יָדִי כְּבוֹד קֹהֶלֶת.
אֶפְשַׁט לְבוּשׁ תֵּבֶל, וְהַדַּעַת - לְבוּשׁ	חוּר לָבְשָׁה אוֹ כְסָתָה בְתְכֵלֶת
כִּי מָאֲסָה נַפְשִׁי, כְּאִלּוּ נוֹאֲשָׁה	לִי מִמְּצֹא כָבוֹד וְהִיא נוֹחֶלֶת
דַּלְתֵי יְגוֹנִים פָּתְחָה אֵלַי, הֲכִי	דַּלְתֵי שְׂשׂוֹנִים אַחֲרֵי נוֹעֶלֶת.
מַה לָאֲנָשִׁים יֹאמְרוּ: אֵיךְ תֶּאֱהַב	כָּבוֹד אֲשֶׁר יְמַל כְּרֹאשׁ שִׁבֹּלֶת ?
הֵן כִּי תְבַקֵּשׁ מַעֲלוֹת שֶׁנִּבְצָרוּ -	בִּדְמֵי בְּנֵי יוֹם חַרְדְּךָ נִגְאֶלֶת!
אָמְרוּ לְמוֹכִיחַי - וּמְנִי יֶחֱשׁוּ,	כִּי שָׁמְעָה אָזְנִי דְבַר בֶּן פֶּלֶת
אִם הָאֲדָמָה לֹא תְשִׂימֵנִי לְרֹאשׁ -	אֵין הָאֲדָמָה אַהֲבָה מַשְׂכֶּלֶת
לוּ יָדְעָה מֵאֶתְמוֹל רוּם מַעֲלוֹת	נַפְשִׁי - לְרַגְלַי הָיְתָה נוֹפֶלֶת!
עַל הַיְקָר אֶחְמֹל, וְהָאֵל יַעֲנֶה	נֶפֶשׁ אֲשֶׁר עַל הַיְקָר חוֹמֶלֶת
אוּלֵי אֱלֹהִים שָׁם בְּפִי דָבָר כְּמוֹ	אֶבֶן יְקָרָה - וַתְּהִי נַחֶלֶת
כַּשִּׁיר אֲשֶׁר יוּשַׁר - וְיָרַח אַף אֱנוֹשׁ	מִבֵּין אֲמָרָיו חֶלְבְּנָה וּשְׁחֵלֶת
לוּ כַּצְרִי הַזֶּה בְּבֵית לוֹט יָדְעוּ	אַנְשֵׁי סְדוֹם - הִתְדַּפְּקוּ עַל דֶּלֶת!

Although the irony is marked, there is not here the lightness
of touch which Ibn Gabirol evinced in the wine-poem, and
which is also to be seen in some of his liturgical pieces written
con brio for joyful occasions, such as a wedding, or the theme
of spring in the hymns for the dew-litany on Passover (see
pp. 80–81). But where social poetry is concerned, Ibn
Gabirol is at his greatest when, mirth and witticism laid aside,
his fantastic dexterity with double entendre and reapplied
quotation combine with his magisterial use of metre to give

power to the message that he is concerned to convey. Nowhere is this more apparent than in his great elegy on the death of Yequthiel ibn al-mutawakkil, for the circumstances of whose death in 1039 see pp. 20f.[19] That date is given in the body of the poem by means of a pun on the Hebrew word *teth = giving*, or *paying* [*sc.* the penalty] by his murderers one year later: the double *taw* of *teth* bearing the numerical value of 800, i.e. the 800th year of the fourth millennium of the Jewish calendar, which commenced in 240 CE. The poem also contains valuable evidence regarding the social history of Jews in eleventh-century Spain, and regarding its ideal of philanthropic leadership. Allowance may have to be made for some exaggeration by Ibn Gabirol of the political importance of Yequthiel, whom the Arab chroniclers do not name. But the starkness of the initial words, *biymey yequ'thiel*, ought immediately to call to mind the beginning of the Song of Deborah (after its exordium), *biymey shamgar ben 'anath* (in the days of Shamgar son of Anath),[20] and so hint—as unmistakably as would the initial bars of Beethoven's *Eroica*—that, for the poet at least, the subject of his dirge is a person of epic stature.[21]

'Twas in Yekúthiél's time, which is past,
And passing, symbol-wise, itself must show
That heaven and earth, divinely formed, at last
Shall fade, and in their fading, hence must go.

Pause, then, reflect. Who is this Time, that lays
Snares never yet conceived, hales folk hence, then
Sending yet others hither, makes the days
His hucksters, plying a brisk trade in men?

I cannot make it out, no more than they
Could make it out whom History dubs wise:
Does flesh, disdainful, shoo the soul away,
Or spirit press for her release, to rise?

They're fools who will insist the world's a dream,
Forgetting facts; they're right, yet fail to see
That dreams prate idly, just like folk, who seem
To say a lot, while holding back the key.

The world's cram full of booby-traps, bedecked
In camouflage to dupe the ruder sort:
While kings' fond leagues with Death have none effect,
And nobles' best-laid plans he brings to nought.

Their peoples' call they heed not, till Death's call
Barks out his summons; then none can rebel,
As in the slave-mart pomp and pride soon fall
From prince and prelate, both knocked down to Hell.

Down in a trice, their strength unclutched, they drop;
No prized possession now can bring relief
Or pleas in mitigation—would they stop
Proceedings, not a silk will touch their brief.

Naked they wend their way, stripped of their gains,
That cash they banked in towering piles: the sweets
Of wealth and honour vanished, there remains
The tattered relic of their winding-sheets.

Into the dark they go, their vigour cast
Aside, each ear split open now; confined
Deep down beneath their vaults they hear, at last,
The iron gates of Earth clang shut behind.

Hold hard, Death: stay your hand—why terrorize
Each wretched draft made yours for dungeoning?
Though creatures see in you a judge, who tries,
Each sentence has an unexpected sting.

Some, once their own best friends, stumble, by you
But tapped; life's stumblers clutch your friendly grasp.
Playboys and toughs may sneer, yet through and through
They shudder, struck with panic by your rasp.

If crackling flames set forest tracts ablaze,
And charréd cedars mark where lightning struck,
What hope has groundsel, that beside the ways
The passer-by uproots with but a pluck?[22]

The world's awry, my friends: I see it wears
A mask too sour for me to recognize.
Ignore me, then, if I give way to tears
Of bitterness—chide not, nor criticize.

My lips do chatter—do not ask me why,
When shattered lies the screen that lent me shade:
Yekúthiél is dead, whose wealth could buy
The dying health, and send them on, remade.

Strike down the capital—the thresholds quake;
The pillar falls—its moulded cusps must burst.[23]
A murky smudge leaves Heaven's lights opaque,
And Earth's remaining span is henceforth cursed.

Each day—I didn't know before—displays
Its power to choose, or spurn. Now of all men
The choicest they have snatched; which shows that days
Get into trouble, and give birth to pain.

But all they give me is a brazen stare;
Their crime exposed, they blench not: never sign
A contract, never trust them—they did snare
A covenanted envoy, near-divine.

Some maniacal vow, perhaps, inspires
Their lust to smash all beauty where they raid.
If so, then every jot their oath requires
Is settled: they are quit, but he has paid.

Come, lords of minstrelsy, to conclave: find
Your resolution, clear your thoughts, pass on
To vote me aid; haste, steady me—my mind
Strays, riveted on him, and he is gone.

Tears, weeping's heirs, their duty skimped, run dry,
Then flow—like periodic streams.[24] The heart
Of adamant must be that could defy
Such pain as this, nor yet be riv'n apart.

No danegeld such an onslaught might avert,
A tragedy to sear all hearts: let blight
Blast breasts unmoved—constriction, numbing hurt
Derange them, pluck their hearts clean out with fright!

Despised be Earth, till sympathy shall rock
Her very fundaments: noise not his fate
In God's most favoured Land, lest sorrow shock
Her hills, their naked grief disconsolate.

My people, mourn: fled is the angel, stark
Ruined God's shrine, arms gone, the treasure sacked.
Cry round the town: 'Lost, God's triumphant Ark!
The tablets signed by God's own hand are cracked!'

Spring's month, once sign of miracles, is changed;
Long grow the shadows, once thy shade. Irate
Forth from his lair the beast this day is ranged:
Round Zion hungry lions sit—and wait.

This day, thy diadem of glory falls;
Thy altar's starved of sacrifice, and slow
Curls smoke from temple's inmost courts, from halls
Of study where, hate-gorged, did roar the foe.

Exiled this day the Maid of Judah goes,
While foemen loot. Oblivion henceforth hide
Saul's fate, and Jonathan's, Josiah's woes,
Gedáliah, and those Ten who, steadfast, died.[25]

In darkness lie both sun and moon expunged.
Let no man gape in wonder: could their lead
Fathom my grief, then both in Hell had plunged,
Their fragments scattered wide on Ocean's bed.

All music ceased, all merriment, when bonds
Were shackled on his feet: axe-toppled lies
The pine that soared o'er tangled bush, its fronds
Festooned with needles, reaching for the skies.

Prince of a hundred summers saving one
He falls, a prey for howling hordes to rend.
To Israel's God all praise—His will be done
Whose judgment holds unswerving to the end.

His servant's blood, that from the ground did cry,
He heard, and venged him on their godless spite.
The year, full-circling, spelled[26] their doom, to tie
Their deadfall to their victim's mourning-night.

Yekúthiél! Our rock, that once did fling
Marauders headlong, our Gibraltar![27] Cheer
Shone from thy mast, the footsore beckoning
Homeward, above the skyline pointing clear.

Yekúthiél! Thine was the olive's shade,
The cedar's, flourishing on Lebanon:
An emperor, each morning on parade
Amid his Guards, inspiring his men on.

A noble tree, whereon might every bird
Gather and nest. His shoulder bore the weight
Of government; preferment on his word
Did hang, for men deserving of the state.

His counsel silenced councillors, their own
Made foolish by his argument: aye, kings
Sat muted, chin in hand; for him the drone
Of courtiers, hushing, stifled vapourings.

Alack! Plucked is the peg that did secure
Our tent, which now slumps over, guy-ropes slack.
Alack! Our vineyard can no more endure,
Its muscat all too viciously pruned back.

My heart grieves with the pipes' lament, and deep
Within its weeping echoes Zion's wail
For every thud that battered down the keep
My people thought too high for foe to scale,

Till all the clambering tendrils round her hill
Are mined, as by some vine-dresser's dread snip;
Leaving the bare foundations, and a spill
Of rubble, fit for dumping down the tip.

Would he might watch again, each day, how fare
His nurslings—earning slights, or men's respect!
O for his leading-rein of loving care,
The hand that steadied, when my steps were checked!

O for his championship against the sneer
Of the cabal's intrigue, their plots to block!
Bare-fanged, the lions snarl: would he were here
To save the sorry remnant of the flock!

Weep, David's seed, for robes of sceptred state,
Weep, all of Aaron's line, for priestly tire,
Weep, Levi's house, for choirs now desolate
And on the willow hang your broken lyre.

Hard-headed business-folk, weep for the stone
That lent to yours the lustre of its name;
Weep, studious lawyers, who in Babylon
Gave rulings—power no longer backs your claim.

Weep, sages, all your kingly poise let down,
Mourn your ambassador's sage counsel: mourn,
You merchant-guildsmen, each his golden gown,
The mace that did your dignity adorn.

Weep for the precious silver of his hair
That purchased honour for all bent by age;
Weep, migrant misfits, grateful for the fare
For droppers-in beneath his foliage.

Weep, you who hunger: mourn that lavish board
To share whose dainties made your boast go round.
Mourn, all that thirst, weep for the cloud that poured
Late rain down lips that gasped like parchéd ground.

My people, weep a leader. Your good name,
The power your hand might wield—he was their stay.
The harp within your heart must thrum the same
Relentless note, till grief drains life away.

Grief wrings all hands, each face bears mourning's slash,
No loins ungird their sack: by silence mocked
A crowd waits on, all heads bestrewn with ash,
Round gates of righteousness forever locked.

Tears leave a groaning trail where stalking fear
Has dazed far-flung fraternities, that tossed
To Earth's perimeter, felt he was near,
Now orphaned, with a father-figure lost.

Now that his life's passed by, we understand
The fruits of our by-passing God's decrees.[28]
If we forget his kindness, our right hand
Forget its cunning, till Earth's own demise.

My people! Feel no more the scourge's maim,
Let sorrow's cup no more intoxicate
Your wits, that uncontrolled expose your shame:
Fear not—from Scripture comfort take, and wait.

'Stealthy comes help when faltering Israel quails.'[29]
Like Aaron's holocausts,[30] this, too, shall mean
Atonement through blood—Yekúthiél's:
'Before the Lord your God ye shall be clean.'

Destined is he, awaked with the elect,
To stand amongst the multitude at last:
Gone now the saints who could, by faith, protect,
Gone—since Yekúthiél's time, which is past.

‎– ∪ – – ∪ – – – ∪ –   　　　‎– – – ∪ – – – – ∪

‎בִּימֵי יְקוּתִיאֵל אֲשֶׁר נִגְמְרוּ 　　אוֹת כִּי שְׁחָקִים לַחֲלֹף יִצֹּרוּ!

‎שִׂימוּ לְבַבְכֶם תֵּדְעוּ כִּי הַזְּמָן 　　יָכִין לְעַם שִׂיחוֹת וְלֹא נוֹצָרוּ

‎יִקְחוּ יְמוֹתָיו עַם וְגַם עַם יִתְּנוּ 　　עַד אֲחַשֵּׁב כִּי עִם אֱנוֹשׁ יִסְחָרוּ

‎לֹא אֲדָמָה זֹאת כַּאֲשֶׁר לֹא יָדְעוּ 　　כָּל אַנְשֵׁי לֵבָב אֲשֶׁר נִזְכָּרוּ:

‎אִם הַנְּפָשׁוֹת הַגְּוִיּוֹת מָאֲסוּ 　　אוֹ הַנְּשָׁמוֹת לַעֲלוֹת יִפְצָרוּ.

‎מַה גּוֹאֲלֵי הָאוֹמְרִים: תֵּבֵל חֲלוֹם! 　　אֵיךְ שָׁכְחוּ דָבָר וְלֹא זָכָרוּ:

‎כֵּן הוּא כְּדִבְרֵיהֶם, אֲבָל הוּא מֵאֲשֶׁר 　　שָׁוְא דִּבְּרוּ לָאִישׁ וְלֹא נִכְפָּרוּ!

‎הוּכַן בְּקִרְבָּהּ לַתְּלָאוֹת מַאֲרָב 　　וּכְמִפְּנֵי הַבּוֹעֲרִים נִסְתָּרוּ

‎כָּפַר בְּרִית מַלְכֵי אֲדָמָה עִם שְׁאוֹל 　　גַּם מַחְשְׁבוֹת הָרוֹזְנִים הוּפָרוּ

‎מַה קָּרְאוּ עַמִּים וְלֹא עָנוּ, עֲדֵי 　　קָרָא שְׁאוֹל לָהֶם וּפִיו לֹא מָרוּ!

‎שָׁבַת גְּאוֹן עַזִּים וְשָׂרִים שָׁחֲחוּ 　　כִּי כַעֲבָדִים אֶל שְׁאוֹל נִמְכָּרוּ

‎פִּתְאֹם לְפֶתַע יָרְדוּ יַחַד לַבּוֹר 　　לֹא מָצְאוּ כֹחַ וְלֹא עָצָרוּ

‎לֹא מָצְאוּ מֵלִיץ יְכַפֵּר בַּעֲדָם 　　מִכָּל סְגֻלָּתָם אֲשֶׁר אָצָרוּ

‎אֲשֶׁתוֹלְלוּ יַחַד וְרֵיקָם הָלְכוּ 　　מִתּוֹעֲפוֹת כַּסְפָּם אֲשֶׁר צָבָרוּ

‎לֹא נֶאֱשַׁר מִכָּל כְּבוֹדָם בִּלְעֲדֵי 　　הֵם הַבְּלוֹאִים בַּאֲשֶׁר נִקְבָּרוּ

‎בָּאוּ בְמַחְשַׁכִּים וְאָזְנָם פִּתְחָה 　　תַּחַת בְּרִיחִים בַּעֲדָם סָגָרוּ!

‎כַּתֵּר מְעַט, מָוֶת, וְיָדֶיךָ אֱסֹף! 　　מַה תַּעֲרֹץ דַּלִּים בְּיָד נִסְכָּרוּ?

‎דְּמוּ יְצוּרִים כִּי בְצֶדֶק תִּשְׁפְּטֵם – 　　וּדְרָכְךָ לֹא כֵן כְּמוֹ שָׁעָרוּ

‎כִּי בָךְ אֲנָשִׁים נֶעֱזָרִים כָּשָׁלוּ 　　וּבָךְ אֲנָשִׁים כּוֹשְׁלִים נֶעֱזָרוּ

‎אִם לָעַג עַזִּים וְעָלֵיזִים לָךְ – 　　הִנֵּה מְאֹד מִפַּחְדְּךָ סָמָרוּ

‎אֵשׁ בָּאֲרָזִים נָפָלָה – מַה יַּעֲשׂוּ 　　אֵפוֹא אֲזוֹבֵי קִיר בְּיָד נִקְצָרוּ?

‎אֶרְאֶה פְּנֵי תֵבֵל, יְדִידִי, זוֹעֲפִים 　　יִתְנַכְּרוּ אֵלַי וְלֹא נִכָּרוּ –

‎עַל כֵּן שְׁעוּ מִנִּי, אֲמָרֵר בַּבְּכִי 　　מַה תִּקְצְפוּ עָלַי וּמַה תִּגְעָרוּ?

אַל תִּשְׁאֲלוּ עַל מֶה שְׂפָתַי צָלְלוּ –
אָבַד יְקוּתִיאֵל, אֲשֶׁר הָאוֹבְדִים
כַּפְתּוֹר אֲשֶׁר הָכָּה וְסִפִּים רָעֲשׁוּ
חֹשֶׁךְ וְצַלְמָוֶת מְאוֹרִים נִגְאָלוּ
לֹא יָדְעוּ נַפְשִׁי, אֲבָל הַיּוֹם לְבַד,
עַד לָקְחוּ מִבְּחַר אֱנוֹשׁ – וָאֵדְעָה
אָכֵן לְעֻמָּתִי פְּנֵיהֶם חֻזְּקוּ
אַל תַּאֲמֵן בָּהֶם וְאַל תִּכְרֹת בְּרִית
אִם נָדְרוּ נֶדֶר לְהַשְׁחִית כָּל יְקָר
הוּסְרוּ, הוּעֲדוּ, הַמּוּשָׁלִים
חוּשּׁוּ לְעֶזְרָתִי וְיָדֵי חַזְּקוּ
גַּם הַדְּמָעוֹת גָּרְעוּ חֹק נַחֲלָה
אַךְ הַלְּבָבוֹת כַּשָּׁמִירִים חָזְקוּ
הוֹיָה אֲשֶׁר לֹא תוּכְלוּ עוֹד כַּפְּרָה
יִקְפֹּצוּ, יַנְתְּסוּ, יְנָתְּצוּ
יִתְבּוֹלְלוּ, יִתְמוֹלְלוּ, יִתְגּוֹלְלוּ
תֵּקַל בְּעֵינֵינוּ – עֲדֵי יִתְפַּלְצוּן
אַל תַּעֲבִירוּ קוֹל בְּאֶרֶץ הַצְּבִי
עַמִּי, סְפֹד, כִּי הַכָּרוּב סָר מִדְּבִיר
וּזְעַק לְפִי קֶרֶת וְהֵילֵל, כִּי אָרוֹן
נֶהְפַּךְ לְךָ נִיסָן, אֲשֶׁר הָיָה לְנֵס,
הַיּוֹם אֲשֶׁר עָלָה אֲרִי מִסֻּבְּכוֹ
הַיּוֹם עֲטֶרֶת עַם צְבִי בּוֹ נָפָלָה
הַיּוֹם יְסוֹד הֵיכָל פְּנִימִי הֶעֱרָה
הַיּוֹם בְּקֶרֶב מוֹעֲדֵי אֵל שָׁאָגוּ

כִּי מֵעֲלֵי רֹאשִׁי צְלָלַי סָרוּ
בּוֹ עָתְקוּ חַיִל וְנַם גָּבְרוּ
יָכִין אֲשֶׁר נָפַל וְגָלוֹת סָרוּ!
וִימֵי אֲדָמָה אַחֲרָיו יוּאָרוּ
אִם יְמָאֲסוּ יָמִים וְאִם יְבְחָרוּ
כִּי יָלְדוּ אָוֶן וְעָמָל הָרוּ
כִּי אֶדְעָה פִּשְׁעָם וְלֹא יֵחָרוּ!
כִּי עַל דְּמוּת מַלְאָךְ בְּרִית קָשָׁרוּ
בּוֹ שֻׁלְּמוּ נְדָרָם אֲשֶׁר נָדָרוּ
הִתְנַגְּשׁוּ, הִתְקַדְּשׁוּ, הַבָּרוּ!
כִּי מַחְשְׁבוֹתַי אַחֲרָיו מֵאָסָרוּ
כִּי כַאֲפִיקֵי נַחֲלָה נִגְרוּ –
כִּי נָשְׂאוּ כָזֹאת וְלֹא נִגְזָרוּ!
הוֹיָה אֲשֶׁר לָהּ כָּל לְבָבוֹת חָרוּ
יְמָאֲסוּ, יַנְתְּסוּ, יָתְרוּ
יִתְהוֹלָלוּ, יִתְחוֹלָלוּ, יֵאָרוּ
לָהּ מוֹסְדֵי אֶרֶץ וְיִתְפּוֹרָרוּ!
פֶּן יִרְגְּזוּן הָרִים וְיִתְעַרְעָרוּ!
וּכְלֵי קְרָב וּכְלֵי יְקָר נִפְזָרוּ
נִלְקַח וְלוּחוֹת הַבְּרִית נִשְׁבָּרוּ –
נָסוּ צְלָלֶיךָ וְנַם עָבָרוּ –
הַיּוֹם אֲרָיוֹת עַל אֲרִיאֵל צָרוּ
הַיּוֹם תְּמִידֵי מִזְבֵּחַ הוּסָרוּ
הַיּוֹם בְּתוֹכוֹ מוֹקְדִים בָּעָרוּ
הָאוֹמְרִים לָהֶם „עָרוּ עָרוּ"

73

הַיּוֹם בְּתוּלַת בַּת יְהוּדָה הָגְלָתָה   הַיּוֹם שְׁלָלָהּ אוֹיְבִים בָּזָרוּ

נִשְׁכַּח כְּאָב שָׁאוּל וְיוֹנָתָן בְּנוֹ   וּכְאָב בְּנוֹ אָמוֹן אֲשֶׁר דָּקָרוּ

וּכְאָב גְּדַלְיָה בֶן אֲחִיקָם אַחֲרָיו   וּכְאָב עֲשֶׂרֶת שׁוֹפְטִים אָסָרוּ!

אַל תִּתְמְהוּ, אַנְשֵׁי אֲדָמָה, עַל דְּבַר   שֶׁמֶשׁ וְיָרֵחַ אֲשֶׁר קָדָרוּ:

לוּ חָרְדוּ לְקָצֶה כְאָבִי - יָרְדוּ   לְקָצֶה תְהוֹם וּלְפִי שְׁאוֹל נִפְזָרוּ!

שָׁבַת מְשׂוֹשׂ תֻּפִּים וְהַגִּיל נֶאֱסַף   יוֹם רָתְקוּ רַגְלָיו וְיוֹם נֶאֱסָרוּ

נָפַל בְּרוֹשׁ עַל בֵּין עֲבוֹתִים גָּבְהָה   קוֹמַת סְעַפּוֹתָיו אֲשֶׁר נִצְמָרוּ

נָפַל שְׁנַת תִּשְׁעִים וְתֵשַׁע שַׂר גְּבִיר   בִּידֵי מְרֵעִים אַחֲרָיו נָעָרוּ

יִגְדַּל לְעוֹלָם שֵׁם אֱלֹהֵי יַעֲקֹב   כִּי מִשְׁפְּטֵי צִדְקוֹ מְאֹד יָשָׁרוּ:

רָאָה דְמֵי עֲבָדוֹ לְפָנָיו צוֹעֲקִים   וַיִּדְרְשֵׁם מִיַּד רְשָׁעִים זָרוּ

יוֹם תֵּת פְּקֻדָּתָם שְׁנַת תֵּ"ת הָיְתָה   בַּיּוֹם אֲשֶׁר שׂוּחָה לְפָנָיו כָּרוּ

הָיָה יְקוּתִיאֵל כְּסֶלַע יָקְתְאֵל   בּוֹ נִשְׁמְטוּ זָרִים וְגַם זוֹרָרוּ

הָיָה יְקוּתִיאֵל כְּתֹרֶן הָעֲלָה   עַל הַר, אֲשֶׁר בּוֹ עוֹבְרִים אָשׁרוּ

הָיָה יְקוּתִיאֵל כְּזֵית רַעֲנָן   אוֹ כַאֲרָזִים בַּלְּבָנוֹן פֵּרוּ

הָיָה יְקוּתִיאֵל כְּמֶלֶךְ בְּגְדוּד   אֶל אָהֳלוּ הַמַּחֲנוֹת צָפָרוּ

שָׁם נִקְבְּצוּ דַיּוֹת וְשָׁמָּה קֻּנְּנוּ   כָּל צִפֳּרֵי כָנָף וְשָׁם דָּגָרוּ

מְשׁרַת מְלָכִים עַל כְּתֵפָיו הָיְתָה   וּלְפִי דְבָרוֹ הַגְּבִירִים שָׁרוּ

וּלְמוֹעֲצוֹתָיו יִדְּמוּ הַיּוֹעֲצִים   וּלְמַחְשְׁבוֹתָיו נוֹאֲלוּ, נִבְעָרוּ

שָׂמוּ מְלָכִים כַּף לְפִיהֶם, וַהֲמוֹן
יָתֵר אֲשֶׁר מֵאֲהֳלֵנוּ נִגְדְּעָה -
גֶּפֶן אֲשֶׁר שׂוֹרֵק בְּכַרְמִי נִטְּעָה -
לְבִי לְצִיּוֹן כַּחֲלִילִים יֶהֱמֶה
תִּזְעַק: אֲהָהּ, כִּי נָפְלָה חוֹמָה אֲשֶׁר
סָרוּ נְטִישֶׁיהָ וְנִגְלָה הַיְסוֹד
מִי יִתְּנֵנִי עוֹד וְיִפְקֹד יוֹם לְיוֹם
מִי יְמָשְׁכֵנִי בַּעֲבוֹתוֹת אַהֲבָה
מִי יַעֲמֹד לִפְנֵי עֲדַת מִתְקוֹמְמִים
מִי יַעֲרֹךְ בַּד לְהָשִׁיב צוֹרֲרִים
מִי יַהֲרֹס שַׁגֵּי כְפִירִים שׁוֹאֲגִים
יִבְכּוּ בְּנֵי דָוִד עֲלֵי אֶרֶץ יָקָר
יִבְכּוּ בְּנֵי אַהֲרֹן עֲלֵי אֵפוֹד וְעַל
יִבְכּוּ בְּנֵי לֵוִי עֲלֵי כִנּוֹר, אֲשֶׁר
יִבְכּוּ מְתֵי אֶרֶץ עֲלֵי כֶתֶם חֲלִי
יִבְכּוּ פְלִילֵינוּ בְּשִׁנְעָר אַחֲרָיו
יִבְכּוּ מְלָכֶיהָ עֲלֵי צִיר נֶאֱמָן
יִבְכּוּ גְבִירֶיהָ עֲלֵי מִקֵּל כָּאָר

שָׂרִים בְּמִלֵּיהֶם לְךָ עָצָרוּ
הָהּ לַחֲבָלֶיהָ אֲשֶׁר הֻתָּרוּ!
הָהּ לַעֲנָפֶיהָ אֲשֶׁר נִזְמָרוּ!
וּלְקוֹל בְּכִיתָהּ רַחֲמַי נִכְמָרוּ
בָּהּ נִשְׂגְּבוּ עַמִּי וּבָהּ נִבְצָרוּ
בָּהּ, וַאֲבָנֶיהָ לַגַּיְא הֻגָּרוּ!
אִם יִכְבְּדוּ בָנָיו וְאִם יִצְעָרוּ?
מִי יִתְמְכֵנִי עֵת צְעָדַי צָרוּ?
יִתְיָעֲצוּ עָלַי וְיִתְאַמָּרוּ?
כִּי יַעֲרִימוּ סוֹד וְיִתְעוֹרָרוּ?
לִטְרֹף שְׁאָר צֹאן אוֹבְדוֹת נָעָרוּ?
בּוֹ לָבְשׁוּ יֶשַׁע וְעֹז אָזָרוּ
אוּרִים וְגַם תֻּמִּים אֲשֶׁר יָקָרוּ
בּוֹ נִצְּחוּ שִׁירוֹת וְגַם שׁוֹרָרוּ
יִתְהַלְּלוּ בִשְׁמוֹ וְיִתְפָּאָרוּ
כִּי אָזְלַת יָדָם וְכָל חָסָרוּ
יִוָּעֲצוּ אִתּוֹ וְיִצְטַיָּרוּ
תָּעֹז יְמִינָה רִי וְיִתְחַבָּרוּ

יִבְכּוּ קְרוּדֶיהָ עֲלֵי עֵץ רַעֲנָן
יִבְכּוּ רְעֵבֶיהָ עֲלֵי שֻׁלְחָן אֲשֶׁר
יִבְכּוּ צְמֵאֶיהָ עֲלֵי עָנָן אֲשֶׁר
יִבְכּוּ בְנֵי עַמִּי עֲלֵי נָגִיד אֲשֶׁר
קִרְבָּם כְּכִנּוֹר יֶהֱמֶה מֵאֵין דְּמִי
הִתְנוֹדְדוּ, הִתְגּוֹדְדוּ, גַּם הֶעֱלוּ
גַּם יָשְׁבוּ דוּמָם וְשַׂק לֹא פִתְּחוּ
יִרְהוּ וְיֶחֱרְדוּ לְשָׁמְעוֹ מִקְצוֹת
יִשְׂאוּ נְהִי נִהְיָה וּפָרָה יִצְעֲקוּ
לֹא יָדְעוּ, עַד כִּי שְׁנוֹתָיו חָלְפוּ
תִּשְׁכַּח יְמִינָם, אִם חֲסָדָיו יִשְׁכְּחוּ
שֵׁבֶט בְּנֵי אוֹ כוֹס עֲלֵיכֶם עָבְרָה
אַל תִּפְחֲדוּ, כִּי הַנְּבוּאָה דִּבְּרָה:
הִנֵּה יְקוּתִיאֵל יְכֻפַּר פִּשְׁעֲכֶם
יִכּוֹן וְיַחֲשֵׁב לָאֵל דָּמוֹ כְּדַם
יָקִיץ וְגַם יַעֲמֹד לְגוֹרָלוֹ בְּיוֹם
פַּסּוּ אֱמוּנִים וַחֲסִידִים גָּמְרוּ -

יַאַסְפוּ תַחְתָּיו וְיִתְגּוֹדְרוּ
יִתְעַדְּנוּ נֶגְדּוֹ וְיִתְיַמְּרוּ
פִּיהֶם לְמַלְקוֹשׁ יַעֲרֹף פָּעֲרוּ
בּוֹ נוֹסְפוּ יָדַם וּבוֹ נִזְכָּרוּ
עַד כִּי כְבֵדָם שָׁפְכוּ וַיְעָרוּ
אֵפֶר בְּרָאשֵׁיהֶם וְשַׂק חָגָרוּ
עַל שַׁעֲרֵי צֶדֶק אֲשֶׁר נִסְגָּרוּ
אֶרֶץ מְגוּרֵיהֶם אֲשֶׁר בָּהּ גָּרוּ
כִּי כַיְתוֹמִים אַחֲרָיו נִשְׁאָרוּ
כִּי חָלְפוּ תוֹרוֹת וְחֹק עָבָרוּ
עַד יִפָּחוּ הָרִים וְעַד יוּסָרוּ!
אַל תִּשָּׁבְרוּ בָהּ עוֹד וְאַל תִּתְעָרוּ
בְּכָשְׁלָם עֵזֶר מְעַט נֶעֱזָרוּ!
לִפְנֵי אֲדֹנָי מַלְכְּכֶם תִּטְהָרוּ
עוֹלוֹת, עֲלֵי יַד אַהֲרֹן הַקְטָרוּ!
יִצָּרְפוּ רַבִּים וְיִתְבָּרָרוּ
בִּימֵי יְקוּתִיאֵל אֲשֶׁר נִגְמָרוּ!

This poem, consummately constructed with its end in its beginning like fate's dread leviathan biting its own tail, is organized so successfully that it conceals the circumstance that the reflective passages which it contains could stand independently, similarly to some of the paired quatrains in Tennyson's *In Memoriam*. I suspect that some of them may stem from thoughts noted by Ibn Gabirol over the years in a kind of commonplace-book, for use where it should prove appropriate to set them, cast into the metrical form of their adoptive context. In spite of the personal affection for Yequthiel, and the appreciation of his public role that the elegy clearly reflects, its mood is a sure indication that the natural habitat of Ibn Gabirol's essential self was in the atmosphere of those relatively rare hours of contemplation that obligations towards his patron, and towards the Jewish community generally, allowed him to snatch; and one thinks of the situation of Goethe, after his return from Italy to Weimar. Personal temperament, a Neoplatonic understanding of the illusory value of the actualities of everyday life, and Ibn Gabirol's own personal vicissitudes combined to make him what he was. The essentially positive, and spiritually confident aspect of his view of the world and of man's situation therein, within the context of the divinely ordained scheme of things, would find expression in his *Royal Crown* (pp. 117f.). The following short poem of resignation in face of the inevitable loneliness of one who finds reflection upon that scheme an all-absorbing vocation, may be considered its complement:[31]

Blank mind—like[32] brawn's bulk blocks all else from sight,
   And counsel—secret as the soul within:
   The world's well-wishers snared in evil's gin,
And joylessness on earth our human plight:

The slave's fist raised to strike his lord in spite,
  Whilst maid her very queen would discipline,
  Son threatening parents twain in froward sin,
Daughter disdaining dam, her own sire's right.[33]

Mine eye hath scanned the world: the world's sons hold
That best which whirls as nonsense, raving mad;
Man must bear toil while life shall onward roll,
Until he bears the weight of worms and mould
As earth at last returns to earth, and glad
The soul soars upward, homing on the Soul.

‒ ‒ ‒ ∪ ‒ ‒ ‒ ∪ ‒ ‒ ∪   ‒ ‒ ∪ ‒ ‒ ‒ ∪ ‒ ‒ ‒ ∪

וְגוּף נִרְאֶה וְנֶפֶשׁ נַעֲלָמָה   וְלֵב נָבוּב וְתוּשִׁיָּה סְתוּמָה

וְלֹא שָׂשׂוֹן לְאָדָם בָּאֲדָמָה   וְאֶרֶץ - שׁוֹחֲרֶיהָ יִמְצְאוּן רַע

וְשִׁפְחָה יִסְּרָה מַלְכָּה, וְאָמָה   וְעֶבֶד יַהֲרֹג הַיּוֹם אֲדוֹנָיו

וְכֵן הַבַּת בְּאָבִיהָ וְאִמָּה   וּבֵן יָקוּם עֲלֵי אָבִיו וְאִמּוֹ

אֲשֶׁר הַטּוֹב בְּעֵינִי כֹל - מְהוּמָה!   יְדִידִי, רָאֲתָה עֵינִי בְתֵבֵל

וְיִשָּׂא אַחֲרִיתוֹ גוּשׁ וְרִמָּה   יְמֵי חַיֵּי אֱנוֹשׁ יִשָּׂא עֲמָלִים

וְתַעַל הַנְּשָׁמָה לַנְּשָׁמָה.   וְתָשׁוּב הָאֲדָמָה לָאֲדָמָה

6

LITURGICAL POETRY

THE 244 pieces admitted by Jarden to the canon of Ibn Gabirol's liturgical compositions[1] were, for the most part, written with a specific occasion in view, as introductions, etc., to various high-lights in the statutory service, making play with biblical allusions appropriate to the day concerned and articulating its especial significance. They vary from 'symphony-length' items such as the *Royal Crown* (pp. 106f., 117f.), or his *'azharoth* for Pentecost, a versified summary of the 613 precepts—248 positive and 365 negative—that comprise the Jewish law,[2] said to have been composed by Ibn Gabirol when he was sixteen years old, to items of four lines constructed around his shorter acrostic signature *SheLoMoH*. To describe these miniature poems as gems is not an idle figure of speech: they evince the genius of the intaglio-cutter, who knows that he must express the essential lines of his scene, on a stone small enough to set into a signet ring, so vividly that they will themselves suggest much more than they state, e.g. the set of a lion's jaws that almost makes audible his roar.

Ibn Gabirol's intellectual love of God was perhaps no less intense than Spinoza's, but, unlike Spinoza, he had not rejected the possibility of a providential care divinely exercised over man and in particular Israel; and he was therefore able to accept the ceremonial institutions of Judaism as symbols, that might elicit from the Jew at worship the acknowledgment of his spiritual opportunities and the affirmation of his response to them. And although it is the sublime universalism associated with the Jewish New Year festival, and the intensity with which the Day

79

of Atonement asserts the paradox of a Deity not subject to change who can nevertheless forgive man's sin, that inspired Ibn Gabirol to compose hymns at which the very angels might marvel, he does not fail to touch the profound theological meaning of the joyful occasions of the Jewish year in those pieces written in *allegro* mood, for celebration of festivals.

The spring feast of Passover brings together the themes of Israel's historic beginnings as a people delivered from Egypt, the renewal of nature, and, corresponding to these two, faith in a future redemption from exile and in the reality of some meaningful existence beyond the grave. In the climate of Palestine/Israel, where, until less than thirty years ago the water-supply had always been precarious, it is not surprising that the Hebrew Bible should make metaphorical play with water to symbolize several of these motifs: and their nexus is brought into sharp focus in the additional service for the first day of Passover, when the prayer for rain that has been recited during the winter months is discontinued and is replaced, through the summer, with a prayer for dew. The change is introduced with liturgical ceremoniousness, as the following pieces by Ibn Gabirol testify. They are inserted to introduce the statutory items in the regular form of the *'amidah*, or prayer *par excellence*.

The first two benedictions of the *'amidah* concern, respectively, providential history from patriarchal times onward ('blessed art Thou . . . the shield of Abraham'), and the resurrection ('blessed . . . who revivest the dead'). Ibn Gabirol wrote prefaces for each of them:[3]

> Crushed was thy folk, whom Egypt's sun did burn,
>   And now by roaming wearied: grant them rest
> With thy dew freshened, let their sap return;
>   Thou, God dost answer those who are oppressed,
> When comes the time that thy grace is revealed
>   To them that trust thee Thou dost prove a shield.

שְׁזוּפַת שֶׁמֶשׁ לְחוּצַת פַּתְרוּסִים
מְרֻדֵּיךְ תְּנוֹבֵב בְּטַלְלֵי רְסִיסִים
הָאֵל הָעוֹנֶה בְּעֵת רָצוֹן עֲמוּסִים
מָגֵן הוּא לְכָל הַחוֹסִים

Thy spirit send: our corpse to life recall,
Our fairest land to pristine youth restore;
From Thee our fruit stems, that art good to all:
Surely Thou wilt revive us, as of yore.

שַׁלַּח רוּחָךְ לְהַחֲיוֹת גְּוִיֵנוּ
לְקַדְמוּתָהּ תְּשׁוֹבֵב נַחֲלַת צְבִיֵנוּ
מִמְּךָ טוֹב לַכֹּל יִמָּצֵא פִּרְיֵנוּ
הֲלֹא אַתָּה תָּשׁוּב תְּחַיֵּנוּ

By way of heightening the intensity of congregational
prayer at the moment when, for the first time in the spring
season, the formula 'Thou who art mighty to save dost cause
the dew to descend' is declared, Ibn Gabirol wrote a longer
recitative poem which weaves together with the theme of
dew the twelve months of the year from *Nisan* (March–April)
to *'Adar* (February–March), the twelve tribes of Israel, the
prophets, the twelve signs of the Zodiac, and the biblical
passages in which dew is referred to either literally or as a
simile of divine beneficence. It is too long to quote in full, but
the first and last sections are here cited:[1]

With dew stored up by Thee, the earth to purify,
Invigorate those heaped to rot, like straw once threshed,
For Abraham's sake, who Thee his son did not deny,
Make Reuben, under *Aries* his sign, refreshed.

With dew of blessing make to tinkle mountain rills,
Down slopes covered in produce sweet, by light caressed.

In April bless a people fainting from their ills,
And to thy promise look, which said they should be
blessed.

As it is written,[5] 'Therefore God give thee of the dew of heaven, and of the fatness of the earth, and of plenty of corn and wine'.

בְּטַל   אָצוּר לְבָרֵר וְלַלְּבֵּן
אַמֵּץ נָדוֹשׁ כְּהַדּוֹשׁ מַתְבֵּן
לְמַעַן   אָב לֹא חָשַׁךְ בֵּן
תְּאַמֵּץ בְּמַזַּל טָלֶה רְאוּבֵן

בְּטַל   בְּרָכָה יִרְעֲפוּ גְבוֹהִים
בְּמַעֲדַנֵּי אֶרֶשׁ נְגוֹהִים

בְּנִיסָן   בָּרֵךְ עַם כָּמֵהִים
בְּבִרְכַּת וְיִתֶּן לְךָ הָאֱלֹהִים

ככתוב ויתן לך האלהים מטל השמים ומשמני הארץ
ורב דגן ותירוש (בראשית כז כח)

With dew spread north, south, east, and west, thine
oath fulfil,
For Obadiah: hasten on the march of time;
As he prophets concealed, whom tyrants sought to kill,[6]
Let *Pisces* bring to Benjamin glory sublime.

With dew ransom my root, to bloom at life's return;
On Passover, accept my cry: In March sustain
Thy folk with kindness, whom their foes as refuse
spurn;
The doctrine I should hear, let fall like gentle rain.

As it is written,[7] 'my doctrine shall drop as the rain, my speech shall distil as the dew, as the small rain upon the tender herb, and as the showers upon the grass'.

בְּטַל   שְׁבוּעָה לִשְׂמֹאל וְיָמִין
לְקָרֵב לָנוּ קֵץ הַיָּמִין
לְמַעַן   מְלִיצִים מִצַּד הַסְמָּין
תְּהַדֵּר בְּמַזַּל דָּגִים בִּנְיָמִין

בְּטַל   הַפְרֵה שֳׁרָשַׁי וּפְרָחַי
קַח שַׁוְעָתִי בְּחַג פִּסְחִי
בַּאֲדַר   טָפֵל נָתוּן לְסָחִי
וְאָז יַעֲרֹף כַּמָּטָר לִקְחִי

ככתוב יערף כמטר לקחי תזל כטל אמרתי
כשעירים עלי דשא וכרביבים עלי עשב (דברים לב ב)

The Song of Songs is associated with Passover, and prominent in the imagery of its liturgical hymns; both because of
the atmosphere of spring that breathes through the book; and
thanks to the tradition which, ascending to late antiquity,
reads it as a love-idyll, involving estrangement, reconcilia-
tion, and patience in awaiting a long-postponed consumma-
tion, between God and Israel, his chosen bride. That is the
background to the following two poems, the first of which is
cast in the form of a dialogue, the first speaker being Israel:[8]

'That gate long closed, unchain,
   And through it send to me
My hart,[9] come back again,
   That long ago did flee,[10]
Returned to my embrace,
   My bedfellow to be,[11]
And leave, for me to trace,
   Entranced, the scent of Thee.'

'Fair bride, who is this swain
   Thou wouldst I send to thee?'[12]
'Fresh-skinned, to Him pertain
   Features a joy to see.

He is the One whose face
   I draw, my Lover He,
And Friend,[13] mine by his grace:
   Anoint Him, King to be!'

‏‏– –   – ‿ – –   – –   – ‿ – –
‏שַׁעַר אֲשֶׁר נִסְגַּר קוּמָה פְּתָחֵהוּ

‏– –   – ‿ – –   – –   – ‿ – –
‏וּצְבִי אֲשֶׁר בָּרַח אֵלַי שְׁלָחֵהוּ

לְיוֹם בּוֹאֲךָ עָדַי לָלוּן בְּבֵין שָׁדַי

שָׁם רֵיחֲךָ הַטּוֹב עָלַי תְּנִיחֵהוּ

מִי זֶה דְמוּת דּוֹדֵךְ כַּלָּה יְפֵה פִיָּה

כִּי תֹאמְרִי אֵלַי שְׁלָחָה וְקָחֵהוּ

הַהוּא יְפֵה עַיִן אָדֹם וְטוֹב רֹאִי

דּוֹדִי וְרֵעִי זֶה קוּם נָא מְשָׁחֵהוּ

The next poem is assigned to the last day of Passover, the
dominating theme of which is the messianic future, faith in
which must be able to surmount the distance of its vista, and
resist the temptation to indulge in eschatological calculations
that inevitably sap Jewish morale and strain such faith when
the expected date proves illusory. As regularly in the Middle
Ages, Esau/Edom/Se'ir (here further identified with *sa'ir*, the
quasi-demonic he-goat) stands for the Roman empire and, by
extension, Christendom as its successor, just as Ishmael
frequently typifies the world of Islam. It is the messiah who is
here addressed:[14]

How long wilt thou lie in the tomb,
   Thou sprig of Jesse's root?[15]
Winter is past:[16] arise and bloom
   With buds that promise fruit.

Why should a slave rule princes' seed,
   And Christian Edom win
A royal throne that was decreed
   For his own younger twin?[17]

I have a thousand years incurred
   Of servitude, disgraced

In exile, like some lonely bird
    That haunts the empty waste.[18]

No white-robed angel[19] might I find
    That could the date reveal
When comes the end: God bade one bind
    It hidden, under seal.[20]

```
  – –  – –  ◡ – –  – –  – ◡ – –        – –  – –  ◡ – –  – –  – ◡ – –
```

שֹׁרֶשׁ בְּנוֹ יִשַׁי עַד אָן תְּהִי נִקְבָּר   הוֹצֵא לְךָ פֶּרַח כִּי הַסְּתָו עָבָר

לָמָּה יְהִי עֶבֶד מוֹשֵׁל בְּבֶן שָׂרִים   תַּחַת מְלֹךְ צָעִיר שָׂעִיר הֲלֹא נָבָר

מִנִּי זְמַן אֶלֶף שָׁנִים אֲנִי נֶעֱבָד   אֲדָמֶה בְּתוֹךְ גָּלוּת קָאַת בְּתוֹךְ מִדְבָּר

הַאֵין לְבוּשׁ בַּדִּים לִשְׁאֹל וְאֵיךְ יִגְלֶה   הַקֵּץ וְאֶל צִנָּה סָתוּם חָתֹם דָּבָר

The same bridal imagery based on the Song of Songs also informs the following poem, which is liturgically assigned not to Passover, but to the last day of the Tabernacles complex of festivals (*Simhath Torah*), when the annual reading of the Pentateuch is completed and at once recommenced amid symbolism drawn from the ritual surrounding the wedding-ceremony. It is, indeed, frequently used in Sephardic communities as a wedding-hymn, since in Judaism marriage is ideally the assertion of the divine election of Israel and the declaration of intention to uphold and transmit the values and responsibilities that that election entails:[21]

'Mid alien tents still must thou dwell, forlorn,
    Out on the heath? Nay, up, to Carmel's top,
My fairest maid, on Bashan's heights to gaze,
    Our garden bower to scan
    Laid out ere time began:
See how, for thee, its beds with lilies blaze.'

'Why, then, my heart's desire, hast Thou forsworn
    So long my garden close, elsewhere to crop,
A lonely hart, in foreign fields to graze?
    Our garden screened shall keep

The joys we taste: aye, sleep,
Lull'd on thy true-love's breast, at peace, always.'

‒ ‒ ‒ ‿ ‒ ‒ ‒ ‒ ‿ ‒ ‒   ‒ ‒ ‒ ‿ ‒ ‒ ‒ ‒ ‿ ‒ ‒

עָמְדִי לְרֹאשׁ כַּרְמֶל צְפִי לְהַר בָּשָׁן   שׁוֹכַנְתְּ בַּשָּׂדֶה עִם אָהֳלֵי כוּשָׁן

וּרְאִי עֲרוּגָתֵךְ כִּי נִמְלְאָה שׁוֹשָׁן   לַבֵּן אֲשֶׁר נֶחְמַס כַּלָּה שְׂאִי עֵינֵךְ

לִרְעוֹת בְּגַן יָקְשָׁן תַּחַת צֲצֵי דִישָׁן   מַה לָּךְ יְפֵה עַיִן כִּי תַעֲזֹב גַּנִּי

וּבְחֵיק יְפַת עַיִן תִּשְׁכַּב וְגַם תִּישָׁן   הָבָה רְדָה לַגַּן תֹּאכַל מְגָדִים שָׁם

The following two poems are specimens of a genre known as the *reshuth*, i.e. introduction,[22] to a passage of particular prominence in the statutory liturgy, in this case the doxology beginning *Nishmath* ('the breath of all that lives shall praise Thee, etc.') which on sabbaths and festivals follows the early morning reading of psalms. The last word of the *reshuth*, *neshamah* (*breath* or *soul*) anticipates the first word, *nishmath*, of the doxology:[23]

My spirit's genuflexions match my knee
    As I approach Thee fearful and prostrate,
Well knowing that in thy sight I may be
    Reckoned no more than some invertebrate.
Thou fillest the whole world: can those like me
    Find means to praise Thee, infinitely great?
Thy glory heaven's angels do not see,
    Comparison with whom I cannot rate.
Yet, for that goodness Thou dost shew, to Thee
    My soul would fain her gratitude equate.

שְׁפַל רוּחַ שְׁפַל בֶּרֶךְ וְקוֹמָה   אֶקְדֶּמְךָ בְּרֹר פַּחַד וְאֵימָה

לְפָנֶיךָ אֲנִי נֶחְשָׁב בְּעֵינַי   כְּתוֹלַעַת קְטַנָּה בָּאֲדָמָה

מְלֹא עוֹלָם אֲשֶׁר אֵין קֵץ לְגָדְלוֹ   הֲכָמוֹנִי יְהַלֶּלְךָ וּבַמֶּה

הֲדָרְךָ לֹא יְכִילוּן מַלְאֲכֵי רוּם   וְעַל אַחַת אֲנִי כַּמָּה וְכַמָּה

הֲטִיבוֹת וְהִגְדַּלְתָּ חֲסָדִים   וְלָךְ תַּגְדִּיל לְהוֹדוֹת הַנְּשָׁמָה

The companion piece is inspired by a discussion in the Talmud[24] as to the reason for the five-fold occurrence in Psalm 103 of the words 'bless the Lord [O my soul]' (*barekhi naphshi*). One explanation offered is as follows:

'The reason why David used this formula five times is because of a correspondence between the Holy One, blessed be He, and the nature of the soul. God fills the cosmos, as the soul fills the human body; as God though all-seeing is invisible, so the soul sees but cannot be seen; God sustains the whole cosmos, and similarly the soul sustains the body; God, and the soul, are alike pure; and just as God resides in the most intimate of interior chambers, so similarly the soul. It is therefore appropriate for something in which these five qualities inhere to offer praise to the One in whom they are likewise inherent.'

My one[25] true self, to God in worship bend,
Thou soul endowed with reason,[26] haste thy flight
In reverence to serve Him, every night,
Each day, think on that world that waits thy end:[27]
Nor chase vain bubbles, thou that canst pretend
To liveliness like God's own life; from sight,
Like him, concealed; be He that formed thee hight
Purest, canst thou thy pure perfection tend:

His arm sustains the welkin, even so
Dost thou thy frame, that but for thee were dumb.
To thy Rock, then, my soul, thy singing raise,
Who made nought like to thee on earth below,
That Rock to whom shall all within me come
Blessing the One whom all that breathe do praise.[28]

```
  --U  -:-U  ---U          --U  ---U  ---U
```

וְרוּצִי לַעֲבֹד אוֹתוֹ בְּאֵימָה   שְׁחִי לָאֵל יְחִידָה הַחֲכָמָה

וְלָמָּה תִרְדְּפִי הֶבֶל וְלָמָּה   לְעוֹלָמֵךְ פְּנִי לֵילֵךְ וְיוֹמֵךְ

אֲשֶׁר גֶּעֱלָם כְּמוֹ אַתְּ נַעֲלָמָה   מְשׁוּגָלָה אַתְּ בְּחַיָּתֵךְ לְאֵל חַי

דְּעִי כִּי כֵן טְהוֹרָה אַתְּ וְתַמָּה   הֲלֹא אִם יוֹצְרֵךְ טָהוֹר וְנָקִי

כְּמוֹ תִשְׂאִי גְוִיָה גֶאֱלָמָה   חֲסִין יִשָּׂא שְׁחָקִים עַל זְרוֹעוֹ

Liturgical tradition assigns the foregoing poems for use on
the New Year festival and the Day of Atonement respectively, and the first of them, in pointing to the insignificance of
man beside the transcendent greatness of God, hints at the
examination of conscience and the spiritual self-appraisal
which the Jew should carry out particularly during the
penitential season. The next poem, which is also found in
some Sephardic rites for the Day of Atonement and is
sometimes chanted at funerals, was suggested by the words of
Eliphaz in Job 4.19. The realistically negative assessment of
human spirituality is balanced by the conclusion: that link
which binds man (and Israel, as quintessential man) to
God—a relationship expressed by the Hebrew word *ḥesed*, a
loyalty and solidarity infused by love—means that despite his
own failures, man has a claim on God which he may advance
without incongruity:[29]

To what will you aspire, who live your day
In houses built on sand, in frames of clay?
Man's rated not a whit more worth than beast:[30]
Worms all—we each must learn that worms we stay.

Shall we, that cower behind a plaster shield,[31]
Raise high our hearts like masters of the field?
No vantage may be man's, for whom at last
The grave is all a thousand years could yield.

And if he strut, self-willed in deed and thought,
By the wry hap of nemesis he's caught,[32]
Seared to a sorry cinder in the flames
Of Hell he lies, where gold avails him naught.

Thou that art man, thou caitiff all forlorn,
Ope wide thine eyes! Whence cam'st thou, hither
                                   borne,
And whither hence must go?[33] Like Jonah's gourd,
Fruit of a single night, and gone by morn.[34]

Better had God not formed that human pair
To harvest trouble. And yet wouldst thou dare
To aim at greatness in thy little plot
Whilst round thee, camouflaged, there lies—the snare?

Dropped from the womb thou cam'st, and fall thou
                                   must
For aye, to turn law-breaker for a crust:[35]
And shouldst thou think to linger for a trice,
Why, instant pocks shall dog thy leprous lust.

Thy body shines like sunlight, all afire
So long the spirit's present to inspire
The flesh with breath: so soon the soul goes forth,
Naught then remains of thee save noisome mire.

Glory thou canst not hoard. He that shall spend
Thy erstwhile wealth's a stranger:[36] thou must wend
Thy way now empty, reckless heretofore
Of greed's worthless beginning, and worse end.

Let then the wicked leave his way[37] to turn
Towards his King in penitence and learn
How He, magnanimous, may yet respond
To hide him whom His anger else must burn.

So you, who blustered boastful, crowd ye nigh,
Of God now mindful, for past deeds to sigh,[38]
And glancing heavenward on contrite palms
Offer your hearts, raised up to Him on high.[39]

Alack, our sin-stained soul! What shall we say
Who, grazing wind, like sheep have gone astray?[40]
How seek for grace whose head in sin is swamped
Too manifold to raise our face, and pray?

But Thou, all-sovereign of skies and land,
From out despondent slough draw up thy band:
Though set in stubbornness our neck, forbear,
Nor from stiffneckedness relax thy hand;

Thine, thine alone is pity: pour it free
For folk who knock thy door so urgently.
Since Thou—none else—it be that art our Lord,
To whom, then, should our eyes turn, save to Thee?[41]

לָמָה תִשְׂאוּ עָיִן	שׁוֹכְנֵי בָתֵּי חֹמֶר
מִן הַבְּהֵמָה אָיִן	וּמוֹתַר הָאָדָם
כִּי אֲנַחְנוּ תוֹלַעַת	לָנוּ יֵשׁ לָדַעַת
וְאֵיךְ יִנְבַּהּ לִבֵּנוּ	לְנֶב חֹמֶר גַּבֵּנוּ
וְאַחֲרִיתוֹ לַקֶּבֶר	מַה יִּתְרוֹן לַגֶּבֶר
וְלוֹ חַי שָׁנִים אָלֶף	וְזֶה יִהְיֶה לוֹ חֵלֶף
יִבָּלַע בַּחֲמַת קֶרִי	הֲלֹא אִם יֵלֵךְ מֶרִי
וְלֹא יוֹעִיל הַזָּהָב	וְיִשָּׂרֵף בַּלַּהַב

פְּקַח עֵינֶיךָ וּרְאֵה   הָאָדָם הַנִּכְאָה
וְאָנָה מוֹצָאֶךָ   מֵאַיִן בּוֹאֶךָ

נִמְשַׁל לַקִּיקָיוֹן   קִצְּךָ עָנִי וְאֶבְיוֹן
וְעַד בֹּקֶר לֹא חָיָה   שֶׁבִּן לַיְלָה הָיָה

וְעָמָל לֹא קָצַרְתָּ   טוֹב אֲשֶׁר לֹא נוֹצַרְתָּ
וְאַתָּה בְּתוֹךְ הַמּוֹקֵשׁ   וְאֵיכָה גְדוֹלוֹת תְּבַקֵּשׁ

וְתִפְשַׁע עַל פַּת לֶחֶם   נוֹפֵל אַף מֵרֶחֶם
אֲזַי תִּמָּצֵא כָל גֶּנַע   וְאִם תִּתְמַהְמַהּ רֶגַע

בְּעוֹד יֵשׁ בּוֹ הָרוּחַ   בְּשָׁרְךָ כְּאוֹר זָרוּחַ
נִשְׁאָר טִיט וָרֶפֶשׁ   וְעֵת תֵּצֵא הַנֶּפֶשׁ

מְאוּמָה מִכְּבוֹדֶךָ   רְאֵה כִּי אֵין בְּיָדֶךָ
וְאַתָּה תֵלֵךְ רֵיקָם   לְזָרִים חֵילְךָ יוּקַם

לַתַּאֲוָה הַקְשַׁבְתָּ   בְּכָל זֹאת לֹא חָשַׁבְתָּ
מַה תַּעֲשֶׂה בְּאַחֲרִיתָה   וְאִם תֵּטִיב רֵאשִׁיתָה

וְיָשֹׁב לִפְנֵי מַלְכּוֹ   יַעֲזֹב רָשָׁע דַּרְכּוֹ
וּמֵחֲרוֹנוֹ יִסָּתֵר   אוּלַי צוּר יֵעָתֵר

וְזִכְרוּ וְהִתְאוֹשָׁשׁוּ   יְהִירִים הִתְקוֹשָׁשׁוּ
אֶל אֵל בַּשָּׁמַיִם   שְׂאוּ לֵבָב וְכַפַּיִם

וְאוֹי עַל נַפְשׁוֹתֵינוּ   הָהּ עַל חַטֹּאתֵינוּ
וְנָס כַּצֹּאן תָּעִינוּ   כִּי רוּחַ רָעִינוּ

וַעֲוֹנוֹת עָבְ ו וָ אֹשׁ   **וּמַר יְבַקֵּשׁ וּפַח נֶפֶשׁ**
וְאֵיךְ נִשָּׂא פָנֵינוּ   מְאֹד רַבּוּ עֲוֹנֵינוּ

מוֹשֵׁל רוּם וָתַחַת   דְּלֵה עַמְּךָ מִשַּׁחַת
חֲסָדֶיךָ אַל תֶּרֶף   וְאִם הִקְשִׁינוּ עֹרֶף

לְעַם דּוֹפְקֵי דְלָתֶיךָ   הָפֵק חֶמְלָתֶךָ
וְעָלֶיךָ עֵינֵינוּ   כִּי אַתָּה אֲדוֹנֵינוּ

Beside the foregoing we may set the following, the mood of which is somewhat more positive in that it focuses on the potentialities of the rational soul[42] and thus adumbrates that component of the *Royal Crown* which constitutes the linchpin of its whole structure (pp. 150f.). The word *qinyan[ekh]* which completes the first stanza (its rendering repeated as a refrain in the English version), is the key to the poem; literally meaning *acquisition*, it here has a technical meaning, viz. a capacity which, not being inherent, has been derived from outside. In philosophical Hebrew writing it renders the Arabic *malka*[43] and corresponds to the Latin *habitus*, an *acquired perfect state*, all three terms deriving ultimately from the Aristotelian term ἕξις (literally [*coming into*] *possession*).[44] The poem is thus concerned with human failure to realize spiritual faculties and recognize opportunities for their application and development; and its metaphor of death dressing vines is one of the most powerful in Ibn Gabirol's *œuvre*:[45]

> Forget, my Soul, thy toil, nor brood, in thrall
> To fears in this oblivion-fated hell:
> Tomorrow shall the corse that housed thee dwell
> Beneath the netherworld's abyss, where all
> (As if it ne'er had been) slips past recall.
> Nay, reason's thine, my Soul; so use it well,
> E'en though thou dreadest death, his pangs to quell,
> And trust in God: success may so befall
> Thee wending to thy Liege thy homeward way,
> And thou shalt save thy very self that day
> Whereon thou lookest thy reward to see
> For all thou wast, and hadst the pow'r to be.

> Why then, my Soul, why with surprise concussed
> In indignation art thou habited
> Mid this world's turmoil? Once the spirit's fled
> Dumb lies the body, fundamental dust,
> When thou to that returnest (as thou must)

Nor takest in thy hand the slightest shred
Of wealth or glory:[46] nay, soon must be sped
Thy roaming hence, as though by wander-lust
Drawn on, yet like some migrant bird's, thy quest
One day shall bring thee fluttered to thy nest[47]—
The day thou lookest thy reward to see
For all thou wast, and hadst the pow'r to be.

Shouldst thou, my most perplexed Soul, respect
Aught that this brief-spanned world regards as dear,
Where royal pomp turns in an instant sheer
Perplexity, and what seems to reflect
A state of health, doth deadly aim direct
Disguised? Choice though its treasures do appear,
'Tis to deceive: its goodness melts, a smear
Oozing frustration's slime its sole effect.
Of all that's thine, others shall have the sum:
What profit, then, thy wealth, when there is come
The day thou lookest thy reward to see
For all thou wast, and hadst the pow'r to be?

Life is a vine, whose dresser, Death, doth prune;
He picks the fruit, and marks at every pace
The striding tendrils' march, to check the race.
Return, my Soul, seek Him that formed thee: soon,
Too soon, this little day slips past his noon
To wane, and long's the road that thou must trace
Back to his courts. Sufficient for thy case,
O wayward Soul, dry crusts,[48] from strife immune.
Forget[49] thy pain, yet mind thy waiting tomb,
Fearful of judgment on that day of doom
Whereon thou lookest thy reward to see
For all thou wast, and hadst the pow'r to be.

Tremble, made humble by thine abject need,
Like to a dove whom fear makes palpitate:
Yet mindful always of that sublimate

Divinely granted rest hereafter, plead
Each hour, each fleeting moment intercede
With God, our dwelling-place,[50] aye, supplicate,
Seeking with tears unceasing to placate
His face: win his goodwill, so thou dost speed
His will, not thine.[51] Then shall his cavalcade
Of angels lead thee to thy garden's shade
The day thou lookest thy reward to see
For all thou wast, and hadst the pow'r to be.

- - -   - - - -
- - -   - - - -

שְׁכָחִי יְגוֹנֵךְ   נֶפֶשׁ הוֹמִיָּה

לָמָּה תִפְחֲדִי   מִמְּצוּקֵי נָשְׁיָה

מָחָר גּוּפֵךְ   יִשְׁכֹּן תַּחְתָּיהָ

הַכֹּל נִשְׁכַּח   כְּאִלּוּ לֹא הָיָה

נֶפֶשׁ הַשְׂכִּילִי   וּמְמֻנָּת חֻלִּי

וְלָאֵל הוֹחִילִי   אוּלַי תּוֹעִילִי

וְנַפְשֵׁךְ תַּצִּילִי   בְּשׁוּבֵךְ אֶל קוֹנֵךְ   יוֹם תְּצַפִּי פְּעֻלַּת קִנְיָנֵךְ

לָמָּה וְלָמָּה   נֶפֶשׁ נִדְהָמָה

תִּלְבְּשִׁי שְׁמָמָה   עֲלֵי תֵבֵל אֲדָמָה

כְּצֵאת הַנְּשָׁמָה   גּוּיָה נֶאֱלָמָה

בְּשׁוּבֵךְ אֶל יְסוֹדֵךְ   לֹא תַשְׂאִי בְיָדֵךְ

מְאוּמָה מִכְּבוֹדֵךְ   יוֹם יָחִישׁ נוֹדֵךְ   כְּצִפּוֹר אֶל קִנֵּךְ

מַה לָּךְ נְסוּכָה   בְּדֶרֶךְ לֹא מְשׁוּכָה

אֲשֶׁר בָּהּ מְלוּכָה   תֵּהָפֵךְ מְבוּכָה

תִּרְמֶה אֲרוּכָה   וְהִיא קֶשֶׁת דְּרוּכָה

כָּל יְקָרָהּ כָּזָב   וְכָל טוּבָהּ אַכְזָב

וְהוּא נָמֵס וְזָב   וְלַאֲחֵרִים נֶעֱזָב   וּמַה יּוֹעִיל הוֹנֵךְ

הַחַי גֶּפֶן   וְהַמָּוֶת בּוֹצֵר

וּבַאֲשֶׁר יֵלֵךְ   צְעָדָיו הוּא נוֹצֵר

שׁוּבִי נַפְשִׁי   לְבַקֵּשׁ הַיּוֹצֵר

הַיּוֹם קָצֵר   וְרָחוֹק הֶחָצֵר

94

נֶפֶשׁ שׁוֹבֵבָה   דַּי לָךְ בְּפַת חֲרֵבָה

וְשִׁכְבִי מַעֲצֵבָה   וְזִכְרִי מַצֵּבָה   וְגוּרִי יוֹם דִּינֵךְ

חִרְדִי כְיוֹנָה   עֲנִיָּה אֶבְיוֹנָה

זִכְרִי בְכָל עֵת   מְנוּחָה עֶלְיוֹנָה

קְרָאִי מְעוֹנָה   בְּכָל רֶגַע וְעוֹנָה

בְּכִי תָמִיד לְעֵינָיו   וְהִתְחַנְּנִי לְפָנָיו

וְהָפִיקִי רְצוֹנָיו   וְאָז מַלְאֲכֵי מְעוֹנָיו   יְבִיאוּךְ אֶל גַּנֵּךְ

As the foregoing poems illustrate, one of the poles around which Ibn Gabirol's presentation of Neoplatonism in religious terms revolved was his marked sense of man's pusillanimous response to his spiritual vocation and failure to integrate therein his God-given faculty of reason. The other is his fascination with the divine transcendence, the reality of which lies beyond human imagination, let alone perception, but a glimpse of which may be caught from contemplation of the world of the angels: for as he wrote when describing the sun in the *Royal Crown* (p. 130),

> 'As practised eyes, by slaves' grand style impressed
> Know that their lord's magnificence exceeds.'

The following poem uses as its launching-pad the talmudic tradition of seven heavens[52] whilst glancing at Solomon's prayer for the dedication of the temple,[53] ' . . . the heaven of heavens cannot contain Thee'; but the key-word is *me'od, very much*—a mere adverb, which would normally be quite inadequate to carry such weight, but which is here rendered powerful by its repetition, in a climactic position, in a series of biblical quotations led off by Psalm 104.1, 'O Lord my God, Thou art very great':[54]

> Ne'er the seven heavens' fold
> Shall contain Thee, who dost hold

95

Skies Thyself unheld, of old
Since Thou madest them extoll'd—
Still by them thy praise is told:
    All must decay save thou, inviolate,[55]
    Lord God—my God—Thou art supremely great.[56]

Awe-tongued angels, standing nigh
Deep within thy courts on high
Praise Thee with averted eye
Lest their roving vision spy
That which none shall dare descry:
    Though praise befits the grandeur of thy state[57]
    Lord God—my God—Thou art supremely great.

Who could utter, day and night,
Ceaseless praise to tell thy might?
Such praise silence must recite,
Since thy Name transcends the height
Reached by hallelujah's flight:[58]
    My soul knows well her praise inadequate,[59]
    Lord God—my God—Thou art supremely great.

Vast thy majesty's extent,
Glory past all measurement;
Couldst Thou dwell in dome or tent,
Who in circumambient
Spheres art not, nor shall be pent?
    Thy strength, surpassing ours, is consummate:[60]
    Lord God—my God—Thou art supremely great.

Four heraldic creatures glide,
Mystic mounts that bear thy pride;[61]
Call thy flock home to thy side
From four quarters, justified
By redemption's year, and guide
    Sheep sore troubled, ill, emaciate:[62]
    Lord God—my God—Thou art supremely great.

שִׁבְעָה שְׁחָקִים לֹא יְכַלְכְּלוּךְ
לָהֶם תִּסְבֹּל וְהֵם לֹא יִסְבְּלוּךְ
מִיּוֹם בְּרָאתָם עוֹד יְהַלְלוּךְ
הֵמָּה יֹאבֵדוּ וְאַתָּה תַעֲמֹד   יְיָ אֱלֹהַי גָּדַלְתָּ מְאֹד

לְךָ יַעֲרִיצוּן סַפְסְרֵי מְרוֹמִי
וְשִׁנְאָן יוֹדֶה בְּהֵיכָל פְּנִימִי
יְרֵאִים חַוֹּת בָּךְ וּמִי יַחֲוֶה סִי   כִּי גָדוֹל יְיָ וּמְהֻלָּל מְאֹד

מִי זֶה יְמַלֵּל מִבְּלִי דוּמָם
עֻזְּךָ לְהַלֵּל לַיְלָה וְיוֹמָם
וְשִׁמְךָ עַל כָּל בְּרָכָה מְרוֹמָם   וְנַפְשִׁי יוֹדַעַת מְאֹד

הֲדַרַת כְּבוֹדְךָ גָּדְלָה וְרַבָּה
וְאֵיכָה תִשְׁכֹּן בְּאֹהֶל וְקֻבָּה
שְׁאֵתְךָ לֹא יוּכַל גַּלְגַּל מְסִבָּה   כִּי עָצַמְתָּ מִמֶּנּוּ מְאֹד

חֲסִין נֶאְדָּר בְּאַרְבַּע חַיּוֹת
זְרוּיִים תָּקַבֵּץ מֵאַרְבַּע זָוִיּוֹת
קֶרֶא שָׁנָת גְּאָלָה לְתוֹעִים כְּשֵׂיוֹת   דַּלּוֹת וְרָעוֹת תֹּאַר מְאֹד

But of all Ibn Gabirol's descriptions of the celestial world, surely the following poem must be reckoned the most sublime, its numinous quality rivalling—perhaps surpassing —that in the inaugural visions of Isaiah and Ezekiel themselves. One is reminded of the words reputedly uttered by Handel after he had written the Hallelujah Chorus: 'I did think I did see all heaven before me, and the great God Himself.'[63]

The framework of the poem is constituted by its refrain, from Psalm 29.1, the truncated verse evoking the memory of its bracketed conclusion: 'give unto the Lord, ye sons of the mighty, give [unto the Lord glory and strength]'. The various divisions of the angelic host are described as parading with music in review order, and I have suggested elsewhere[64] that the whole pattern is based on familiarity with the military aspect of court protocol in Muslim Spain. Presumably Ibn Gabirol will have had occasion, through his obligations to Yequthiel in Saragossa and Samuel Ha-nagid in Granada, to visit the royal court from time to time; but even if he did not, the citizenry in both places will have had opportunities to view military displays held in honour of victories, accessions, etc. A description survives of one such which, although it took place decades before Ibn Gabirol's birth, was (it seems) long remembered: it concerns the accession of Ḥakam II in 961, on the death of 'Abderraḥman III. Judah Ibn Gabirol, Solomon's father, came from Cordoba, but if Solomon was born in 1021/2 (see p. 18), Judah could scarcely have had first-hand knowledge of something that happened in 961. But amongst those participating in the accession ceremonial described below will almost certainly have been Ḥasdai ibn Shaprut (see pp. 9f.), the minister of the late Caliph, and contemporary Jewish pride in his participation in so prestigious a ceremony may well have served to impress its magnificence on subsequent Jewish folk-memory:[65]

'. . . There entered [the city-palace of Az-zahra, near Cordoba] some of the pre-eminent figures of the forces, so timed as to meet the arrival of [the new Caliph's] brothers . . . They came down, according to their various degrees of dignity . . . to take their seats . . . Ḥakam took his seat upon the royal throne, in the centremost of the gilded edifices on the south front that looked out on to the terrace of polished stone. The first to approach him were his brothers, who formally pronounced him caliph . . . thereafter came the viziers, their sons and brothers, and then the commandants of the household troops and the several branches of the palace staff . . . there were ranged in the assembly at which he occupied his throne the chiefest of the nobles to his right and left . . . wearing splendiferous robes of mourning-attire and being girded with swords. They

were followed by the pages of noble birth, wearing
full-length coats of mail and armed with ornamental
swords . . . Round the . . . perimeter were posted
gentlemen-at-arms, being "slav" [i.e. European] eunuchs
of noble birth, dressed in white, all of them sword in hand
. . . Then came the archers, with their . . . bows at the
shoulder . . . the unmutilated slaves heavily armed with
flashing weapons.'

It is to be emphasized that there is no need to insist that the
following poem was directly modelled on folk-memory of
the scene portrayed in the foregoing. It is cited as typical of
the ceremonial occasions likely to have come within Ibn
Gabirol's ken, on which, it is claimed, he based his marvel-
lously vivid picture of the perpetual pomp and pageantry
of the angel's adoration of God:[66]

Gleaming hierarchs[67] of heaven, flashing with their blades
of fire[68]
Like to burnished armour[69] shining, incandescent their
attire,
Proud they march with sound of storm-wind, past the
throne that towers higher,
They whom vision showed the prophet ranged antiphonal[70]
in choir:
Eager in love to pronounce Him all-holiest they combine,
Glory and strength, ye angels, glory to God assign.[71]

Thine the high-borne, mystic creatures 'neath thy throne[72]
that unmoved stays,
Lively, light-refracting angels, rainbow-girt in lustrous
rays,[73]
Four battalions acknowledge thine effulgence in their praise,
Some in solemn, awe-struck measures, others blither voices
raise,
Champions posted day-long, night-long to guard thy
shrine:
Glory and strength, ye angels, glory to God assign.

99

Chief of massed brigades that guard the basis of thy throne,
'tis told,
In command is Michael, princely archangel,[74] proud to
behold;
At thy right they stand paraded, with their chariots
thousandfold,[75]
They escort Thee, thronging, asking how should space thy
dwelling hold:[76]
　When to the veil[77] they bow them, to Thee 'tis they
incline,
　Glory and strength, ye angels, glory to God assign.

Ranking second on the left flank stands a regiment erect
Led[78] by Gabriel, their marshal—famed the gaze his eyes
project;
Seraphs by the thousand mustered, troops of mightiest effect,
Thus on either side surrounding guards thy sacred throne
protect,
　Quarried from fire,[79] yea, fire-girt, their steeds of fire
divine:
　Glory and strength, ye angels, glory to God assign.

Third, the massed bands, bird-like piping music, intricately
planned
Sound mosaics—God's conductor, Nuriel,[80] surmounts the
stand:
Making heaven's vault vibrate[81] they march and
countermarch, a band
Asking loud, 'Where is He,[82] timeless,[83] skies and earth
who did expand?'
　But to glimpse thy majesty, all day, all night they pine:
　Glory and strength, ye angels, glory to God assign.

Fourth in line, arrayed in splendour, through their pomp
thine to attest,[84]
Others joined with Raphael hymn thine epic tale and thy
behest,

Weaving plainsong into garlands,[85] prayers to crown with
might thy crest:
Four divisions singing psalms unceasing thus declare Thee
bless'd,
Linked by Thee in vigour lest they weary, and decline:[86]
Glory and strength, ye angels, glory to God assign.

Scintillating, all assembled, harmonized their songs unite,
For that battered folk Thou bearest since the womb[87] grace
to excite;
Schooled by fear, with feet aligned[88] they stand, their
voices raised in might,
Bright as flames from goldsmiths' firing[89] all thy holiness
recite,
Sweet-strained, responding 'Holy!' with acclamation
trine:[90]

Glory and strength, ye angels, glory to God assign.

— — —	— — —	— — —
כְּנִיצוֹצִים יְלָהֲבוּ	שַׁאֲנַנִּים	שְׁנְאַנִּים
כְּעֵין קָלָל יִצְהָבוּ	מַעֲטֵיהֶם	לַהֲטֵיהֶם
בְּקוֹל רַעַשׁ יִרְהָבוּ	מִתְנַשֵּׂא	מוּל כִּסֵּא
לְהַקְדִּישׁ אֵל יֶאֱהָבוּ	זֶה אֶל זֶה	הֵן בְּמַחֲזֶה
	הָבוּ לַיִי בְּנֵי אֵלִים הָבוּ	
בְּתַחְתִּית כֵּס הַנִּקְבָּע	עֶלְיוֹת	לְךָ חַיּוֹת
אֲזוּרֵי זִיו הַנִּצְבָּע	וְחַשְׁמַלִּים	וְאֶרְאֶלִּים
יְהוֹדוּן מַחֲנוֹת אַרְבַּע	וְהִלָּתָךְ	תְּהִלָּתְךָ
לְךָ נֶ... וְשִׂיו... יַבַּע	וְזֶה יַמְרִיץ	זֶה יַעֲרִיץ
בְּמִשְׁמַרְתָּם נִצְבּוּ	יוֹם וָלַיִל	בְּנֵי חַיִל
בְּרֹאשׁ מַחֲנוֹת הַמּוֹנֶיךָ	הַנֶּאֱמָר	מְכוֹן מִשְׁמָר
מִיכָאֵל גְּאוֹנֶךְ	בְּיַד הַשַּׂר	הֲלֹא נִמְסַר
יַעֲמֹד עַל יְמִינֶךָ	לְרַבְבוֹת	בְּמֶרְכָּבוֹת
דְּרֹשׁ אַיֵּה מְעוֹנֶךָ	וְיִלָּוּ	וִיקֽקוּ
לְךָ יִסְגְּדוּ וְיִקְרְבוּ	לְמוּל פַּרְגּוֹד	וְשָׁם סָגוֹד
עַל יָרֵךְ שְׂמֹאל נִזְקָף	הַמִּשְׁנֶה	הֲמוֹן מַחֲנֶה

גַּבְרִיאֵל הַנִּשְׁקָף	וּנְשִׂיאוֹ	וְעַל צְבָאוֹ
וְחַיִל כָּבֵד מְאֹד נִתְקַף	לַאֲלָפִים	בְּשָׂרָפִים
וְכִסֵּא קָדְשְׁךָ מָקֵף	וְאֵלֶּה פֹּה	זֶה אֵיפֹה
וְסוּסֵי אֵשׁ יִרְכָּבוּ	אֲזוּרֵי אֵשׁ	גְּזוּרֵי אֵשׁ
צְבָא מַחֲנֶה שְׁלִישִׁיָּה	וְשִׁיר יְרַצֵּף	קוֹל יִצְפְּצֵף
עוֹמֵד בָּם לְתַלְפִּיָּה	שַׂר הָאֵל	וְנוּרִיאֵל
יְרוֹפַף חוּג הָעֲלִיָּה	וְשָׁעֲטָתָם	לְשָׁאֵטָם
יוֹצֵר רוּם וְתַחְתִּיָּה	מְקוֹם אֶהְיֶה	בְּקוֹל אַיֵּה
כָּל הַיּוֹם יִתְאָבוּ	הַנֶּהְדָּר	רְאוֹת נֶאְדָּר
בָּרְבִיעִית יָעִידוּ	לְךָ שָׁהוֹד	טְכוּסֵי הוֹד
עִם רְפָאֵל יַגִּידוּ	וְזִמְרָתְךָ	וְאִמְרָתְךָ
לְךָ יִקְשְׁרוּ וְיַעֲנִידוּ	וְכֶתֶר עֹז	וְצִיץ מָעֹז
יַתְמִידוּ וְיַצְמִידוּ	שִׁיר וּמִכְתָּם	וְאַרְבַּעְתָּם
לְבַל יִינְעוּ וְיִדְאָבוּ	וְנִבְרָתָם	חֻבַּרְתָּם
לְךָ יַחַד יְרַגְּנוּ	נִקְבָּצִים	נִיצוֹצִים
רַגְלֵיהֶם יְכוֹנְנוּ	וְיִרְאָתְךָ	בְּאֵימָתְךָ
לְעֻמָּתְךָ יְחַגְּנוּ	הַחֲמוּסִים	בְּעַד עֲמוּסִים
קְדֻשָּׁתְךָ יְשַׁנְּנוּ	כְּמוֹ בָזָק	בְּקוֹל חָזָק
וּכְבוֹד אֵל יְדוֹבֵבוּ	יְשַׁלֵּשׁוּ	יְקַדְּשׁוּ

We may conclude this sample by citing a piece which illustrates well the artificiality of distinguishing between 'sacred' and 'secular' poetry criticized above (p. 54). Although excluded by Jarden from his recent edition it has been generally reckoned as belonging to Ibn Gabirol's canon,[91] and will be found in Sephardic prayer-books for Passover concluding the series of hymns inserted into the prayers for dew (see pp. 80f.), and also in the corresponding position in the liturgy for the eighth day of Tabernacles, when after the end of summer, prayers for rain are re-introduced. Its concluding reference to God as the poet's *shield* indicates that it was designed to precede the benediction of God as 'Shield of Abraham' (p. 80). The words *garon* . . .

be-qor'i lo' niḥar ('my throat is not parched through crying in prayer') recall the beginning of Ibn Gabirol's well-known poem *niḥar be-qor'i geroni*,[92] but since the phrase is adapted from Psalm 69.4(3) too much evidential weight should perhaps not be allowed to this. More to the point is the metrical accuracy and purity of rhyme;[93] and these, like the sentiments, are thoroughly in character with Ibn Gabirol. The poem may be compared to Horace's prefatory ode to Maecenas, in which he avers that whilst others find satisfaction in chariot-racing, estate-management whether for pure investment or as a basis for a political career, etc., for him the poet's garland and the simple pleasures of the countryside so elevate him, that he fancies himself sharing the company of the very gods:[94]

> Thou didst inspire my tongue; Thyself preferred
> That gift, O Lord, that I before Thee lay,
> The songs that Thou upon my lips hast stirred—
> Tribute more choice than trafficking might pay.[95]
>
> Thou, from my childhood's dawn, before thy face
> Didst plot the course my feet should keep, nor stray:[96]
> Thou hast endowed with chords of music's grace
> This throat, unparched[97] whene'er to Thee I pray.
>
> Yea, Thou—none else—hast purged my passion clean
> Like wool left white,[98] its flecks all washed away,
> And so 'tis Thou hast set me where, serene,
> No palpitating fears my heart can sway.[99]
>
> Thou, Lord, didst shelter[100] all my yesterdays,
> My morrow's Shelter, shelter my to-day:
> Thee, Thee alone against the world's forays
> I own my Shield[101]—Lord, brook no more delay.[102]

לְשׁוֹנִי בּוֹנֶנְתָּ   אֱלֹהַי וַתִּבְחַר   בְּשִׁירִים שֶׁשַּׂמְתָּ   בְּפִי טוֹב מִמִּסְחָר

וְנֶגְדְּךָ כּוֹנֶנְתָּ   צְעָדַי מִמִּשְׁחָר   וְלִי גָרוֹן תַּתָּה   בְּקָרְאִי לֹא נִחַר

וְיִצְרִי הִלְבַּנְתָּ   כְּמוֹ צֶמֶר צַחַר   וְלָכֵן לֹא שַׁתָּה   לְבָבִי בִי סְחַרְחַר

הֱיֵה סִתְרִי עַתָּה   כְּאֶתְמוֹל וּלְמָחָר   וּמִגִּי אַתָּה   אֱלֹהַי אַל תְּאַחַר

7

THE ROYAL CROWN

THE theme of Ibn Gabirol's *Royal Crown* (*kether malkhuth*) is the problem of the human predicament: stated in conventional theological terms, the frailty of man and his proclivity to sin, in tension with a benign providence that has to leave room for the operation of man's free will and also make available to him, with the option, the means of penitence. Translated into terms of Neoplatonic psychology, this corresponds to the situation of the immortal soul, which— thanks to its proximity to its source—is of the finest of all created matter in the cosmos; but which finds itself confronted by evil and by moral temptation through being caught up amongst the toils of the sub-lunary world (see p. 115) whose matter, having degenerated at each successive stage of emanation, has arrived at the ultimate degree of coarseness. The poem is consequently printed in prayer-books of the Sephardic rite for the Day of Atonement, and among North African Jewish communities (and their offshoots in Israel and elsewhere) it is still read communally around dawn, before the morning service of the Day. In congregations in northern Europe and the west the custom has largely lapsed, but the *Royal Crown* is still printed for private penitential reading.

The poem, which in mentioning the *fountain of life* in *cento* IX glances at the title of Ibn Gabirol's philosophical *summa*, has distinct points of contact with the *Meqor ḥayyim*, e.g. the characteristics of the divine oneness (*cento* II) and God as foundation (*yesod*), i.e. prime existent (*cento* I). Indeed, the whole scheme of the *Meqor ḥayyim* shimmers behind the *Royal Crown* without being brought into the centre of the picture. It is for the most part presupposed, the occasional explicit pointer hinting at its compatibility and consistency with the traditional Jewish theological thought and imagery, which had been (appropriately) excluded from mention in the philosophical treatise. More than this: the impression is conveyed that traditional Jewish piety, with its theology expressed not in abstract propositions, but through an exuberance of moralizing anecdotage, is not adequate for the philosopher, unless it be intellectually stiffened by the scheme of the *Meqor hayyim* itself or of another speculative endeavour equivalent thereto. Writing for the Jewish believer, the poet hopes (he is too much of a realist to assume) that just as a philosophical scheme is in the forefront of his own mind, it may at least hover at the back of the reader's, awaiting that poetic synthesis with the Hebrew Bible that it is no business of a professionally philosophical tract to provide.

Some will feel that nevertheless there must always remain a tension between the God presupposed by faith, concerned with providence and love, and the only Deity that philosophy can find room for.[1] In Schlanger's words,[2] although for Ibn Gabirol it is the same God who is under discussion in considering both religious and philosophical truth, the totality of the Deity is not the same in each case. The philosopher who happens also to be a believer subscribing to a specific religious faith has to face up to the dilemma that while reason is not, ultimately, identical or perhaps even reconcilable with the axioms of his own particular system of belief, he cannot appeal to mystery for a solution without forfeiting his title to be considered a philosopher. If the result in the case of the *Royal Crown* gratifies the intellectual pretensions of the believer while leaving the philosopher essentially dissatisfied, that inadequacy will not, perhaps, force itself so powerfully upon a modern reader, for whom the Neoplatonic metaphysics and the ptolemaic cosmology as presupposed in the poem (see pp. 113f.) are both obsolete. The challenge, however, can be translated into modern philosophical concepts and terminology, and the believer who would also claim to be a philosopher may not ignore it. But presumably it will always be but a minority of believers whose relentless intellectual integrity insists that they face up to the challenge. Ibn Gabirol felt the call to do so, and apparently convinced himself that he had successfully surmounted it. Those who feel unable to agree will surely concede that so noble a failure justifies Ibn Gabirol's claim that the attempt itself marks his own greatest achievement. Hence the title that he chose for it—the *Royal Crown, kether malkhuth*—culled from the biblical account of the coronation of Queen Esther.[3]

The poem's movement swings—as might be anticipated from a Neoplatonist—alternatively 'downwards' and inwards from God and universal matter, to matter in its most gross state in the sub-lunary world (see p. 115), and thence through man (indeed, through the individual Jew at prayer), the climax of creation, 'upwards' again and outwards towards that source whence, in a series of progressively less finetextured manifestations, concrete matter emanated. The symmetry of the whole is delicately pointed by its enclosure (after the exordium) between two significant quotations. Psalm 139.14, 'marvellous are thy works; and that my soul knoweth right well', introduces two key concepts: the ultimate divine mystery, and the vocation of the soul to respond thereto: by prosecuting intellectual investigation up to its limit, and by learning to appreciate intuitively the force, and the providential purpose, of what lies beyond its intellectual reach. The final word comes from Psalm 19.15, 'let the words of my mouth, and the meditation of my heart, be acceptable [*le-raṣon*: i.e. conforming to thy will] in thy sight, O Lord, my strength and my redeemer'. Spiritual serenity is within the reach of those who can resolve to make the best of their opportunities in the future, and not least of their intellectual potential: *hegyon libbi* means, in biblical Hebrew, *the musing of my heart*, but the words have an overlaid semantic stratum thanks to the medieval use of *hegyon* in the sense of *logical thought*.

Here follows an analysis of the structure of the poem.

1st section (centos I–IX).
I Praise of God, acknowledgement of his surpassing mystery, and of the fact that man's spiritual striving in this world must await recompense in the next. The divine properties: II unique unity, III undefinable existence, IV life outside time, V transcendent greatness, VI power, paradoxically self-restrained, VII light more dazzling than human vision can sustain, VIII the divine essence uncompromised through purblind worship of false gods, since their worshippers are unknowingly seeking the true God, whose properties constitute an undifferentiable mystery, IX divine wisdom (corresponding to intelligence and will in *Meqor ḥayyim* v, 12–16) as the instrument of creation that imprints on created matter its various forms.

2nd Section (centos X–XXIX). Description of the scheme of creation, beginning at its centre—the sub-lunary sphere—and proceeding through the ten outer spheres that constitute Ibn Gabirol's cosmological scheme (see p. 115), up to the Throne of Glory which, corresponding to universal matter, lies 'beyond' them all: the astrological propensities of each sphere, as willed by God, being described. (See diagram, p. 114.)
X Earth's globe and the four elements, earth and water being (notionally) hemispheres, together enclosed by the spheres of air and fire.
XI The Moon.
XII The moon as chronometer; orbital positions causing mutual eclipse by moon and sun.
XIII Mercury.
XIV Venus.
XV The Sun.

XVI The annual movement of the sun between the poles, and its effect on the length of the day.

XVII The effect of the relative positions of the sun and moon on the extent and intensity of the moon's light, pictured in terms of the pursuit of an elusive maiden, and an eventually consummated union (see p. 182, n. 52).

XVIII Mars.

XIX Jupiter.

XX Saturn.

XXI The Zodiac (fixed stars).

XXII The twelve zodiacal signs as mansions of the planets, and as astrological champions of their respective peoples.

XXIII The ninth, all-encompassing sphere (see p. 115).

XXIV The tenth sphere, that of the intelligence, postulated by Ibn Gabirol.

XXV The tenth sphere as the radiative source of souls, and more especially of the angels.

XXVI The Throne of Glory, beyond the outermost sphere, as 'mystery and basic stuff' (i.e. universal matter).

XXVII The place beneath the Throne for the souls of the departed righteous.

XXVIII The forces of nature stored for providential purposes, both benign and punitive.

XXIX The soul of man, created from the radiance of the divine glory (see p. 185, n. 140).

3rd section (*centos* XXX–XXXII). There is no marked division between the preceding section and this; but the Throne having been reached, with the implication that the divine Glory Itself transcends even the Throne, and it having been stated that the human soul originates from that Glory, the stage is set for the 'return' journey, to the situation of the soul embodied in the individual worshipper.

XXX The [rational] soul, in virtue of its faculty of intelligence, is immortal and is subject to purgatory.

XXXI Breathed into man's body by God, it distinguishes

him from the rest of creation, and exercises a tutelary care over the particular body to which it is assigned.

XXXII Man's organs, and the faculties derived from them for divine service: culminating in the poet's tongue, the function of which it is to set forth God's praise. Although God's transcendence renders this beyond attainment, the endeavour is not pointless or hopeless for those who have undergone genuine religious experience; and the attempt may prove the means by which one obsessed with his own sense of guilt may achieve atonement with the God whose character he tries to understand.

4th section (centos XXXIII–XL). The final part of the poem, consisting of confession, petition, thanksgiving, and the expression of confidence, may be subdivided as follows:

A. Confession of guilt and unworthiness (*centos* XXXIII–XXXVII(a)).

XXXIII(a)–(b) Overcome by the contrast between God's transcendence and his own insignificance and proclivity to sin, the worshipper nevertheless summons up resolution to approach God in prayer.

XXXIV Confessional, transforming the statutory alphabetical form from the first person plural to the singular.

XXXV(a)–(b) Rehearsal of God's bountiful providence manifested to man from birth and throughout the vicissitudes of life; and

XXXV(c) its culmination in the gift of faith (in Judaism), which sets those who have it apart from others who, lacking faith and so also morality, can but deride.

XXXVI Despite the poet's sense of unworthiness, he gives thanks for the gift of a soul—originally pure, but defiled through the failure to resist the inclination to evil. Having hitherto failed in all endeavours to overcome this, despite reliance on God's supporting mercy, he must now leave it to that mercy to take the initiative.

XXXVII(a) Petition to God to suppress the evil inclination's workings, and to quash the sentence of punishment which, though due, would leave the worshipper spiritually unprepared for death.

B. Soliloquy on the frailty of man's nature (*centos* XXXVII(b)–(d))

XXXVII(b) Man's feebleness, physical and moral, and the ineffectuality of his frantic attempts, when in peril, to purchase safety with insincere expressions of regret.

XXXVII(c) The hazards of human life from the cradle to the grave, and the unfeeling toll exacted by the elements and by time.

XXXVII(d) Abandoning soliloquy, the poet remonstrates with God: how could man, thus handicapped, ever achieve genuine penitence? Taking this into consideration, let God forbear to punish, and instruct him how to order his remaining life aright.

C. Petition, remonstrance, and admission of moral failure (*centos* XXXVIII–XL(a))

XXXVIII(a) Appeal to God's concern for his own credit, which must preclude his abandoning his worshipper. Flight from God's anger is but flight to God's own mercy. May the limitations of the human condition be borne in mind, and let not God dismiss the poet spiritually unprepared for his journey. When depart he must, let his shortcomings be balanced against the harassments of his past life.

XXXVIII(b) Acknowledgment that suffering—particularly of the Jew in exile—is remedially imposed by God: may God's mercy cause Him to relent, before suffering destroys the worshipper.

XXXVIII(c) Remonstrance—the poet's utter insignificance does not merit a divine surveillance that marks the least fault. God himself originally fashioned him, and it is pointless for God to see his own handiwork destroyed.

XXXIX May God effect a sincerity of repentance and change of heart that will be proof against temptation; and thus, spiritually regenerate, may the poet share in the messianic redemption and witness the rebuilding of the temple.

XL(a)None the less, he remains acutely aware of his own moral failure, being unable to lay claim either to good works, to response to God's loving care or to any genuine sense of penitence.

D. Conclusion of confidence (*centos* XL(b)–(d))

XL(b) Reliance upon God's grace, and on his constant visitation motivated by good-will and not by fault-finding; petition for cleansing from sin in this life, and for a share in the glory and serenity of that to come.

XL(c) When death comes may he find himself amongst the martyrs and the righteous privileged to feast their eyes on the divine Glory, and spiritually mature enough to say 'I give Thee thanks that though Thou wast angry with me, thine anger was turned away, and Thou comfortest me' (Isaiah 12.1).

XL(d) Final acknowledgment of the obligation to utter praises of thanksgiving, expressed in terms which, echoing the statutory liturgy, blend the individual's search for atonement with the collective prayer of Israel; and concluding with the citation of Psalm 19.15 (see p. 107) as indication that, within that act of collective worship to which the philosopher may bring his own insights, he can attain spiritual serenity.

What sources did Ibn Gabirol use for the detail that he so felicitously integrated into his *Royal Crown*? The Jewish sources may, of course, be taken for granted. For the sort of readership and fellow-worshippers that he had in mind, a knowledge of the Bible close to his own mastery of it could be presupposed, and probably also in regard to the relatively few rabbinic allusions. But the Neoplatonic metaphysics had to be complemented by a cosmology which would be accorded respect as being in accordance with contemporary scientific opinion, and for this Jewish sources, or Hebrew translations of Arabic ones, were not yet available. In one of his hymns Ibn Gabirol was content to allude to the talmudic tradition of seven heavens,[4] but what was required in the *Royal Crown* was the astronomical system formulated (on the basis of earlier work of Aristotle and others) by Ptolemy of Alexandria in the second century CE, which was generally recognized until the time of Copernicus (1473–1543) at least. For access to such information Ibn Gabirol turned to an encyclopaedic compilation made, perhaps in Basra, in the late tenth or early eleventh century, known as the *Epistles of the Brethren of Purity* (*Rasā'il iḥwān aṣ-ṣafā*), and also, as has recently been shown, to the work of the astronomer Al-farghani (Alfraganus, died 820 CE). Details regarding the use of these sources, which ascend to Ptolemy's *Planetary Hypotheses*, have been set out by me elsewhere,[5] and no more is repeated here than is necessary for the following of the structure of the second section of the *Royal Crown* (see pp. 125–41, and diagram, p. 114).

The suggestion that in the planning of his *Royal Crown* Ibn Gabirol was influenced by the pseudo-Aristotelian tract *On the Cosmos* (*de mundo*) has in the past been seriously overstressed, and ought no longer be entertained after Blau's article of 1974.[6] To be sure, its author declares his intention[7] of 'making a theology to take account of the nature, position and motion of [the cosmos]'; but it is not one that would have commended itself to Ibn Gabirol, whose scientific data are fuller (and later) than those found in the *de mundo*: and the most that could be claimed is that it constituted a challenge to Ibn Gabirol to produce something that would make clear that the divine will is the ultimate cause underlying the cosmos, instead of postulating the Deity as the controller of its whole mechanism. But there may even be some doubt as to whether the *de mundo* was known to Ibn Gabirol at all. It had been translated into Arabic in Aleppo in the middle of the tenth century,[8] but it is significant that Ibn Gabirol's elder contemporary Al-biruni (973–1048) knew it from the Syriac version only.[9]

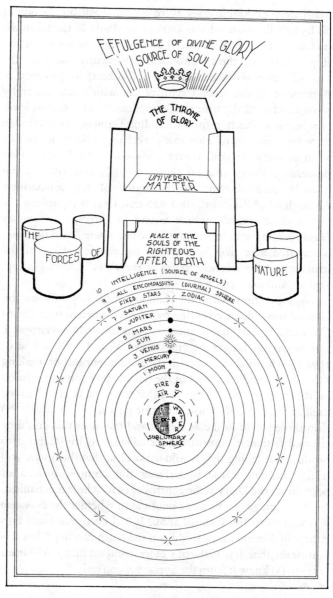

The system is one of a series of concentric spheres round the earth, which is assumed to be the centre of the universe. In the sub-lunary sphere sense-perception leads to the postulation of certain axioms, notably that of the four elements (earth, air, fire, water) of which all things are allegedly composed. In regard to the higher spheres, metaphysics and (carefully modified) astrology tend to merge, and the astronomical data given regarding the volume and the periodicity of the planets are surprisingly accurate (see below, tables). The order—Moon, Mercury, Venus, Sun (considered a planet of the Earth), Mars, Jupiter, Saturn, the Zodiac—in which Ibn Gabirol rehearses details of these eight spheres, is conventional, as is also the assumption of a ninth, diurnal all-encompassing sphere (Arabic *muḥiṭ*) that imparts motion to all the others within itself. The tenth sphere is a postulation of Ibn Gabirol's own: regarded by him as the location of intelligence (for the cardinal role of which in the *Meqor ḥayyim* see *Part v*: 1 p. 50), it is declared in *cento* XXV to be the radiative source of the angels.

TABLE I

Comparative Volume of Planets Relative to Earth

	Ibn Gabirol	*Ptolemy*[11]	Recent Computation
Earth	1	1	1
Moon	$\frac{1}{39}$	$\frac{1}{40}$	0.02
Mercury	$\frac{1}{22,000}$	$\frac{1}{19,683}$	0.055
Venus	$\frac{1}{37}$	$\frac{1}{44}$	0.88
Sun	170 (variant 175):1	$166\frac{1}{3}$:1	1.3×10^6:1
Mars	$1\frac{5}{8}$:1	$1\frac{1}{2}$:1	0.15
Jupiter	75:1	$82\frac{1}{4} + \frac{1}{20}$:1	1,318:1
Saturn	91:1	$79\frac{1}{2}$:1	769:1
Fixed Stars	107 (variant 170):1	$94\frac{1}{6} + \frac{1}{8}$:1	—

In referring to the size of the planets, Ibn Gabirol uses the term *guph* (body), except for Mercury, where *middah* =

TABLE II

Periodicity of the Heavenly Bodies

		Recent Computation	
	Ibn Gabirol	*Sidereal Period*	*Synodic Period*
Moon	29 days (variant $29\frac{1}{2}$ + a 'further known number of parts') (*ḥalaqim yedu 'im*)'	27.322 days	29.53 days
Mercury	10 days (variant 10 months)	87.969 days	115.88 days
Venus	11 months (variant 12 months)	224.7 days	583.92 days
Sun	1 year	—	—
Mars	18 months	686.98 days	779.94 days
Jupiter	12 years	4,332.59 days (11.89 years)	398.88 days
Saturn	30 years	10,759.2 days (29.89 years)	378.09 days
Fixed Stars	36,000 years (variant 36(?) years)	—	—

measure occurs. His figures refer to the volume, and not to the diameter. Although his sources gave information regarding both, it would seem that his decision to cite volume arose from aesthetic considerations regarding Hebrew terminology. Table I sets out the figures comparatively.

Table II compares Ibn Gabirol's figures regarding the time taken by each of the heavenly bodies to complete its circuit with modern calculations (broadly speaking, Ibn Gabirol's figures and those of his sources are in agreement, or the differences can be explained).[12] The differences between sidereal periods and the synodic periods tabulated here is as follows. *Sidereal period* expresses the time of revolution of the planet about the sun with respect to some fixed star. *Synodic period* expresses the time for the planet to return to the same apparent position with respect to the sun. In the case of the moon, it is the period from new moon to new moon.

We may conclude this introduction to the *Royal Crown* with a brief note regarding its poetic form. Apart from the short metrical exordium, the poem is composed in the rhymed free-running lines which medieval Hebrew copied from Arabic (*saj'*), the rhyme providing a mechanism for clause-division. In view of the highly inflected character of Hebrew thanks to its use of suffixed terminations, mere assonance is easily achieved, and would lack the necessary weight to act as a device for punctuation. Sephardic convention, with which one may contrast the less demanding conventions of such modern Hebrew poets as can trouble themselves to rhyme at all, consequently requires that rhymes must be 'masculine', i.e. any rhymed suffix must be preceded by the same root-letter as occurs in the matched ending. Ibn Gabirol's virtuosity displays itself in the length of his rhyme series, and in the tense expectancy that he can thereby generate in the mind of the listener or reader, as with each biblical quotation he strikes not a mere single note, but a chord.

This medium serves well enough for letter-writing or literary essays, such as Judah Al-ḥarizi's belletristic *maqamas*, but on its own would scarcely provide a diction sublime enough for the subject-matter of the *Royal Crown*. That it succeeds is due to the brilliance with which Ibn Gabirol steers every paragraph of his severely classical language, replete with allusions to the Hebrew Bible, to a climactic quotation which summarizes and illuminates all that has gone before as though a firework had suddenly lit up the sculptured front of a medieval cathedral. Those who have learned to appreciate the beauty, and to be moved by the message of the *Royal Crown* will understand my comparison of it to a tall ship under full sail, sweeping majestically across a deep-blue ocean with her canvas perfectly trimmed to the wind along a course the turns in which she negotiates seemingly without effort, to arrive at last at her haven with each detail in her rigging standing out against the glow of a setting sun.

This is the first English translation of the complete *Royal Crown* in poetic form, although verse renderings of parts of it appeared nearly a century ago by Elsie Davis[13] and Alice Lucas.[14] I have written elsewhere[15] of the parallel between the Jewish poets of medieval Spain and the English metaphysical poets of the sixteenth century, and the model that each group affords for translating the work of the other. I have chosen Spenser's nineteen-line stanza as my own basic unit here, but have elaborated means of both extending it and, occasionally, shortening it where I needed to do so. There is good reason for rendering the *Royal Crown* into what many readers will no doubt consider a precious medium to adopt at the end of the twentieth century. The English of King James' version of the Bible was already archaic when that version was published (1611); and the choice of medium may remind anyone who is inclined to forget it that Solomon ibn Gabirol enjoyed the great advantage of knowing that tradition and vocation alike directed him to compose his poetry in a language not his vernacular. Appropriately for its author, the *Royal Crown* constitutes perhaps the supreme example in Hebrew literature of the inter-penetrative integration of matter and form.

EXORDIUM

Perchance my prayer may prove some worth
For fellow-men to learn on earth
Therefrom what uprightness must be
If 'guiltless'[16] *they would make their plea;*
Marvels I tell, that briefly told
God's lively mysteries unfold.
First of my hymns this I acclaim:
The Royal Crown[17] *shall be its name.*

———————　　　　———————

בְּתִפְלָתִי יִסְכָּן גֶּבֶר　　　כִּי בָהּ יִלְמַד יֹשֶׁר וּזְכוּת
סִפַּרְתִּי בָהּ פִּלְאֵי אֵל חַי　　　בְּקָצְרָהּ אַךְ לֹא בַאֲרִיכוּת
שַׂמְתִּיהָ עַל רֹאשׁ מַהֲלָלִי　　　וּקְרָאתִיהָ כֶּתֶר מַלְכוּת

I

Mysterious are Thy works, my soul well knows:
Thine, Lord, is majesty, all pomp and power,
Kingship whose splendour yet more splendid grows
O'ertopping all in glory and wealth's dower.[18]
To Thee celestial creatures, and the seed
Of earth-sprung kind concede
They all must perish, Thou alone remain,
The secret of whose strength doth quite exceed
Our thought, as Thou transcendest our frail plane.
All might is thine, swathed in a mystic shawl,
The fundament of all:
Hid from philosophers thy name: of Thee
That force which poised the universe on nought;
Thou canst bare secrets, in thy searchlight caught,
Thy love prevails, for all thy creatures free.
Thine, too, that goodness in so rich a hoard
For them that fear Thee stored.
Wonders are thine no mind may comprehend,
And life for which decay shall ne'er decree the end.

Whilst loftiest heights sink dwarfed beneath thy throne
Remotest stratosphere secretes Thy glade:
Thine's an existence of whose light our own
Is but the shadow, lightened by Thy shade.
Twin worlds are Thine—twixt them a frontier stone,
The first for deeds, that in the next are paid:[19]
Rewards the just shall win Thou hast concealed,
Knowing their worth, shy as that babe whom sedge did
shield.[20]

נִפְלָאִים מַעֲשֶׂיךָ וְנַפְשִׁי יוֹדַעַת מְאֹד.

לְךָ יְיָ הַגְּדֻלָּה וְהַגְּבוּרָה וְהַתִּפְאֶרֶת וְהַנֵּצַח וְהַהוֹד.

לְךָ יְיָ הַמַּמְלָכָה וְהַמִּתְנַשֵּׂא לְכֹל לְרֹאשׁ וְהָעֹשֶׁר וְהַכָּבוֹד.

לְךָ בְּרוּאֵי מַעְלָה וּמַטָּה יָעִידוּ כִּי הֵמָּה יֹאבֵדוּ וְאַתָּה תַעֲמֹד.

לְךָ הַגְּבוּרָה אֲשֶׁר בְּסוֹדָהּ נִלְאוּ רַעְיוֹנֵינוּ לַעֲמֹד, כִּי עָצַמְתָּ מִמֶּנּוּ מְאֹד.

לְךָ חֶבְיוֹן הָעֹז הַסּוֹד וְהַיְסוֹד.

לְךָ הַשֵּׁם הַנֶּעְלָם מִמְּתֵי חָכְמָה, וְהַכֹּחַ הַסּוֹבֵל הָעוֹלָם עַל בְּלִימָה, וְהַיְכֹלֶת לְהוֹצִיא לָאוֹר כָּל תַּעֲלוּמָה.

לְךָ הַחֶסֶד אֲשֶׁר גָּבַר עַל בְּרוּאֶיךָ, וְהַטּוֹב הַצָּפוּן לִירֵאֶיךָ.

לְךָ הַסּוֹדוֹת אֲשֶׁר לֹא יְכִילֵם שֵׂכֶל וְרַעְיוֹן, וְהַחַיִּים אֲשֶׁר לֹא יִשְׁלַט עֲלֵיהֶם כִּלָּיוֹן,
וְהַכִּסֵּא הַנַּעֲלָה עַל כָּל עֶלְיוֹן, וְהַנָּוֶה הַנִּסְתָּר בְּרוּם חֶבְיוֹן.

לְךָ הַמְּצִיאוּת אֲשֶׁר מִצֵּל מְאוֹרוֹ נִהְיָה כָל הוֹיָה, אֲשֶׁר אָמַרְנוּ בְּצִלּוֹ נִחְיָה.

לְךָ שְׁנֵי הָעוֹלָמִים אֲשֶׁר נָתַתָּ בֵּינֵיהֶם גְּבוּל, הָרִאשׁוֹן לְמַעֲשִׂים וְהַשֵּׁנִי לִגְמוּל.

לְךָ הַגְּמוּל אֲשֶׁר גָּנַזְתָּ לַצַּדִּיקִים וַתַּעְלִימֵהוּ, וַתֵּרֶא אוֹתוֹ כִּי טוֹב הוּא וַתִּצְפְּנֵהוּ.

II

Thy Name is One—of all the primes the Prime,
Base of all algebraic argument,
A Unity beyond account, sublime,
That leaves the schoolmen lost in wonderment:
Uniquity, that neither wanes nor grows,
No plus, no defect knows:
Oneness not gained from accident, nor told,
On which no change, no factor may impose

Nor attribute, nor surrogate; to hold
In logic's bounds that Oneness strict defined
Eludes my wearied mind.
And so, methinks, to watch my way were best
That no offence be by my tongue expressed:[21]
One, ne'er brought low, for fall Thou art too high—
Not one of twain who falls unless his twin be nigh.[22]

אַתָּה אֶחָד רֹאשׁ כָּל מִנְיָן, וִיסוֹד כָּל בִּנְיָן.

אַתָּה אֶחָד וּבְסוֹד אַחְדוּתְךָ חַכְמֵי לֵב יִתְמָהוּ, כִּי לֹא יָדְעוּ מַה הוּא.

אַתָּה אֶחָד וְאַחְדוּתְךָ לֹא יִגְרַע וְלֹא יוֹסִיף, לֹא יֶחְסַר וְלֹא יַעֲדִיף.

אַתָּה אֶחָד וְלֹא כְאֶחָד הַקָּנוּי וְהַמָּנוּי, כִּי לֹא יַשִּׂיגְךָ רִבּוּי וְשִׁנּוּי, לֹא תֹאַר
וְלֹא כִנּוּי.

אַתָּה אֶחָד וְלָשׂוּם לְךָ חֹק וּגְבוּל נִלְאָה הֶגְיוֹנִי, עַל כֵּן אָמַרְתִּי אֶשְׁמְרָה דְרָכַי
מֵחֲטֹא בִלְשׁוֹנִי.

אַתָּה אֶחָד גָּבַהְתָּ וְנַעֲלֵיתָ מִשְּׁפֹל וּמִנְפֹּל, וְאִילוֹ הָאֶחָד שֶׁיִּפֹּל.

III

Thou dost exist, we say, though never ear
Gathered report of Thee, nor mortal eye
Hath glimpsed Thee; what existence, then, is here,
Whereof we cannot ask whence, how, and why?
Exist Thou dost—a sole, unpartnered *Ens*:
Or e'er time did commence,
E'er space there was, didst Thou thy pitch select.
Thou art a hidden mystery, whom sense
Can reach not, thine existence to reflect,
Searching for what Itself must secret keep:
Shall any find? Nay, ours to sigh ''tis, deep, too deep!'[23]

אַתָּה נִמְצָא וְלֹא יַשִּׂיגְךָ שֵׁמַע אֹזֶן וְלֹא רְאוֹת עָיִן, וְלֹא יִשְׁלַט בְּךָ אֵיךְ וְלָמָּה
וְאָיִן.

אַתָּה נִמְצָא אֲבָל לְעַצְמְךָ, וְאֵין לְאַחֵר עִמָּךְ.

אַתָּה נִמְצָא וּבְטֶרֶם הֱיוֹת כָּל זְמַן הָיִיתָ, וּבְלִי מָקוֹם חָנִיתָ.

אַתָּה נִמְצָא וְסוֹדְךָ נֶעְלָם וּמִי יַשִּׂיגֶנּוּ, עָמֹק עָמֹק מִי יִמְצָאֶנּוּ.

IV

Thou livest—yet from no established date
Or point in time thy Life did forward roll,
No infused spirit made Thee animate
Nor soul, who art the very Soul of soul;
Thy Life is not like man's, a breath to spend,[24]
With worms to mark its end:
A living mystery art Thou, to give
Him joy eternal who could comprehend,
And eat the tree's immortal fruit, and live.[25]

אַתָּה חַי וְלֹא מִזְּמָן קָבוּעַ, וְלֹא מֵעֵת יָדוּעַ.
אַתָּה חַי וְלֹא בְנֶפֶשׁ וּנְשָׁמָה, כִּי אַתָּה נְשָׁמָה לַנְּשָׁמָה.
אַתָּה חַי וְלֹא כְחַיֵּי אָדָם לַהֶבֶל דָּמָה, וְסוֹפוֹ עָשׁ וְרִמָּה.
אַתָּה חַי וְהַמַּגִּיעַ לְסוֹדְךָ יִמְצָא תַעֲנוּג עוֹלָם, וְאָכַל וְחַי לְעוֹלָם.

V

We call Thee Great—beside whom, what men think
Is greatness, straight must shrink,
Superiority is made seem small;
Thy greatness outstrips thought, exceeds in pride
The chariots[26] mystics build for Thee to ride,
Past praise, past greatness—Greatest, far, of all.[27]

אַתָּה גָדוֹל וּמוּל גְּדֻלָּתְךָ כָּל גְּדֻלָּה נִכְנַעַת, וְכָל יִתְרוֹן מִגְרַעַת.
אַתָּה גָדוֹל מִכָּל מַחֲשָׁבָה, וְגֵאֶה מִכָּל מֶרְכָּבָה.
אַתָּה גָדוֹל עַל כָּל גְּדֻלָּה, וּמְרוֹמַם עַל כָּל בְּרָכָה וּתְהִלָּה.

VI

Mighty art Thou, whose creatures ne'er aspire
Thy Might—unchanged, entire—
To emulate:[28] so ample is thy Might
That in thy raging wrath Thou canst refrain

And grant thy pardon in thine own despite,[29]
Long-suffering with those whom sin doth stain:
Thy Might means love for all that Thou hast made,
Primeval love, in mighty deeds for aye displayed.[30]

אַתָּה גִבּוֹר וְאֵין בְּכָל יְצִירוֹתֶךָ וּבְרִיּוֹתֶיךָ, אֲשֶׁר יַעֲשֶׂה כְמַעֲשֶׂיךָ וְכִגְבוּרוֹתֶיךָ.
אַתָּה גִבּוֹר וּלְךָ הַגְּבוּרָה הַגְּמוּרָה, אֲשֶׁר אֵין לָהּ שִׁנּוּי וּתְמוּרָה.
אַתָּה גִבּוֹר וּמֵרֹב בַּאֲוָתָךְ תִּמְחֹל בְּעֵת זַעְפֶּךָ, וְתַאֲרִיךְ לַחַטָּאִים אַפֶּךָ.
אַתָּה גִבּוֹר וְרַחֲמֶיךָ עַל כָּל בְּרוּאֶיךָ כֻלָּם, הֵמָּה הַגִּבּוֹרִים אֲשֶׁר מֵעוֹלָם.

VII

Thou art that Light whose supramundane ray
The soul may look upon, so be she pure,
But intervening sin doth overlay
With clouds, till Thou dost lurk from her, obscure:
The light to which this world is as a screen,
But in God's City seen;[31]
Eternal Light, the intellect for Thee
Yearns love-lorn whilst, myopic, she may glean
Nought but blurred vision—more she cannot see.[32]

אַתָּה אוֹר עֶלְיוֹן וְעֵינֵי כָל נֶפֶשׁ זַכָּה יִרְאוּךָ, וְעַנְנֵי עָווֹנִים מֵעֵינֶיהָ יַעְלִימוּךָ.
אַתָּה אוֹר נֶעְלָם בָּעוֹלָם הַזֶּה וְנִגְלֶה בָעוֹלָם הַנִּרְאֶה, בְּהַר יְיָ יֵרָאֶה.
אַתָּה אוֹר עוֹלָם וְעַיִן הַשֵּׂכֶל לְךָ תִכְסֹף וְתִשְׁתָּאֶה, אֶפֶס קָצֵהוּ תִרְאֶה וְכֻלּוֹ לֹא
תִרְאֶה.

VIII

Thou very God, Thou, Lord of Lords,[33] dost hold
Beneath thy sway controlled
Beings celestial and those below:
All creatures are thy witnesses, in bond
Each to thy Name with service to respond,
And each pays homage to thine honour so.
And though men worship other things, their act

Doth not from Thee detract
Since, in their striving, Thee they seek to find
But lose the royal road to stray, mistaken, blind;
Some sunk in quagmires, some ensnared, misled
By fancy, think them in their Promised Land;
While clear-eyed servants, marching straight ahead[34]
Nor right nor left, shall in the King's court[35] stand.
On thy Godhead and Unity are stayed
Thy creatures all, each formed by thine own hand.
Spell not mystic Divinity undone:
God, Being, Oneness, uncreated—all is One.[36]

אַתָּה הוּא אֱלֹהֵי הָאֱלֹהִים וַאֲדוֹנֵי הָאֲדוֹנִים, שַׁלִּיט בָּעֶלְיוֹנִים וּבַתַּחְתּוֹנִים.
אַתָּה אֱלוֹהַּ וְכָל הַבְּרוּאִים עֲדֶיךָ, וּבִכְבוֹד זֶה הַשֵּׁם נִתְחַיֵּב כָּל נִבְרָא לְעָבְדֶךָ.
אַתָּה אֱלוֹהַּ וְכָל הַיְצוּרִים עֲבָדֶיךָ וְעוֹבְדֶיךָ, וְלֹא יֶחְסַר כְּבוֹדֶךָ, בִּגְלַל עוֹבְדֵי
בִלְעָדֶיךָ, כִּי כַוָּנַת כֻּלָּם לְהַגִּיעַ עֲדֶיךָ, אֲבָל הֵם כְּעִוְרִים מְגַמַּת פְּנֵיהֶם דֶּרֶךְ
הַמֶּלֶךְ וְתָעוּ מִן הַדֶּרֶךְ: זֶה טָבַע בִּבְאֵר שַׁחַת, וְזֶה נָפַל אֶל פַּחַת, וְכֻלָּם חָשְׁבוּ
כִּי לְחֶפְצָם נָגָעוּ, וְהֵם לָרִיק יָגָעוּ, אַךְ עֲבָדֶיךָ הֵם כְּפִקְחִים, הַהוֹלְכִים דֶּרֶךְ
נְכֹחִים, לֹא סָרוּ יָמִין וּשְׂמֹאל מִן הַדֶּרֶךְ, עַד בּוֹאָם לַחֲצַר בֵּית הַמֶּלֶךְ.
אַתָּה אֱלוֹהַּ סוֹמֵךְ הַיְצוּרִים בֵּאלֹהוּתֶךָ, וְסוֹעֵד הַבְּרוּאִים בְּאַחְדוּתֶךָ.
אַתָּה אֱלוֹהַּ וְאֵין הֶפְרֵשׁ בֵּין אֱלֹהוּתְךָ וְאַחְדוּתְךָ, וְקַדְמוּתְךָ וּמְצִיאוּתְךָ, כִּי הַכֹּל
סוֹד אֶחָד, וְאִם יִשְׁתַּנֶּה שֵׁם כָּל אֶחָד, הַכֹּל הוֹלֵךְ אֶל מָקוֹם אֶחָד.

IX

Wise art Thou—aye, from Thee doth wisdom flow,
A fount of life:[37] that wisdom which is thine
The mind of brutish man can never know,
A wisdom, demiurge[38] of thy design
Or e'er prime matter was, delighting Thee[39]
Primeval equally;
Wisdom no master taught Thee, not acquired.
And, emanating from her, came to be
Matter[40] so predisposed as Thou inspired
Even as artists work, and out from void

Was being's stuff decoyed
Like light leaps out from eye, to object drawn:[41]
Nor tool nor vessel had that master-mind
Yet dredged it from light's source, shaped, cleansed,
                                            refined,

Called non-being to fissiparous spawn,
Bade substance fix itself, bade cosmos stand
Congealed, of heaven's tracts the measure spanned,[42]
And laced, with powered loops, a tent for spheres,
To charge the lowest hem, for each to each
                                            adheres.[43]

אַתָּה חָכָם וְהַחָכְמָה מְקוֹר חַיִּים מִמְּךָ נוֹבַעַת, וְחָכְמָתְךָ נִבְעַר כָּל אָדָם מִדָּעַת.
אַתָּה חָכָם וְקַדְמוֹן לְכָל קַדְמוֹן, וְהַחָכְמָה הָיְתָה אֶצְלְךָ אָמוֹן.
אַתָּה חָכָם וְלֹא לָמַדְתָּ מִבַּלְעָדֶךָ, וְלֹא קָנִיתָ חָכְמָה מִזּוּלָתֶךָ.
אַתָּה חָכָם וּמֵחָכְמָתְךָ אָצַלְתָּ חֵפֶץ מְזֻמָּן, שַׂמְתּוֹ כְּפוֹעֵל וְאָמָּן, לִמְשֹׁךְ מֶשֶׁךְ הַיֵּשׁ
מִן הָאַיִן, כְּהִמָּשֵׁךְ הָאוֹר הַיּוֹצֵא מִן הָעַיִן, וְשׁוֹאֵב מִמְּקוֹר הָאוֹר מִבְּלִי דֳלִי, וּפוֹעֵל
הַכֹּל בְּלִי כֶּלִי, וְחָצַב וְחָקַק, וְטָהַר וְזִקַּק, וְקָרָא אֶל הָאַיִן וְנִבְקַע, וְאֶל הַיֵּשׁ
וְנִתְקַע, וְאֶל הָעוֹלָם וְנִרְקַע, וְתִכֵּן שְׁחָקִים בַּזֶּרֶת, וְיָדוֹ אֹהֶל הַגַּלְגַּלִּים מְחַבֶּרֶת,
וּבְלוּלְאוֹת הַיְכֹלֶת יְרִיעוֹת הַבְּרִיאוֹת קוֹשֶׁרֶת, וְכֹחָה נוֹגַעַת עַד שְׂפַת הַבְּרִיאָה
הַשָּׁפָלָה הַחִיצוֹנָה הַיְרִיעָה הַקִּיצוֹנָה בַּמַּחְבֶּרֶת.

X

Who may declare the might Thou didst display
In making Earth an orb, one half dry land,
The other half of water,[44] and didst lay
The wind to circle round her in a band
Whirling continuous,[45] and round the wind
A sphere of fire entwined,
Four elements from one foundation,[46] one
The parent source whence all do flow, combined
In permutations ever new begun,
Divided in four streams, each several head
From Eden's watershed?[47]

מִי יְמַלֵּל גְּבוּרוֹתֶיךָ בַּעֲשׂוֹתְךָ כַּדּוּר הָאֶרֶץ נֶחֱלָק לְשָׁנַיִם, חֶצְיוֹ יַבָּשָׁה וְחֶצְיוֹ
מָיִם, וְהִקַּפְתָּ עַל הַמַּיִם גַּלְגַּל הָרוּחַ, סוֹבֵב סוֹבֵב הוֹלֵךְ הָרוּחַ, וְעַל סְבִיבוֹתָיו
יָנוּחַ, וְהִקַּפְתָּ עַל הָרוּחַ גַּלְגַּל הָאֵשׁ, וְהַיְסוֹדוֹת הָאֵלֶּה אַרְבַּעְתָּם לָהֶם יְסוֹד
אֶחָד, וּמוֹצָאָם אֶחָד, וּמִמֶּנּוּ יוֹצְאִים וּמִתְחַדְּשִׁים, וּמִשָּׁם יִפָּרֵד וְהָיָה לְאַרְבָּעָה
רָאשִׁים.

XI

Thy grandeur who shall tell? Thou didst confine
Fire's sphere within a sphere, the firmament
Wherein the Moon snuffs in some solar scent
Of radiance, and part from her doth shine;
She beats her bounds in nine-and-twenty days[48]
Full orbit, in her ways
Mysterious, be her secrets deep or slight,[49]
In mass to Earth's as one to thirty-nine.
As each month new events she doth excite
In this our world, benignant or malign,
Always her own Creator's will[50] she heeds,
That she may show to all mankind his mighty deeds.[51]

מִי יְחַנֶּה גְדֻלָּתְךָ בְּהַקִּיפְךָ עַל גַּלְגַּל הָאֵשׁ גַּלְגַּל הָרָקִיעַ וּבוֹ הַיָּרֵחַ, וּמִזִּיו הַשֶּׁמֶשׁ
שׁוֹאֵף וְזוֹרֵחַ, וּבִתְשָׁעָה וְעֶשְׂרִים יוֹם יִסֹּב גַּלְגַּלּוֹ, וְיַעֲלֶה דֶרֶךְ גְּבוּלוֹ, וְסוֹדָיו מֶהֶם
פְּשׁוּטִים וּמֶהֶם עֲמֻקִּים, וְגוּפוֹ פָחוּת מִגּוּף הָאֶרֶץ כְּחֵלֶק מִתִּשְׁעָה וּשְׁלֹשִׁים
חֲלָקִים, וְהוּא מְעוֹרֵר מִדֵּי חֹדֶשׁ בְּחָדְשׁוֹ חִדּוּשֵׁי עוֹלָם וְקוֹרוֹתָיו, וְטוֹבוֹתָיו
וְרָעוֹתָיו, בִּרְצוֹן הַבּוֹרֵא אוֹתוֹ לְהוֹדִיעַ לִבְנֵי הָאָדָם גְּבוּרוֹתָיו.

XII

Shall any tell thy praise, who didst appoint
The Moon, that she[52] chief reckoner appears
Of times and feasts; yea, cycles, which conjoint
Should count by signs those greater days, the years?[53]
Night is her realm till she, in time, must wane,
And gloom her splendour stain,

And she be swathed in blackness, lacking light
She borrowed from the sun:[54] yet should the twain
Stand on the Dragon[55] at the fourteenth night,
His line dividing them, by no Sun drenched
In beams, Moon's lamp is quenched;
That all the world observing,[56] this may know,
That though the rank celestial creatures hold
Be noble, yet a Judge keeps them controlled
Who raiseth one and brings another low.
But fallen, still she shines, to life returned[57]
Leaving her darkness spurned:
And when the month's end comes, and Moon to Sun
Doth cleave, perchance both on the Dragon stand as one;
'Tis then the turn of Moon to interfere
And hide the Sun's own light, like some black cloud,
That all may see how kingship doth inhere
In none of heaven's host with all their crowd.
Nay, Him who can eclipse them must they fear
As Lord, before whose sovereignty are cowed
The hierarchs of each next higher sphere.[58]
So men who deemed the Sun their god[59] are bowed
By shame, their thought and words confounded clear,
And own the hand is God's,[60] nor power-endowed
That Sun whose Darkener admits no peer:
His rule as absolute must be allowed—
The Sun's own pensioner, carl of a thegn
He sends, dimmed, no more idolized, Sun shall not
reign.[61]

מִי יַזְכִּיר תְּהִלָּתְךָ בַּעֲשׂוֹתְךָ הַיָּרֵחַ רֹאשׁ לְחֶשְׁבּוֹן מוֹעֲדִים וּזְמַנִּים, וּתְקוּפוֹת
וְאוֹתוֹת לְיָמִים וְשָׁנִים, בַּלַּיְלָה מֶמְשַׁלְתּוֹ, עַד בּוֹא עִתּוֹ, וְחָשַׁךְ יְפַעְתּוֹ, וְיִתְכַּסֶּה
מַעֲטֵה קַדְרוּתוֹ, כִּי מִמְּאוֹר הַשֶּׁמֶשׁ אוֹרָתוֹ. וּבְלֵיל אַרְבָּעָה עָשָׂר אִם יַעַמְדוּ עַל
קַו הַתְּלִי שְׁנֵיהֶם, וְיַפְרִיד בֵּינֵיהֶם, אָז הַיָּרֵחַ לֹא יָהֵל אוֹרוֹ, וְיִדְעַךְ גֵּרוֹ, לְמַעַן
דַּעַת כָּל עַמֵּי הָאָרֶץ כִּי בְּרוּאֵי מַעֲלָה אִם הֵם יְקָרִים, עֲלֵיהֶם שׁוֹפֵט לְהַשְׁפִּיל
וּלְהָרִים, אַךְ יִחְיֶה אַחֲרֵי נִפְלוֹ, וְיָאִיר אַחֲרֵי אָפְלוֹ. וּבְהִדָּבְקוֹ בְּסוֹף הַחֹדֶשׁ עִם

הַחַמָּה אִם יִהְיֶה תְלִי בֵינֵיהֶם, וְעַל קַו אֶחָד יַעַמְדוּ שְׁנֵיהֶם, אָז יַעֲמֹד הַיָּרֵחַ לִפְנֵי
הַשֶּׁמֶשׁ כְּעָב שְׁחוֹרָה, וְיַסְתִּיר מֵעַיִן כָּל רוֹאֶיהָ מְאוֹרָהּ, לְמַעַן יָדְעוּ כָל רוֹאֵיהֶם,
כִּי אֵין הַמַּלְכוּת לִצְבָא הַשָּׁמַיִם וְחֵילֵיהֶם, אֲבָל יֵשׁ אָדוֹן עֲלֵיהֶם, מַחְשִׁיךְ מְאוֹרֵיהֶם,
כִּי נָבֹהַ מֵעַל גָּבֹהַ שׁוֹמֵר וּגְבֹהִים עֲלֵיהֶם, וְהַחוֹשְׁבִים כִּי הַשֶּׁמֶשׁ אֱלֹהֵיהֶם, בָּעֵת
הַזֹּאת יֵבוֹשׁוּ מִמַּחְשְׁבוֹתֵיהֶם, וְיִבָּחֲנוּ דִבְרֵיהֶם, וְיֵדְעוּ כִּי יַד יְיָ עָשְׂתָה זֹּאת וְאֵין
לַשֶּׁמֶשׁ יְכֹלֶת, וְהַמַּחְשִׁיךְ אוֹרָהּ לוֹ לְבַדּוֹ הַמֶּמְשָׁלֶת, וְהוּא הַשּׁוֹלֵחַ אֵלֶיהָ עֶבֶד
מֵעֲבָדֶיהָ, גְּמוּל חֲסָדֶיהָ, לְהַסְתִּיר אוֹרָהּ, וְלִכְרֹת מִפְלַצְתָּהּ וַיְסִירֶהָ מִגְּבִירָה.

XIII

Thou in thy righteousness (who may rehearse
Its measure?) didst encase Moon's firmament
Within a second sphere, that doth traverse
Its path symmetrical—sans kink, sans dent:[62]
Wherein moves Mercury, that some men call
The Star—his bulk more small
Than Earth's by two and twenty thousand parts,
Each lap of his ten frantic days in all.
'Tis he that stirs dissension in men's hearts,
Complaints and strife; but he doth chance afford
To garner wealth, and hoard:
Obeying Him that fashioned him to be
A slave, and wait upon his Lord's decree;
The Star of wisdom and intelligence,[63]
Fools he turns subtle, lads he shows the way to sense.[64]

מִי יְסַפֵּר צִדְקוֹתֶיךָ בְּהַקִּיפְךָ עַל רְקִיעַ הַיָּרֵחַ גַּלְגַּל שֵׁנִי בְּאֵין בְּאֵין יוֹצֵאת וָפֶרֶץ, וּבוֹ כוֹכָב
הַנִּקְרָא כּוֹכָב וּמִדָּתוֹ כְּחֵלֶק מִשְׁנַיִם וְעֶשְׂרִים אֶלֶף מִן הָאָרֶץ, וּמַקִּיף הַגַּלְגַּל בַּעֲשָׂרָה
חֲדָשִׁים בְּמֶרֶץ, וְהוּא מְעוֹרֵר בָּעוֹלָם רִיבוֹת וּמְדָנִים, וְאֵיבוֹת וּרְגָנִים, וְנוֹתֵן כֹּחַ
לַעֲשׂוֹת חַיִל וְלִצְבֹּר הוֹן, וְלִכְנֹס עֹשֶׁר וּמָמוֹן, בְּמִצְוַת הַבּוֹרֵא אוֹתוֹ לְשָׁרְתוֹ כְּעֶבֶד
לִפְנֵי אָדוֹן, וְהוּא כוֹכַב הַשֵּׂכֶל וְהַחָכְמָה, נוֹתֵן לִפְתָאִים עָרְמָה, לְנַעַר דַּעַת וּמְזִמָּה.

XIV

Thy mysteries shall any comprehend?
Thou, round this second sphere, a third hast placed
Where troops upon a radiant queen attend,
Venus, with bridal decorations graced,[65]
Who in eleven months her course doth fill,
And those possessed of skill
To read her secrets know her measurement
To Earth's one thirty-seventh: by the will
Of her Creator, she renews content
Amid mankind, and ease, and joy, delights
And songs of wedding-nights.[66]
Of ripest fruits the ornament she wears,
Yea, and each several plant that blossom bears,
The Sun's chief produce, all his finest boons,
And choicest fruits maturing through successive
moons.[67]

מִי יָבִין סוֹדוֹתֶיךָ בְּהַקִּיפְךָ עַל גַּלְגַּל הַשֵּׁנִי גַּלְגַּל שְׁלִישִׁי וּבוֹ נֹגַהּ כִּגְבֶרֶת בֵּין
חַיָלֶיהָ, וְכַכַּלָּה תַּעְדֶּה כֵלֶיהָ, וּבְעַשְׁתֵּי עָשָׂר חֹדֶשׁ תְּסֹב גְּלִילֶיהָ, וְגוֹפָהּ כְּחֵלֶק
מִשְּׁבְעָה וּשְׁלֹשִׁים מִן הָאָרֶץ לְיוֹדְעֵי סוֹדָהּ וּמַשְׂכִּילֶיהָ, וְהִיא מְחַדֶּשֶׁת בָּעוֹלָם בִּרְצוֹן
בּוֹרְאָהּ הַשֶּׁקֶט וְשַׁלְוָה, וְדִיצָה וְחֶדְוָה, וְשִׁירוֹת וּרְנָנִים, וּמִצְהֲלוֹת חֻפּוֹת חֲתָנִים,
וְהִיא מְקַשֶּׁרֶת פְּרִי תְנוּבוֹת וּשְׁאָר הַצְּמָחִים, מִמֶּגֶד תְּבוּאוֹת שֶׁמֶשׁ וּמִמֶּגֶד גֶּרֶשׁ
יְרָחִים.

XV

Who hath the wit thy secret to discern,
How, round the sphere of Venus thou didst swing
A fourth, concentric, where the sun doth turn
To join in each full year his circuit's ring?
Eight score and ten times (so proofs demonstrate)
Is he than Earth more great,
And light dispenseth free throughout the skies
That from him, all the stars may radiate;

He doth grant victory, and glorifies
With royal dignity, whose awe brings low
The terror-stricken foe:
He keeps the world amazed, promoting wars
Or peace by new-found wonders, rooting out
Empires, that this may droop and that may sprout,[68]
High-handed in the strength on which he draws;
Yet not his own, but his Creator's will
All-wise, he doth fulfil.
While on his daily course,[69] he homage pays
Unto his King, raising at dawn the head
That bowed at eventide his setting rays;
As docile as a maid, called to the bed
Of some great lord from his seraglio
At night, who yet demure when dawn doth come, must
go.[70]

מִי יַשְׂכִּיל סוֹדְךָ בְּהַקִּיפְךָ עַל גַּלְגַּל נֹגַה גַּלְגַּל רְבִיעִי וּבוֹ הַחַמָּה, וְסוֹבֶבֶת כָּל הַגַּלְגַּל
בְּשָׁנָה תְמִימָה, וְגוּפָה גָדוֹל מִגּוּף הָאָרֶץ מֵאָה וְשִׁבְעָים פַּעַם בְּמוֹפְתֵי שֵׂכֶל וּמִזְמָּה,
וְהִיא חוֹלֶקֶת אוֹר לְכָל כּוֹכְבֵי שָׁמַיְמָה, וְנוֹתֶנֶת תְּשׁוּעָה לַמְּלָכִים וְהוֹד מַלְכוּת
וְאֵימָה, וּמְחַדֶּשֶׁת נִפְלָאוֹת בָּעוֹלָם אִם לְשָׁלוֹם וְאִם לְמִלְחָמָה, וְעוֹקֶרֶת מַלְכָיּוֹת
וְתַחְתָּם אֲחֵרוֹת מְקִימָה וּמְרִימָה, וְלָה יְכֹלֶת לְהַשְׁפִּיל וּלְהָרִים בְּיָד רָמָה, וְהַכֹּל
בִּרְצוֹן הַבּוֹרֵא אוֹתָהּ בְּחָכְמָה, וּבְכָל יוֹם וָיוֹם תִּשְׁתַּחֲוֶה לְמַלְכָּהּ וּבֵית נְתִיבוֹת נִצָּבָה,
וּבַשַּׁחַר תָּרִים רֹאשׁ וְתִקֹּד לָעֶרֶב בְּמַעֲרָבָה, בָּעֶרֶב הִיא בָאָה וּבַבֹּקֶר הִיא שָׁבָה.

XVI

What mind could grasp thy greatness, how the Sun
To be a timekeeper Thou hast designed,
To count the days, as into years they run,
Each instant fixed, each period defined;
And make the fruit-trees bud, beneath the bland
Spell of Orion's band
And genial Pleiades,[71] for richest yield:[72]
Six months he moves towards his northmost stand

Warming the air, the floods, trees of the field
And rocks, whilst every day the longer grows
The further north he goes,
Till round his polar terminus the day
Is six months long, as surest signs can prove;
Thence his predestined path doth southward move
To reach a place whereof the learned say
(From tests they make) that through six months its plight
Is one perpetual night.
So his ways whisper hints[73] that may suggest
The might of his Creator's wondrous deeds;
As practised eyes, by slaves' grand style impressed,
Know that their lord's magnificence exceeds.
As slave, through him is seen the power and state
That are his Lord's, whose gifts he bears as delegate.[74]

מִי יָכִיל גְּדֻלָּתְךָ בַּעֲשׂוֹתְךָ אוֹתָהּ לִמְנוֹת בָּהּ יָמִים וְשָׁנִים, וְעִתִּים מְזֻמָּנִים,
וּלְהַצְמִיחַ בָּהּ עֵץ עוֹשֶׂה פְּרִי וּמְעַדֵּנוֹת כִּימָה וּמוֹשְׁכוֹת כְּסִיל דְּשָׁנִים וְרַעֲנַנִּים,
וְשִׁשָּׁה חֳדָשִׁים הוֹלֶכֶת לִפְאַת צָפוֹן לְחַמֵּם הָאֲוִיר וְהַמַּיִם וְהָעֵצִים וְהָאֲבָנִים, וּכְפִי
קִרְבָתָהּ לַצָּפוֹן יִגְדְּלוּ הַיָּמִים וְיַאַרְכוּ הַזְּמַנִּים, עַד יִמָּצֵא מָקוֹם אֲשֶׁר יִגְדַּל יוֹמוֹ
עַד הֱיוֹתוֹ שִׁשָּׁה חֳדָשִׁים בְּמוֹפְתִים נֶאֱמָנִים, וְשִׁשָּׁה חֳדָשִׁים הוֹלֶכֶת לִפְאַת דָּרוֹם
בְּמַעְגָּלִים נְתוּנִים, עַד יִמָּצֵא מָקוֹם אֲשֶׁר יִגְדַּל לֵילוֹ עַד הֱיוֹתוֹ שִׁשָּׁה חֳדָשִׁים
לְפִי מִבְחַן הַבּוֹחֲנִים, וּמִמֶּנָּה יֵדְעוּ קְצָת דַּרְכֵי בוֹרְאָהּ וְשֶׁמֶץ מִגְּבוּרוֹתָיו, וְעִזּוּזוֹ
וְנִפְלְאוֹתָיו, כִּי מִגְּדֻלַּת הָעֲבָדִים גְּדֻלַּת הָאָדוֹן נוֹדַעַת, לְכָל יוֹדְעֵי דַעַת, וְעַל
הָעֶבֶד יִגָּלֶה תֹּקֶף הָאָדוֹן וּכְבוֹדוֹ, וְכָל טוּב אֲדֹנָיו בְּיָדוֹ.

XVII

Thy signs and wonders—who shall these descry?
Thou didst appoint the Sun to furnish light
To stars, both those pitched low and those raised high
And to the Moon—a spot of palest white
So long she stands straight underneath his ray;[75]
But as she moves away
Of his refulgence doth she catch a glow

While distance brings her opposite the play
Of brightness she receives from him, and so
When face to face they stand, on her doth gleam
His incandescent beam:[76]
But mid-month past, the more she doth pursue
The more doth he, now deviant, evade,
And so her mantled majesty must fade
Till, with her month, her cycle's end is due,
And she creeps secret in her crescent's rim
A day, and more than half, to cleave to him,[77]
And thus renewed, regains her former state,
As out his marriage-chamber comes a groom, elate.[78]

מִי יַכִּיר אוֹתוֹתֶיךָ בְּהַפְקִידְךָ אוֹתָהּ לְהַעֲנִיק אוֹר לְכוֹכְבֵי מַעְלָה : מַטָּה גַם לַלְּבָנָה,
וְאִם תַּחְתֶּיהָ תַּעֲמֹד הַבַּהֶרֶת [בַּהֶרֶת] לְבָנָה, וּכְפִי אֲשֶׁר יִרְחַק מִמֶּנָּה הַיָּרֵחַ, מִזִּיוֹנָהּ
לוֹקֵחַ, כִּי בְרָחֳקוֹ יְקָרֵב לַעֲמֹד נִכְחָהּ, וִיקַבֵּל זַרְחָהּ, עַד יִמָּלֵא אוֹרוֹ בְעָמְדוֹ לְפָנֶיהָ,
וְהֵאִיר אֶל עֵבֶר פָּנֶיהָ, וְכָל אֲשֶׁר יְקָרֵב אַחַר חֲצִי הַחֹדֶשׁ אֵלֶיהָ, הוּא נוֹטֶה מֵעָלֶיהָ,
וְיִרְחַק מֵעֲמֹד נֶגְדָּהּ, וְיֵלֵךְ לְצִדָּהּ, וְעַל כֵּן תֶּחְסַר אַדַּרְתּוֹ, עַד כְּלוֹת חָדְשׁוֹ וּתְקוּפָתוֹ,
וְיָבוֹא בִגְבוּל שְׁפָתוֹ, וּבְהִדְבְּקוֹ עִמָּהּ יָסָתֵר בַּמִּסְתָּרִים, כְּפִי יוֹם וָחֵצִי וַחֲצִי שָׁעָה
וּרְגָעִים סְפוּרִים, וְאַחֲרֵי כֵן יִתְחַדֵּשׁ וְיָשׁוּב לְקַדְמָתוֹ, וְהוּא כְחָתָן יוֹצֵא מֵחֻפָּתוֹ.

XVIII

Who knows thy miracles? 'Tis Thou didst roll
A fifth sphere round the Sun's, where Mars doth stalk,
That red-faced king, in eighteen months' patrol
Full-circuiting his palace sentry-walk,
One and five-eighths the size of Earth, no more,
Yet fierce, a lord of war
Whose soldiers bear their shields deep stained in red:[79]
Battles he wakes, destruction, slaughter, gore,[80]
corpses on which the carrion birds are fed
Wounded that burned by pestilence must lie,
Their sap parched tinder-dry:[81]
He heralds years of dearth, and fires, and rain

Of flint-like hail, and thunderclaps, the slain
Mangled by foes, their sword unsheathed, intent
To speed their feet in evil's course, on bloodshed bent.[82]

מִי יֵדַע פְּלִיאוֹתֶיךָ בְּהַקִּיפְךָ עַל גַּלְגַּל חַמָּה גַּלְגַּל חֲמִישִׁי וּבוֹ מַאֲדִים כְּמֶלֶךְ
בְּהֵיכָלוֹ, וּבִשְׁמוֹנָה עָשָׂר חֹדֶשׁ יָסֹב גַּלְגַּלוֹ, וּמִדָּתוֹ כְּגוּף הָאָרֶץ פַּעַם וָחֵצִי וּשְׁמִינִית
פַּעַם וְזֶה תַּכְלִית גָּדְלוֹ, וְהוּא כְּגִבּוֹר עָרִיץ מָגֵן גִּבּוֹרֵיהוּ מְאָדָּם, וּמְעוֹרֵר מִלְחָמוֹת
וְהֶרֶג וָאַבְדָן, וּמְכֵּי חֶרֶב וּלְחוּמֵי רֶשֶׁף נֶהְפַּךְ לְחֶרֶב לְשֻׁדָּם, וּשְׁנַת בַּצֹרֶת וּשְׂרֵפַת
אֵשׁ וּרְעָמִים וְאַבְנֵי אֶלְגָּבִישׁ וּמְדֻקָּרִים וְשׁוֹלְפֵי חֶרֶב כְּנֶגְדָּם, כִּי רַגְלֵיהֶם לָרַע
יָרוּצוּ וִימַהֲרוּ לִשְׁפָּךְ דָּם.

XIX

Tremendous are thy acts: who could express
How Thou didst set the sphere of Mars within
A sixth, in which there lodgeth righteousness[83]
As through its vastness Jupiter doth spin?
Fifteen and threescore times he multiplies
Earth's breadth by his own size,
And circles round his orbit in twelve years,
The planet of good will and of the ties
Of love, in hearts God-fearingness he stirs,
Repentance, upright dealing, noble ways,[84]
All parts that earn men's praise:
'Tis he that bids the crops yield their increase,
But strife, contention, wars he maketh cease:[85]
His equity—so runs his law—the breach
Shall heal, that he with justice through the world may
reach.[86]

מִי יַבִּיעַ נוֹרְאוֹתֶיךָ בְּהַקִּיפְךָ עַל גַּלְגַּל מַאֲדִים גַּלְגַּל שִׁשִּׁי בִּמְסִבָּה, עֲצוּמָה וְרַבָּה,
צֶדֶק יָלִין בָּהּ, וְגוּפוֹ נָדוֹל מִגּוּף הָאָרֶץ חֲמִשָּׁה וְשִׁבְעִים פַּעַם בְּמִדַּת רָחְבָּהּ, וְסוֹבֵב
הַגַּלְגַּל בִּשְׁתֵּים עֶשְׂרֵה שָׁנָה וְהוּא כּוֹכַב הָרָצוֹן וְהָאַהֲבָה, וּמְעוֹרֵר יִרְאַת הַשֵּׁם וְיֹשֶׁר
וּתְשׁוּבָה, וְכָל מִדָּה טוֹבָה, וּמַרְבֶּה כָל תְּבוּאָה וּתְנוּבָה, וּמַשְׁבִּית מִלְחָמוֹת וְיָירִיב
וּמְרִיבָה, וְדָתוֹ לְחַזֵּק בְּיָשְׁרוֹ כָּל בֶּדֶק, וְהוּא יִשְׁפֹּט תֵּבֵל בְּצֶדֶק.

XX

What man dare of thy grandeur to converse?
Enclosing Jupiter's, Thou didst create
A seventh sphere, where Saturn doth traverse
His orbit, one and ninety times more great
In measure he than Earth, nor comes he back
Round his revolving track
Ere thirty years be passed; he waketh war,
Despoliation, famine, and the sack
Of cities, trains of captives are his law,
Lands ravaged, realms uprooted—by the will
Of One that charged him this strange service to fulfil.[87]

מִי יְשׂוֹחֵחַ גְּדֻלָּתְךָ בְּהַקִּיפְךָ עַל גַּלְגַּל צֶדֶק גַּלְגַּל שְׁבִיעִי וּבוֹ שַׁבְּתַי בִּתְקוּפָתוֹ,
וְגוּפוֹ גָדוֹל מִגּוּף הָאָרֶץ אַחַת וְתִשְׁעִים פַּעַם בְּמִדָּתוֹ, וְסוֹבֵב הַגַּלְגַּל בִּשְׁלֹשִׁים
שָׁנָה בִּמְרוּצָתוֹ, וּמְעוֹרֵר מִלְחָמוֹת וּבִזָּה וּשְׁבִי וְרָעָב כִּי כֵן דָּתוֹ, וּמַחֲרִיב אֲרָצוֹת
וְעוֹקֵר מַלְכֻיּוֹת בִּרְצוֹן הַמַּפְקִיד אוֹתוֹ, לַעֲבֹד עֲבוֹדָתוֹ, נָכְרִיָּה עֲבוֹדָתוֹ.

XXI

Who may reach out to thy transcendent height?
Beyond the sphere of Saturn, Thou hast wrought
An eighth, that in circumgyrating flight
Twelve zodiacal signs it should support,
Broidered as on the belt the High Priest wears;[88]
Cast in its mould, it bears
Those outmost stars of all set in the skies:
But once in six and thirty thousand years
Come they full wheel—so distant each one lies.
All these, five score and seven times the Earth
Exceed in greater girth;
A sphere, though finite, vast: and power resides
In those signs, whence that potency doth flow
That each created thing can wield below
Each after its own kind, as He decides

Who did create them, and the signs hath made
Marshals of their parade:
Each sign he framed proportionate, bestowed
Their names,[89] and ordained each to bear his load.[90]

מִי יַגִּיעַ לְרוֹמְמוּתָךְ בְּהַקִּיפְךָ עַל גַּלְגַּל שַׁבְתַּי גַּלְגַּל שְׁמִינִי בְּמָסַבְּתוֹ, וְהוּא סוֹבֵל
שָׁתַּיִם עֶשְׂרֵה מַזָּלוֹת עַל קַו חֶשֶׁב אֲפֻדָּתוֹ, וְכָל כּוֹכְבֵי שַׁחַק הָעֶלְיוֹנִים יְצוּקִים
בִּיצוּקָתוֹ, וְכָל כּוֹכָב מֵהֶם יַקִּיף הַגַּלְגַּל בְּשִׁשָּׁה וּשְׁלֹשִׁים אֶלֶף שָׁנִים מֵרֹב גַּבְהוּתוֹ,
וְגוּף כָּל כּוֹכָב מֵהֶם מֵאָה וְשֶׁבַע פְּעָמִים כְּגוּף הָאָרֶץ וְזֹאת תַּכְלִית גְּדֻלָּתוֹ, וּמִכֹּחַ
הַמַּזָּלוֹת הָהֶם, נֶאֱצַל כֹּחַ כָּל בְּרוּאֵי מַטָּה לְמִינֵיהֶם, בְּרָצוֹן בּוֹרְאָם וּמַפְקִידָם
עֲלֵיהֶם, וְכָל אֶחָד מֵהֶם עַל מַתְכָּנְתּוֹ בְּרָאוֹ, וּבְשֵׁם קְרָאוֹ, אִישׁ אִישׁ עַל עֲבוֹדָתוֹ
וְעַל מַשָּׂאוֹ.

XXII

What man may thy eternal ways divine?
Thou, for the seven planets designate
Didst make the twelve signs mansions palatine,
Lending thine own strength to invigorate
The *Ram*, paired with the *Bull*, and that third sign
Of *Gemini*, the twain inseparate
Visaged like men,[91] and then the fourth in line
Cancer, and *Leo* whom Thou didst instate
With some part of thy majesty[92] to shine
Close by his sister *Virgo*[93] radiate;
Libra, next whom is placed the serpentine
Scorpio; and that ninth Thou didst create
A warrior bold, ne'er knowing his strength pine,[94]
Who aims his *Bow*, an Ishmael[95] constellate:
Thy might formed[96] *Capricorn*, and did assign
Aquarius, pail in hand, to be their mate:
Last, lonely *Pisces* didst Thou place in trine
That Jonah's whale[97] be seen predestinate.
These fill the zodiac's exalted list,
Twelve princes, each his nation's own protagonist.[98]

מִי יֵדַע הֲלִיכוֹתֶיךָ בַּעֲשׂוֹתְךָ לְשִׁבְעָה כוֹכְבֵי לֶכֶת הֵיכָלוֹת, בִּשְׁתֵּים עֶשְׂרֵה
מַזָּלוֹת, וְעַל טָלֶה וְשׁוֹר אָצַלְתָּ כֹּחַךָ בְּהִתְיַחֲדָם, וְהַשְּׁלִישִׁי תְּאוֹמִים כִּשְׁנֵי אַחִים
בְּהִתְאַחֲדָם, וּדְמוּת פְּנֵיהֶם פְּנֵי אָדָם, וְלָרְבִיעִי וְהוּא סַרְטָן גַּם לָאַרְיֵה נָתַתָּ מֵהוֹדְךָ
עָלָיו, וְלַאֲחוֹתוֹ הַבְּתוּלָה הַקְּרוֹבָה אֵלָיו, וְכֵן לְמֹאזְנַיִם וּלְעַקְרָב אֲשֶׁר בְּצִדּוֹ הוּשַׁת,
וְהַתְּשִׁיעִי הַנִּבְרָא בְצוּרַת גִּבּוֹר כֹּחוֹ לֹא נָשָׁת, וַיְהִי רוֹבֶה קַשָּׁת, וְכֵן נִבְרָא גְּדִי
וּדְלִי בְּכֹחַךָ הַגָּדוֹל, וּלְצִדּוֹ הַמַּזָּל הָאַחֲרוֹן וַיְמַן יְיָ דָּג גָּדוֹל, וְאֵלֶּה הַמַּזָּלוֹת גְּבֹהִים
וְנִשָּׂאִים בְּמַעֲלוֹתָם, שְׁנֵים עָשָׂר נְשִׂיאִים לְאֻמּוֹתָם.

XXIII

Who shall search out those thoughts Thou keepest hid?
Thou to a ninth sphere didst a rank accord
Above the zodiac's, when Thou didst bid
It emanate and rise a noble lord;
All spheres he locks within him, to include[99]
Each one's created brood;
Westward he drives each star in every sphere
From east, against their inclination slewed
By his more potent course[100] compelled to steer.
He bows towards the sundown once each day
His homage thus to pay
To his own King who lets him seem to reign,
A sphere within which cosmos and its breed
Of creatures are but as a mustard seed
In Ocean's vast, upsurging hurricane.
His grandeur nought next greatness that doth cling
To his Creator who is eke his King:
Nay, all that pomp and state, his high degree
As less than nought He reckons, sheer nonentity.[101]

מִי יַחְקֹר תַּעֲלוּמוֹתֶיךָ בְּהַאֲצִילְךָ עַל גַּלְגַּל הַמַּזָּלוֹת גַּלְגַּל תְּשִׁיעִי בְּמַעֲרָכוֹ, הַמַּקִּיף
עַל כָּל הַגַּלְגַּלִּים וּבְרוּאֵיהֶם וְהֵם סְגוּרִים בְּתוֹכוֹ, הַמַּנְהִיג כָּל כּוֹכְבֵי שָׁמַיִם
וְנַגְלֵּיהֶם מִמִּזְרָח לְמַעֲרָב לְתַקֵּף מַהֲלָכוֹ, הַמִּשְׁתַּחֲוֶה בְּכָל יוֹם לִפְאַת מַעֲרָב
לְמַלְכּוֹ וּמַמְלִיכוֹ, וְכָל בְּרוּאֵי עוֹלָם בְּתוֹכוֹ, כְּנִרְגִּיר חַרְדָּל בַּיָּם הַגָּדוֹל לְתֹקֶף
גָּדְלוֹ וְעָרְכּוֹ, וְהוּא וּגְדֻלָּתוֹ נֶחְשָׁב כְּאַיִן וּכְאֶפֶס לִגְדֻלַּת בּוֹרְאוֹ וּמַלְכּוֹ, וְכָל
מַעֲלוֹתָיו וְגָדְלוֹ, מֵאֶפֶס וָתֹהוּ נֶחְשְׁבוּ לוֹ.

XXIV

Who shall perceive the mysteries enshrined
In thy creative acts? Thou didst raise high
Above the ninth, a tenth[102]—the sphere of mind—
Intelligence, the palace court most nigh
Unto Thyself; God's holy tithe,[103] whose height
Soaring sublime, doth quite
Transcend sublimity, where thought doth quail
When it can reach no more, and recondite
Seclusion hides thy glory,[104] fittest veil,
Within the palanquin Thou didst design
Of silver from truth's mine[105]
Fashioned, Intelligence its cloth of gold,
Pillared on righteousness, by Thee controlled
In orbit (for thy might caused it to be),
From Thee to Thee revolving, yearning aye for Thee.[106]

מִי יָבִין סוֹדוֹת בְּרִיאוֹתֶיךָ בַּהֲרִימְךָ עַל גַּלְגַּל הַתְּשִׁיעִי גַּלְגַּל הַשֵּׂכֶל הוּא הַהֵיכָל
לִפְנֵי, הָעֲשִׂירִי יִהְיֶה קֹדֶשׁ לַיָּי, וְהוּא הַגַּלְגַּל הַנַּעֲלֶה עַל כָּל עֶלְיוֹן, אֲשֶׁר לֹא
יַשִּׂיגֵהוּ רַעֲיוֹן, וְשָׁם נְוֵה הַחֶבְיוֹן, אֲשֶׁר הוּא לְךָ לְרוֹכֵב לַעֲרִיפוֹן, מֵכֶף הָוֶמֶת
יָצַקְתָּ אוֹתוֹ, וּמִזְּהַב הַשֵּׂכֶל עָשִׂיתָ רְפִידָתוֹ, וְעַל עַמּוּדֵי צֶדֶק שַׂמְתָּ מְסִבָּתוֹ, וּמִכֹּחֲךָ
מְצִיאוּתוֹ, וּמִמְּךָ וְעָדֶיךָ מְנַמָּתוֹ, וְאֵלֶיךָ תְּשׁוּקָתוֹ.

XXV

Thy thoughts' profundity what man can sound?
From the refulgence of this loftiest sphere,
Intelligence, Thou didst the stuff compound
Of souls, so they all radiate appear,

And some there be, psyches of highest rate,
That on thy will do wait
As angels of thy Presence, mighty lords,
Majestic, gallant officers of state,
All of them wielding whirling, flame-wrapped swords.[107]
Bid by the spirit so:[108]
Hewn as from crystal,[109] each a lively sprite,
Supernal, some thy outer courts frequent,
Some throng thy inner halls, they eyes intent
To watch thy progress—from the fount of light
Drawn, from the sanctum marching group by group,
A space between each troop:
And floating on their banners are displayed
Their coats of arms, designs a master-draughtsman made,[110]
Princes and sergeants, soldiers too, each band
In march and countermarch with tireless tread,
Unseen themselves, yet leaving naught unscanned;
Some quarried out of flame, some that are sped
As whistling winds upon their missions fanned,
And some of fire with water compacted[111]
In harmony, some Seraphim, the brand
Of lightning flash and sparks by comets shed;
Thus ranged by thousand myriads, they stand
In heaven's heights, in turn to bow their head
To Him that drives the storm-clouds[112] four-in-hand;
On guard, their companies distributed
In day and night watches,[113] they sing a planned
Concert of praise to Him round whom is spread
Engirding might:[114] kneeling, together grand
Response they make in awe, and thus 'tis said:
'In gratefulness of heart[115] we understand
Thou art our Lord: Thou hast us fashionéd
By thine own hand, not we,[116] thy slaves, as well
Thy witnesses,[117] who thy creatorship shall tell.'

מִי יַעֲמִיק לְמַחְשְׁבוֹתֶיךָ בַּעֲשׂוֹתְךָ מִזִּיו גַּלְגַּל הַשֵּׂכֶל זֹהַר הַנְּשָׁמוֹת, וְהַנְּפָשׁוֹת
הָרָמוֹת, הֵם מַלְאֲכֵי רְצוֹנֶךָ, מְשָׁרְתֵי פָנֶיךָ, הֵם אַדִּירֵי כֹחַ וְגִבּוֹרֵי מַמְלֶכֶת, בְּיָדָם
לַהַט הַחֶרֶב הַמִּתְהַפֶּכֶת, וְעוֹשֵׂי כָל מְלָאכֶת, אֶל אֲשֶׁר יִהְיֶה שָׁמָּה הָרוּחַ לָלֶכֶת,
כֻּלָּם גְּזָרוֹת פְּנִימִיּוֹת, וְחַיּוֹת עֶלְיוֹנִיּוֹת, חִיצוֹנִיּוֹת וּפְנִימִיּוֹת, הֲלִיכוֹתֶיךָ צוֹפִיּוֹת,
מִמְּקוֹם קָדוֹשׁ יַהֲלֵכוּ, וּמִמְּקוֹר הָאוֹר יִמָּשֵׁכוּ, נֶחֱלָקִים לְכִתּוֹת, וְעַל דִּגְלָם אוֹתוֹת,
בְּעֵט סוֹפֵר מָהִיר חֲרוּתוֹת, מֵהֶם נְסִיכוֹת וּמֵהֶם מְשָׁרְתוֹת, מֵהֶם צְבָאוֹת, רָצוֹת
וּבָאוֹת, לֹא עֲיֵפוֹת וְלֹא נִלְאוֹת, רוֹאוֹת וְלֹא נִרְאוֹת, מֵהֶם חַצּוּבֵי לֶהָבוֹת, וּמֵהֶם רוּחוֹת
נוֹשְׁבוֹת, מֵהֶם מֵאֵשׁ וּמִמַּיִם וּמֶרְכָּבוֹת, מֵהֶם שְׂרָפִים, וּמֵהֶם רְשָׁפִים, מֵהֶם בְּרָקִים,
וּמֵהֶם זִקִים, וְכָל כַּת מֵהֶם מִשְׁתַּחֲוֶה לְרוֹכֵב עֲרָבוֹת, וּבְרוּם עוֹלָם נִצָּבִים לַאֲלָפִים
וְלִרְבָבוֹת, נֶחֱלָקִים לְמִשְׁמָרוֹת, בַּיּוֹם וּבַלַּיְלָה לְרֹאשׁ אַשְׁמוּרוֹת, לַעֲרֹךְ תְּהִלּוֹת
וְשִׁירוֹת, לָגֵאזָר בִּגְבוּרוֹת, כֻּלָּם בַּחֲרָדָה וּרְעָדָה כּוֹרְעִים וּמִשְׁתַּחֲוִים לָךְ, וְאוֹמְרִים
מוֹדִים אֲנַחְנוּ לָךְ, שָׁאַתָּה אֱלֹהֵינוּ, אַתָּה עֲשִׂיתָנוּ, וְלֹא אֲנַחְנוּ, וּמַעֲשֵׂה יָדְךָ כֻּלָּנוּ,
וְכִי אַתָּה אֲדוֹנֵינוּ וַאֲנַחְנוּ עֲבָדֶיךָ, וְאַתָּה בּוֹרְאֵנוּ וַאֲנַחְנוּ עֵדֶיךָ.

XXVI

Who dare to that palladium[118] draw nigh
Which, ere time was, Thou stablished as thine own?
Above the sphere of intellect more high
Hast Thou raised loftiest thy Glory's throne:[119]
There mystery has its abode, the field
Of majesty concealed,
Life's secret and life's base: the intellect
Reacheth its bounds, but there its course must yield;
For soaring upward still, in triumph decked
Upon thy throne of might Thou dost retreat,
Nor may man climb that Sinai's peak to share thy seat.[120]

מִי יָבוֹא עַד תְּכוּנָתְךָ בְּהַגְבִּיהַךְ לְמַעֲלָה מִגַּלְגַּל הַשֵּׂכֶל כִּסֵּא הַכָּבוֹד, אֲשֶׁר שָׁם נְוֵה
הֶחָבְיוֹן וְהַהוֹד, וְשָׁם הַסּוֹד וְהַיְסוֹד, וְעָדָיו יַגִּיעַ הַשֵּׂכֶל וְיַעֲמֹד, וּמִלְמַעְלָה בָּאתָ
וְעָלִיתָ עַל כֵּס תַּעֲצוּמָךְ, וְאִישׁ לֹא יַעֲלֶה עִמָּךְ.

XXVII

What man is there with thy deeds could compete?[121]
Beneath thy throne of Glory Thou has stowed
A place where souls of all thy saints may meet[122]
The pure in spirit, in that bless'd abode
Bound in the bond of life[123] for evermore;
And those careworn and sore
Renew the strength their toil had drained,[124] and rest
Safe from the deluge, from their ark ashore:[125]
There, with amenity unending bless'd,
World without end, the life to come they know
And stages, for the show
Of spectacles, round which the souls, close packed,
Peering in mirrors,[126] hope these may reflect
God's image glimpsed, while they—to show respect—
By being seen[127] perform their pilgrim act:
Within the palace precincts they abide—
Pages, to wait beside
The King's own board,[128] regaled by Him with taste
Of all the intellect's most ripe delight
From his right royal fare:[129] by such fruits graced
Serene repose is theirs, unending right
To joy of heritage[130] so nobly bland
Won from the milk and honey of the promised land.[131]

מִי יַעֲשֶׂה כְּמַעֲשֶׂיךָ בַּעֲשׂוֹתְךָ תַּחַת כִּסֵּא כְבוֹדְךָ, מַעֲמָד לְנַפְשׁוֹת חֲסִידֶיךָ, וְשָׁם נְוֵה
הַנְּשָׁמוֹת הַטְּהוֹרוֹת, אֲשֶׁר בִּצְרוֹר הַחַיִּים צְרוּרוֹת, וַאֲשֶׁר יִיגְעוּ וְיִיעָפוּ, שָׁם כֹּחַ
יַחֲלִיפוּ, וְשָׁם יָנוּחוּ יְגִיעֵי כֹחַ, וְאֵלֶּה בְּנֵי נֹחַ, וּבוֹ נֵעַם בְּלִי תַכְלִית וְקִצְבָּה, וְהוּא
הָעוֹלָם הַבָּא, וְשָׁם מַעֲמָדוֹת וּמַרְאוֹת, לַנְּפָשׁוֹת הָעוֹמְדוֹת בְּמַרְאוֹת הַצּוֹבְאוֹת, אֶת
פְּנֵי הָאָדוֹן לִרְאוֹת וּלְהֵרָאוֹת, שׁוֹכְנוֹת בְּהֵיכְלֵי מֶלֶךְ, וְעוֹמְדוֹת עַל שֻׁלְחַן הַמֶּלֶךְ,
וּמִתְעַדְּנוֹת בְּמֶתֶק פְּרִי הַשֵּׂכֶל וְהוּא יִתֵּן מַעֲדַנֵּי מֶלֶךְ, זֹאת הַמְּנוּחָה וְהַנַּחֲלָה אֲשֶׁר
אֵין תַּכְלִית לְטוּבָהּ וְיָפְיָהּ, וְגַם זָבַת חָלָב וּדְבַשׁ הִיא וְזֶה פִּרְיָהּ.

XXVIII

Who shall thy deep-hid archetype reveal?
In those remotest heights Thou didst dispose
Ranges of magazines,[132] there to conceal
Dread marvels men mythologize, and those
That tell thy might's quintessence stored therein,
A treasure-house, one bin
Whereof holds life, kept for the pure in heart,
One holds salvation for those turned from sin,[133]
One streams of fire and brimstone,[134] set apart
For those who break thy covenant, a heap
Of pits past credit deep
Of unquenched fire, wherein fall God's accursed:[135]
Stacked stores of storm-winds, hurricanes, thick packs
Of crusted ice,[136] intensest cold, and stacks
Of hail, frost, snow, flood-waters when they burst,
And stores of drought, heat,[137] smoke-palls, rime, and cloud
That glowers in banks, dark in its gloomy shroud:
Thou keepest all for their due times, some meant
Benign, some Thou didst stablish for man's chastisement.[138]

מִי יְגַלֶּה צְפוּנוֹתֶיךָ בַּעֲשׂוֹתְךָ בַּמָּרוֹם חֲדָרִים וְאוֹצָרוֹת, בָּהֶם נוֹרָאוֹת סְפוּרוֹת,
וּדְבַר גְּבוּרוֹת, מֵהֶם אוֹצְרוֹת חַיִּים, לַזַּכִּים וּנְקִיִּים, וּמֵהֶם אוֹצְרוֹת יֶשַׁע, לְשָׁבֵי
פֶשַׁע, וּמֵהֶם אוֹצְרוֹת אֵשׁ וְנַחֲלֵי גָפְרִית, לְעוֹבְרֵי בְרִית, וְאוֹצְרוֹת שׁוּחוֹת עֲמֻקּוֹת
לֹא תִכְבֶּה אִשָּׁם, זְעוּם יְיָ יִפָּל שָׁם, וְאוֹצְרוֹת סוּפוֹת וּסְעָרוֹת, וְקִפָּאוֹן וִיקָרוֹת,
וְאוֹצְרוֹת בָּרָד וְקֶרַח וְשֶׁלֶג, וְצִיָּה גַם חֹם וְנוֹזְלֵי פֶלֶג, וְקִיטוֹר וּכְפוֹר וְעָנָן וַעֲרָפֶל,
וַעֲלָטָה וְאֹפֶל, הַכֹּל הֲכִינוֹת בְּעִתּוֹ, אָח לְחֶסֶד וּאֵם לְנוֹשַׁע שִׁמְתּוֹ, וְצוּר לְהוֹכִיחַ
יְסָדְתּוֹ.

XXIX

Thy power's resource could any human mind
Begin to comprehend? Thou of thine own
Glory's refulgence hast a fragment mined
Bright as its parent Rock, so pure a stone,
Picked from a shaft sheer clarity did drill,[139]

In which Thou didst instil
Wisdom of spirit, and didst call it soul;[140]
Formed at the flash of Intellect to thrill
As flaming fire, fanned like a blazing coal
By thy breath—she doeth till and tend[141] man's frame
Sent forth by Thee, a flame
Within his unscorched limbs that gently glows,
For from the soul's own fire his body rose
Concrete, of nought created, made entire
Because the Lord Himself came down thereon in fire.[142]

מִי יָכִיל עָצְמָתְךָ בְּבָרְאֲךָ מִזִּיו כְּבוֹדְךָ יְפְעָה טְהוֹרָה, מִצּוּר נִגְזָרָה, וּמִמַּקֶּבֶת
בֹּר נֻקָּרָה, וְאָצַלְתָּ עָלֶיהָ רוּחַ חָכְמָה, וְקָרָאתָ שְׁמָהּ נְשָׁמָה, עֲשִׂיתָהּ מִלַּהֲבוֹת אֵשׁ
הַשֵּׂכֶל חֲצוּבָה, וְנִשְׁמָתוֹ כְּאֵשׁ בּוֹעֲרָה בָהּ, וְשִׁלַּחְחָתָה בַּגּוּף לְעָבְדֵהוּ וּלְשָׁמְרֵהוּ, וְהִיא
כְאֵשׁ בְּתוֹכוֹ וְלֹא תִשְׂרְפָהוּ, כִּי מֵאֵשׁ הַנְּשָׁמָה נִבְרָא וְיָצָא מֵאַיִן לְיֵשׁ, מִפְּנֵי אֲשֶׁר
יָרַד עָלָיו יְיָ בָּאֵשׁ.

XXX

Thy wisdom who could reach? Thou didst bestow
Upon the soul thy gift, infixed to stay,
The faculty of knowledge, whence doth flow
Her spring of glory: therefore no decay
May master her that shares, perpetuate,
Her basic stuff's estate,
And this her nature's secret doth explain:
The soul, by wisdom[143] made inviolate
Through reason, never dies, yet must sustain
More bitter punishment than death[144] for sins;
So be she pure, she wins
Goodwill, and smiles at doomsday[145]—but defiled,
A waif through anger's storm[146] she strays, exiled
Throughout her impure time, the shrine denied,[147]
All hallowed things untouched, till she be purified.[148]

מִי יַגִּיעַ לְחָכְמָתְךָ בְּתִתְּךָ לַנֶּפֶשׁ כֹּחַ הַדֵּעָה, אֲשֶׁר בָּה תְּקוּעָה, וַיְהִי הַמַּדָּע מְקוֹר
כְּבוֹדָהּ, וְעַל כֵּן לֹא יִשְׁלֹט עָלֶיהָ כִּלָּיוֹן וְתִתְקַיֵּם כְּפִי קִיּוּם יְסוֹדָהּ, וְזֶה עִנְיָנָהּ
וְסוֹדָהּ, וְהַנֶּפֶשׁ הַחֲכָמָה לֹא תִרְאֶה מָוֶת, אַךְ תְּקַבֵּל עַל עֲווֹנָהּ עֹנֶשׁ מַר מִמָּוֶת,
וְאִם טָהֲרָה תָּפִיק רָצוֹן וְתִשְׂחַק לְיוֹם אַחֲרוֹן, וְאִם נִטְמְאָה תָּנוּד בְּשֶׁצֶף קֶצֶף
וְחָרוֹן, וְכָל יְמֵי טֻמְאָתָהּ בָּדָד תֵּשֵׁב גּוֹלָה וְסוּרָה, בְּכָל קֹדֶשׁ לֹא תִגַּע וְאֶל הַמִּקְדָּשׁ
לֹא תָבוֹא עַד מְלֹאת יְמֵי טָהֳרָהּ.

XXXI

Could any match thy bounteous good, that gave
The soul to make the body quick, and made
Her point the path of life,[149] and teach, and save
From ills that might beset it, lending shade?
When Thou didst nip from clay man's mortal clod
Thou breathed the breath of God
In him as soul,[150] a spirit to impart[151]
Wisdom, and make him midst all creatures odd
Set by this reason from the beasts apart,
That man's mind, mounting ever up, might scale
Those heights he doth assail
Closed in thy universe, placed there by Thee
Who from without dost gauge his deeds, and see
All that he would keep hid, Thou dost survey
Descrying both his lining and his overlay.[152]

מִי יִגְמֹל עַל טוֹבוֹתֶיךָ בְּתִתְּךָ הַנְּשָׁמָה לַגּוּף לְהַחֲיוֹתוֹ, וְאֹרַח חַיִּים לְהוֹרוֹתוֹ וּלְהַרְאוֹתוֹ,
לְהַצִּיל לוֹ מֵרָעָתוֹ, קְרַצְתּוֹ מֵאֲדָמָה, וְנָפַחְתָּ בּוֹ נְשָׁמָה, וְאָצַלְתָּ עָלָיו רוּחַ חָכְמָה,
אֲשֶׁר בָּהּ יִבָּדֵל מִבְּהֵמָה, וְיַעֲלֶה אֶל מַעֲלָה רָמָה. שַׂמְתּוֹ בְּעוֹלָמְךָ סָגוּר וְאַתָּה
מִחוּץ תָּבִין מַעֲשָׂיו וְתִרְאֵנּוּ, וְכָל אֲשֶׁר מִמְּךָ יַעְלִימֶנּוּ, מִבַּיִת וּמִחוּץ תְּצַפֶּנּוּ.

XXXII

Who is there, that perceiveth in thy deeds
The mystery? Thou, when Thou didst create
Man's body for thy service, for its needs
Didst furnish organs—eyes, to contemplate

Thy signs, and ears that he might gain report
Of dread deeds Thou hast wrought,
A mind which, though thy mysteries transcend,
Some part of them may grasp within its thought,
A mouth to tell thy praise, a tongue to lend
Its song, that may for those unborn rehearse
Thy epic might in verse;
Even as I this day, thine handmaid's son,[153]
Poor though my numbers be, would fain indite
Of thy sublimity the merest mite
Yet but the lowest fringe have I begun:
What, then, must be that power which crowns thy ways,
Thy primal acts displays?
Such things 'twere life to find, yet from their trace
Those who have ears to hear can recognize thy face
Though never on thy glory they set eyes:
But those who of thy might have ne'er heard tell,
Can such as they thy godhead recognize?
How in their hearts can thy truth come to dwell,
Or serving Thee all thoughts of theirs devise?
Therefore thy servant findeth heart[154] to spell
Thy praise in summary, though fragment-wise,
In his Lord's presence, haply to dispel
Remembrance of his sin[155] what better scheme
Than with such chapter-heads[156] his liege-lord's grace
　　　　　　　　　　　　　　　　　　　　redeem?

מִי יָדַע סוֹד מִפְעֲלוֹתֶיךָ, בַּעֲשׂוֹתְךָ לַגּוּף צָרְכֵי פְעֻלּוֹתֶיךָ, וְנָתַתָּ לּוֹ עֵינַיִם לִרְאוֹת
אוֹתוֹתֶיךָ, וְאָזְנַיִם לִשְׁמֹעַ נוֹרְאוֹתֶיךָ, וְרַעְיוֹן לְהָבִין קְצָת סוֹדוֹתֶיךָ, וּפֶה לְסַפֵּר
תְּהִלָּתֶךָ, וְלָשׁוֹן לְהַגִּיד לְכָל יָבוֹא גְבוּרֹתֶךָ, כָּמוֹנִי הַיּוֹם אֲנִי עַבְדְּךָ בֶּן אֲמָתֶךָ,
הַמְסַפֵּר כְּפִי קֹצֶר לְשׁוֹנִי מְעַט מִזְעָר מְרוֹמְמוּתֶךָ, וְהֵן אֵלֶּה קְצוֹת דְּרָכֶיךָ וּמֶה עָצְמוּ
רָאשֵׁיהֶם, כִּי חַיִּים הֵם לְמוֹצְאֵיהֶם, בָּהֶם יוּכְלוּ כָל שׁוֹמְעֵיהֶם לְהַכִּירֶךָ, וְאִם לֹא
רָאוּ פְּנֵי יְקָרֶךָ, וְכָל אֲשֶׁר לֹא יִשְׁמַע גְּבוּרָתֶךָ, אֵיךְ יַכִּיר אֱלֹהוּתֶךָ, וְאֵיךְ תָּבוֹא
בְלִבּוֹ אֲמִתּוּתֶךָ, וִיכַוֵּן רַעְיוֹנָיו לַעֲבוֹדָתֶךָ, עַל כֵּן מָצָא עַבְדְּךָ אֶת לִבּוֹ לִזְכֹּר לְפָנֵי
אֱלֹהָיו, מְעַט מִזְעָר מֵרָאשֵׁי תְהִלּוֹתָיו, אוּלַי בָּם מְעַוֹּנוֹ יַשֶּׁה, וּבַמֶּה יִתְרַצֶּה זֶה
אֶל אֲדוֹנָיו הֲלֹא בְרָאשֵׁי.

XXXIII(a)

Lord, I am too confounded in my shame
To stand in suppliance before Thee—thine
(Full well I know) is greatness, in that same
Measure that utter lowliness is mine;
As strength omnipotent inheres in Thee,
So feeblest power in me,
Beside thy perfect knowledge mine doth fail,
Its defect therein showing symmetry;
For Thou art One, Thou livest nonpareil
In might, enduring, wise, and great, and God:
And I dust of the earth,[158] a very worm, a clod.

אֱלֹהַי בֹּשְׁתִּי וְנִכְלַמְתִּי לַעֲמֹד לְפָנֶיךָ לְדַעְתִּי, כִּי כְפִי עָצְמַת גְּדֻלָּתְךָ כֵּן תַּכְלִית
דַּלּוּתִי וְשִׁפְלוּתִי, וּכְפִי תֹקֶף יְכָלְתְּךָ כֵּן חָלְשַׁת יְכָלְתִּי, וּכְפִי שְׁלֵמוּתְךָ כֵּן חֶסְרוֹן
יְדִיעָתִי, כִּי אַתָּה אֶחָד וְאַתָּה חַי וְאַתָּה גִּבּוֹר וְאַתָּה קַיָּם וְאַתָּה גָדוֹל וְאַתָּה חָכָם
וְאַתָּה אֱלוֹהַּ וַאֲנִי גוּשׁ וְרִמָּה, עָפָר מִן הָאֲדָמָה,

XXXIII(b)

I am a vessel shameful to the brim,
A mute stone, yea, a shadow that is flit,[159]
A fluttered breeze, blown out ere it can skim,
That comes not back;[160] mine is the spider's spit
Of venom,[161] in a crooked heart devised,[162]
A heart uncircumcised;[163]
In anger all my greatness, in deceit
My skill at forging vanity[164] comprised;
My haughty eye disdains; short-tempered heat
Snorts from my nostrils, speech upon my lip
Impurity doth drip,[165]
On twisted ways my feet[166] haste to transgress.[167]
And what, in all, am I? What use pretence
My life hath any worth, or what defence
Lies in my strength and claim of righteousness?
Of all my yesterdays nought is the sum:

What, then, when death is come?[168]
From nought came I, and hence return to nought:[169]
And so, all royal courtesies ignored
I come before Thee,[170] brazen-faced in thought
Unclean, mid lust that uncontrolled hath whored
Set on its idols, in its passion caught;
My soul unpurged,[171] my heart a filthy hoard,
Distraught at death's approach, my body's pain
A riff-raff,[172] agues that still wax yet ne'er shall wane.

כְּלִי מָלֵא כָלְמָּה, אֶבֶן דּוּמָה,

צֵל עוֹבֵר רוּחַ הוֹלֵךְ וְלֹא יָשׁוּב, חֲמַת עַכְשׁוּב, עֲקֹב הַלֵּב, עֶרֶל לֵב, גְּדָל חֵמָה,
חוֹרֵשׁ אָוֶן וּמִרְמָה, גְּבַהּ עֵינַיִם, קְצַר אַפַּיִם, טְמֵא שְׂפָתַיִם, נֶעְקָשׁ דְּרָכַיִם, וְאָץ
בְּרַגְלָיִם. מָה אֲנִי מֶה חַיַּי וּמַה גְּבוּרָתִי, וּמַה צִּדְקָתִי, נֶחְשַׁב לְאַיִן כָּל יְמֵי הֱיוֹתִי,
וְאַף כִּי אַחֲרֵי מוֹתִי, מֵאַיִן מוֹצָאִי, וּלְאַיִן מוֹבָאִי. וְהִנֵּה בָאתִי לְפָנֶיךָ אֲשֶׁר לֹא
כַדָּת בְּעַזּוּת פָּנִים, וְטָמֵאת רַעְיוֹנִים, וְיֵצֶר זוֹנֶה, לְגִלּוּלָיו פוֹנֶה, וְתַאֲוָה מִתְגַּבְּרָה,
וְנֶפֶשׁ לֹא מְטֹהָרָה, וְלֵב טָמֵא, אוֹבֵד וְנִדְמֶה, וְגוּף נָגוּף מָלֵא אֲסַפְסוּף, יוֹסִיף וְלֹא
יָסוּף.

XXXIV

I know, Lord, sin is mine too manifold
To count, trespass for memory too great;
Yet I recall of them some part, which told
Can but a drop in Ocean's tracts equate:
Perchance confessing these I may assuage
Their Ocean's surging rage,[173]
And Thou, in heaven hearing me, forgive.[174]
As trespasser[175] against thy sacred page
Spurning what Thou ordained imperative,
With heart and mouth insinuating flaws
I have abhorred thy laws;
Perversely I have done, and evil wrought;
I have been arrogant; I have been quick
To violence, falsehood have I daubed thick,
Counsel I gave with boundless evil fraught;
Lies have I uttered, scorn I have displayed,

I have rebelled, and made
Reviling blasphemies my speech, and shown
My stubbornness; iniquity I own:
I have been froward where I should obey,
And I have vexed Thee, meeting Thee stiff-necked;
At thy reproof all I did e'er betray
Was sick, blank conscience; wrong did I effect,
My ways I made corrupt, and I did stray
From paths designed for me: I did deflect
And shun thy precepts: aye, in my distress
Justice is thine: truth was thy part, mine wickedness.[176]

אֱלֹהַי יָדַעְתִּי כִּי עֲוֹנוֹתַי רַבּוּ מִסְפֹּר, וְאַשְׁמוֹתַי עָצְמוּ מִלְּזְכֹּר, אַךְ אֶזְכֹּר מֵהֶם
כְּטִפָּה מִן הַיָּם, וְאֶתְוַדֶּה בָהֶם אוּלַי אַשְׁבִּיחַ שְׁאוֹן גַּלֵּיהֶם וְדָכְיָם, וְאַתָּה תִשְׁמַע
הַשָּׁמַיִם וְסָלָחְתָּ. אָשַׁמְתִּי בְּתוֹרָתֶךָ, בָּזִיתִי בְמִצְוֹותֶיךָ, גָּעַלְתִּי בְלִבִּי וּבְמוֹ פִי,
דִּבַּרְתִּי דֹפִי, הֶעֱוֵיתִי וְהִרְשַׁעְתִּי, זַדְתִּי, חָמַסְתִּי, טָפַלְתִּי שֶׁקֶר, יָעַצְתִּי רַע לְאֵין חֵקֶר,
כִּזַּבְתִּי, לַצְתִּי, מָרַדְתִּי, נִאַצְתִּי, סָרַרְתִּי, עָוִיתִי, פָּשַׁעְתִּי, צָרַרְתִּי וְעֹרֶף הִקְשֵׁיתִי,
קַצְתִּי בְתוֹכַחוֹתֶיךָ, רָשַׁעְתִּי, שְׁחַתִּי דַרְכִי, תָּעִיתִי מִמַּהֲלָכֶי, עָבַרְתִּי מִמִּצְוֹותֶיךָ
וְסַרְתִּי, וְאַתָּה צַדִּיק עַל כָּל הַבָּא עָלַי כִּי אֱמֶת עָשִׂיתָ וַאֲנִי הִרְשָׁעְתִּי.

XXXV(a)

Lord, I must stand crestfallen to recall
To mind how oft I caused thy wrath to burn;
Thou didst accord me bounties, yet for all
Of them I made Thee ill return.
Thou didst create me, not to fill some need,
'Twas thine own goodwill's deed[177]
Compelled by none, that purest love did give,
And ere I was, thy mercy did precede
And spirit breathed in me,[178] to make me live
Nor didst Thou then abandon me forlorn,
Into this world new-born.
Nay, Thou didst raise me with a father's care,
Or like the child a foster-parent rears,[179]
And on my mother's breast, secure from fears,[180]

Laid me, and drenched me with delights to spare;
When I essayed to stand, strength didst Thou lend;
Upon thine arms didst bear me; Thou didst ten
My infant footsteps, steadying;[181] a school
Thou wast to me for wisdom, and strict conduct's rule.[182]

אֱלֹהַי נָפְלוּ פָנַי בְּזָכְרִי כָּל אֲשֶׁר הִכְעַסְתִּיךָ, כִּי עַל כָּל טוֹבוֹת שֶׁגְמַלְתַּנִי רָעָה גְמַלְתִּיךָ,
כִּי בְרָאתַנִי לֹא לְצֹרֶךְ רַק נְדָבָה, וְלֹא בְהֶכְרֵחַ כִּי אִם בְּרָצוֹן וְאַהֲבָה, וְטֶרֶם הֱיוֹתִי
בְחַסְדְּךָ קִדַּמְתָּנִי, וְנָפַחְתָּ רוּחַ בִּי וְהֶחֱיִיתָנִי, וְאַחֲרֵי צֵאתִי לַאֲוִיר הָעוֹלָם לֹא
עֲזַבְתָּנִי, אֲבָל כְּאָב חוֹמֵל גִּדַּלְתָּנִי, וּכְאוֹמֵן אֶת הַיוֹנֵק אֲמַנְתָּנִי, עַל שְׁדֵי אִמִּי
הִבְטַחְתָּנִי, וּמִנְּעִימוֹתֶיךָ הִשְׂבַּעְתָּנִי, וּבְבוֹאִי לַעֲמֹד עַל עָמְדִי חִזַּקְתָּנִי, וְקַחְתַּנִי
עַל זְרוֹעוֹתֶיךָ וַתְרַגְּלְתָּנִי, וְחָכְמָה וּמוּסָר לִמַּדְתָּנִי,

XXXV(b)

Thou savedst me out of straits, and e'er didst screen
With thine own hand, while passing wrath[183] was near,
Concealing me; from perils that unseen
Beset me, thy redemption kept me clear.
Ne'er faint fatigue's attack upon me bore
But Thou wast there before,
With remedy for my distress prepared[184]
Yet didst not let me know:[185] did I ignore
Danger, all careless, Thou it was that cared.
When I midst snarling lions sought a track
'Twas Thou their fangs didst crack[186]
And lead me through: when throes of fever pressed
Sore on me,[187] Thou didst cure me for no fee;
Thy judgments oft surprised the world, but me
Thou didst deliver from the sword, from pest,
From famine, and abundance didst provide:
When I provoked Thee, gently didst Thou chide
Paternal;[188] when I called Thee in dismay
Thou heldst me dear, nor empty e'er turned me away.

וּמִכָּל צָרָה וְצוּקָה חִלַּצְתָּנִי,

וּבְעֵת עָבַר זַעַם בְּצֵל יָדְךָ הִסְתַּרְתָּנִי, וְכַמָּה צָרוֹת נֶעֱלָמוּ מֵעֵינַי וּמֵהֶם גְּאַלְתָּנִי,

וּבְטֶרֶם בּוֹא הַתְּלָאָה הִקְדִּמְתָּ וְטוֹאָהּ, לְמַבְּתִי וְלֹא הוֹדַעְתָּנִי, וּבְעֵת לֹא נִשְׁמַרְתִּי

מִכָּל נֶזֶק אַתָּה שְׁמַרְתָּנִי, וּבְבוֹאִי בֵּין שְׁנֵי אֲרָיוֹת שָׁבַרְתָּ מַלְתְּעוֹת כְּפִירִים וּמִשָּׁם

הוֹצֵאתָנִי, וּבְחוּל עָלַי חֳלָיִים רָעִים וְנֶאֱמָנִים חִנָּם רְפָאתָנִי, וּבְבוֹא שְׁפָטֶיךָ הָרָעִים

עַל הָעוֹלָם מֵחֶרֶב הַצַּלְתָּנִי, וּמִדֶּבֶר מִלַּטְתָּנִי, וּבְרָעָב זַנְתָּנִי, וּבְשֶׁבַע כִּלְכַּלְתָּנִי,

וּבְהַכְעִיסִי אוֹתְךָ כַּאֲשֶׁר יְיַסֵּר אִישׁ אֶת בְּנוֹ יִסַּרְתָּנִי, וּבְקָרְאִי מִצָּרָתִי יָקְרָה נַפְשִׁי

בְּעֵינֶיךָ וְרֵיקָם לֹא הֲשִׁיבוֹתָנִי,

XXXV(c)

Yet on this lavishness more didst Thou heap
In giving me a perfect faith in Thee
As God of truth, so in thy law I keep
My trust as truth's own law, and truth do see
In all thy prophets spoke; nor hast allowed
Amidst that rebel crowd
My lot to fall, who, coarse in mind, blaspheme
Thy name,[189] and do deride thy law, and loud
In voice against thy servants strive, and deem
Thy prophets liars: they who make great show
Of innocence, below
Their surface sly—that pure, refined soul
They flaunt, lies o'er a livid spot;[190] a bowl
Of shame are they, its outside washed in guile
But all contained therein is stuff which doth defile.[191]

וְעוֹד הִגְדַּלְתָּ וְהוֹסַפְתָּ עַל כָּל זֶה בְּתִתְּךָ לִי אֱמוּנָה

שְׁלֵמָה לְהַאֲמִין כִּי אַתָּה אֵל אֱמֶת, וְתוֹרָתְךָ אֱמֶת, וּנְבִיאֶיךָ אֱמֶת, וְלֹא נָתַתָּ **לִי**

חֵלֶק עִם מוֹרְדֶיךָ וְקָמֶיךָ, וְעַם נָבָל נִאֲצוּ שְׁמֶךָ, אֲשֶׁר בְּתוֹרָתְךָ יַלְעִיבוּ, וּבְעוֹבְדֶיךָ

יָרִיבוּ, וּנְבִיאֶיךָ יַכְזִיבוּ, מַרְאִים תֻּמָּה, וְתַחְתֵּיהָ עָרְמָה, מַרְאִים נֶפֶשׁ זַכָּה

וְנִטְהֶרֶת, וְתַחְתֵּיהָ תַּעֲמֹד הַבַּהֶרֶת, כִּכְלִי מָלֵא כְּלִמָּה, רָחוּץ מִחוּץ בְּמֵי עָרְמָה,

וְכֹל אֲשֶׁר בְּתוֹכוֹ יִטַמָּא.

XXXVI

I am too slight to merit all this care,
For ever kindly true, and truly kind,
Which Thou hast shown thy servant:[192] yet I dare
Give thanks to Thee, Lord, for Thou hast assigned
A holy soul, which Thou gave me intact;
But each successive act
Of ill I did, defiled her: 'twas my will
Of lust profane left her obscenely wracked.
Full well I know that though I have done ill
I harmed not Thee, but me—nay, my fell bent
For lust stands forth intent
To challenge me, always at my right hand[193]
Nor lets me catch my breath,[194] or plot to gain
Relief: with halter and with bearing-rein[195]
To lead him, broken, long—how long!—I planned,
And strove to row his barque back to the shore
From the lascivious roar
Of Ocean's storms, in vain:[196] he did frustrate
My plans,[197] and what my lips had vowed, did desecrate.[198]
Integrity I set in each new thought,
Yet he deviseth trouble and deceit;
I plead for peace, but war is his retort[199]
Till he makes me a footstool for his feet,[200]
And shedding blood in peace-time, war hath brought:[201]
How often have I sallied forth to meet
His line, and ranged my worship, one cohort,
Next penitence—two made my host complete:
Alongside which I drew up in support
Thy host of mercies, for 'twas my conceit
When battle with my nature must be fought
Should he at Jabbok's ford one host defeat
The other might escape[201]—so did it sort
As I foresaw: he vanquished me, and beat
My scattered troops, and I have no resort
Save mid thy mercies' host to seek retreat,
Knowing that with their aid he can be caught

And I shall crush him—let theirs be the feat
Of arms, launched for their citadel's redoubt,[203]
Then I, perchance, can deal the blow to drive him out.[204]

קָטֹנְתִּי מִכֹּל הַחֲסָדִים וּמִכָּל הָאֱמֶת אֲשֶׁר עָשִׂיתָ אֶת עַבְדֶּךָ, אָמְנָה יְיָ אֱלֹהַי אוֹדְךָ,
כִּי נָתַתָּ בִּי נֶפֶשׁ קְדוֹשָׁה וּבְמַעֲשַׂי הָרָעִים טִמֵּאתִיהָ, וּבְיִצְרִי הָרַע חִלַּלְתִּיהָ
וְגֵאַלְתִּיהָ, אַךְ יָדַעְתִּי, כִּי אִם הִרְשַׁעְתִּי, לֹא לְךָ רַק לְעַצְמִי הֲרֵעוֹתִי, אֲבָל יִצְרִי הָאַכְזָרִי
נִצָּב עַל יְמִינִי, לְשִׂטְנִי, לֹא יִתְּנֵנִי הָשֵׁב רוּחִי, וּלְהָכִין מְנוּחִי, וְזֶה כַּמֶּה לַהֲבִיאוֹ
בְכֶפֶל רְסָנִי חָשַׁבְתִּי, וְחָתַרְתִּי לַהֲשִׁיבוֹ מַיִם הַתַּאֲווֹת אֶל הַיַּבָּשָׁה וְלֹא יָכֹלְתִּי,
הֲנִיא מַחְשְׁבוֹתַי, וְחִלֵּל מוֹצָא שְׂפָתַי, אֲנִי חוֹשֵׁב מַחְשְׁבוֹת תָּמָּה, וְהוּא חוֹרֵשׁ
אָוֶן וּמִרְמָה, אֲנִי לְשָׁלוֹם וְהוּא לְמִלְחָמָה, עַד שְׂמָנִי לְרַגְלָיו הֲדוֹם, וַיָּשֶׂם דְּמֵי
מִלְחָמָה בְּשָׁלוֹם, וְכַמֶּה פְּעָמִים יָצָאתִי לְהִלָּחֵם עִמּוֹ וְעָרַכְתִּי מַחֲנֶה עֲבוֹדָתִי
וּתְשׁוּבָתִי, וְשַׂמְתִּי מַחֲנֶה רַחֲמֶיךָ לְעֶזְרָתִי, כִּי אָמַרְתִּי אִם יָבוֹא יִצְרִי אֶל
הַמַּחֲנֶה הָאַחַת וְהִכָּהוּ וְהָיָה הַמַּחֲנֶה הַנִּשְׁאָר לִפְלֵטָה וְכַאֲשֶׁר חָשַׁבְתִּי כֵּן הָיָה
גָּבַר עָלַי, וְהֵפִיץ חֵילִי, וְלֹא נִשְׁאַר אֵלָי, כִּי אִם מַחֲנֶה רַחֲמֶיךָ אַךְ אֵדַע כִּי בָם
אֶתְקַפֶּנּוּ, וְיִהְיוּ לִי מֵעִיר לָעֹזְר אוּלַי אוּכַל נַכֶּה בּוֹ וַאֲנָרְשֶׁנּוּ.

XXXVII(a)

Do Thou, Lord, will to curb my cruel pride
Of passion's rage: thy face from my offence,
From each fault where I trespassed, do Thou hide,
Nor with my days but half run hale me hence[205]
Before I make my journey's needs my care
And have time to prepare
Provision for the day when I depart;
For if I leave this world and must repair
Naked to that same place whence I did start,[206]
For what was my creation destinate?
Why was I called by fate
To see this life of toil? It were more worth
For me had I remained,[207] nor come at birth
Forth to secure for sin an enlarged hold
And make transgression by my deeds more manifold.

יְהִי רָצוֹן מִלְפָנֶיךָ יְיָ אֱלֹהַי לְכַף אֶת יִצְרִי הָאַכְזָרִי וְהַסְתֵּר פָּנֶיךָ מֵחַטָאַי וּמֵאֲשָׁמַי,
וְאַל תַּעֲלֵנִי בַּחֲצִי יָמַי, עַד אָכִין צְרָכִי, לְדַרְכִּי, וְצֵידָתִי, לְיוֹם נְסִיעָתִי, כִּי אִם
אֵצֵא מֵעוֹלָמִי כַּאֲשֶׁר בָּאתִי, וְאָשׁוּב עָרֹם לִמְקוֹמִי כַּאֲשֶׁר יָצָאתִי, לָמָה נִבְרֵאתִי,
וְלִרְאוֹת עָמָל נִקְרֵאתִי, טוֹב לִי עוֹד אֲנִי שָׁם, מֵצֵאתִי לְהַגְדִּיל פֶּשַׁע וּלְהַרְבּוֹת
אָשָׁם.

XXXVII(b)

Lord, prithee in thy mercy, not in ire
Judge me, lest Thou reduce me past recall:[208]
For what is man that Thou must needs require
That he be tried at law by Thee at all?
How in the scales of justice canst Thou place
A breath the wind doth chase[209]
It weighs not light nor heavy in the pan;
Shall it advantage Thee, in either case,
To weigh thin air?[210] Nay, since he first began
Afflicted hath he been, by plague possessed,
Smitten of God, oppressed:[211]
At his beginning thistledown, breeze-borne,
And at his latter end chaff in the wind,[212]
His life between but grass that blight did find,
Yet God doth dog him still, though chased and worn.[213]
Right from the womb his grief night-long doth last,
Each day in sighs is passed;
High though he flies to-day, tomorrow flies
Breed on him[214]—stubble frights him,[215] brambles prick, he
dies.

If sated, surfeit leads him to offend,
If famished, for a crust of bread he steals;[216]
Pursuing wealth, swift footsteps doth he bend
Forgetting death doth press hard on his heels;
In troublous times, when he in straits is penned
He jabbers honeyed words, for help appeals
With many vows, but should his troubles end
Once he goes out and new enlargement feels
He voids his vows,[217] and what he did intend

With words, he doth forget; with bolts he seals
His door,[218] that he the stouter may defend,
And all the while death through his chambers reels,[219]
His guards he doubles, yet within the keep
An ambush lies,[220] nor hurdles ward off wolf from sheep.

אָנָּא הָאֱלֹהִים בְּמִדַּת רַחֲמֶיךָ שָׁפְטֵנִי, אַל בְּאַפְּךָ פֶּן תַּמְעִיטֵנִי, כִּי מָה
הָאָדָם כִּי תְרִיגֵנְהוּ, וְהֶבֶל נִדָּף אֵיךְ בְּמִשְׁקָל תְּבִיאֵהוּ, וּבַעֲלוֹתוֹ בְּמֹאזְנֵי מִשְׁפָּט לֹא
יִכְבַּד וְלֹא יֵקַל, וּמַה יִּסְכָּן לָךְ לַעֲשׂוֹת לָרוּחַ מִשְׁקָל, מִיּוֹם הֱיוֹתוֹ הוּא נָגַשׁ
וְנַעֲנֶה, נָגוּעַ מֻכֵּה אֱלֹהִים וּמְעֻנֶּה, רֵאשִׁיתוֹ מוֹץ נֶהְדָּף, וְאַחֲרִיתוֹ קַשׁ נִדָּף,
וּבְחַיָּיו כְּעֵשֶׂב נִשְׁדָּף, וְהָאֱלֹהִים יְבַקֵּשׁ אֶת נִרְדָּף. מִיּוֹם צֵאתוֹ מֵרֶחֶם אִמּוֹ, **יָגוֹן**
לַיְלוֹ וַאֲנָחָה יוֹמוֹ, אִם הַיּוֹם יָדוּם, מָחָר תּוֹלָעִים יָרֻם, הַמּוֹץ יִדְפֶנּוּ, **וְהַקּוֹץ**
יַצְפֶנּוּ, אִם יִשְׂבַּע יִרְשַׁע, וְאִם יִרְעַב עַל פַּת לֶחֶם יִפְשַׁע, לִרְדּוֹף הָעֹשֶׁר · **קַלּוּ**
אֲשׁוּרָיו, וְיִשְׁכַּח הַמָּוֶת וְהוּא אַחֲרָיו. בְּעֵת הַמֵּצַר יָרֵב אֲמָרָיו, וְיַחֲלִיק דְּבָרָיו,
וְיַרְבֶּה נְדָרָיו, וּבְצֵאתוֹ לַמֶּרְחָב יַחֵל דְּבָרָיו, וְיִשְׁכַּח נְדָרָיו, וִיחַזֵּק בְּרִיחֵי שְׁעָרָיו,
וְהַמָּוֶת בַּחֲדָרָיו, וְיַרְבֶּה שׁוֹמְרִים מִכָּל עֵבֶר וְהָאוֹרֵב יוֹשֵׁב לוֹ בַּחֶדֶר, וְהַזְּאֵב
לֹא יַעַצְרֶנּוּ גָדֵר, מִבּוֹא אֶל הָעֵדֶר.

XXXVII(c)

Man comes to birth,[221] nor knows the reason why,
And should he joy, he knows not what doth give
His pleasure cause; so each one's life slips by
And none can know how long he has to live.
A child, his gait is stubborn, and when lust
Begins in him to thrust,[222]
He rangeth, stirred by quest of fortune's goal,
On shipboard, posting through the desert's dust,
Risking in lion's dens[223] his life and soul
Among the beasts[224] that soul which ought instead
Tread paths where angels tread:
And when he thinks that fame success hath brought
And garnered riches,[225] while all seems serene
Comes a despoiler:[226] when upon the scene
His eyes once more he opens, there is nought.[227]
Whate'er the date, with nuisance manifold
Appointment he must hold,

Whate'er the hour, with accident; whate'er
The instant, crisis; each new day brings some new scare:[228]
A little moment doth his ease remain,
Then, in a trice, disaster[229]—war, the fell
Cut of a sword, a bolt clean through his brain
Shot from an arblast:[230] haply griefs, pell-mell
Surround him, or the floods in their disdain
Swamp him unmarked;[231] or dire disease, to swell
With unremitting agonies[232] his pain;
Self-burdened,[233] he finds asps' gall[234] taste in mell,
And as his pain increaseth, so doth wane
His glory;[235] wanton lads, with jeers,[236] expel
Him from his rule,[237] aye, e'en his sons complain,
His own loins' issue; friends, estranged, rebel
Nor heed his greeting, till from his domain
He goes to death's domain at his hour's knell,
Doffing his silk-worm's braid[238] and vermail stain
To don the earthworm's mantled vermicel,
And dust returns to dust, a couch to find
In that same element whence his own stuff was mined.[239]

יִנְאֶה וְלֹא יֵדַע לָמָּה, וְיִשְׂמַח וְלֹא יֵדַע

בַּמֶּה, וְיִחְיֶה וְלֹא יֵדַע בַּמֶּה. בְּיַלְדוּתוֹ, הוֹלֵךְ בִּשְׁרִירוּתוֹ, וְכַאֲשֶׁר תָּחֵל רוּחַ
הַתַּאֲוָה לְפַעֲמוֹ, יִתְעוֹרֵר לֶאֱסֹף חַיִל וְהוֹן וְיִסַּע מִמְּקוֹמוֹ, לִרְכֹּב אֳנִיּוֹת, וְלִרְדֹּף
בַּצִּיּוֹת, וּלְהָבִיא נַפְשׁוֹ בִּמְעוֹנוֹת אֲרָיוֹת, וְהִיא מִתְהַלֶּכֶת בֵּין הַחַיּוֹת. וּבְחָשְׁבוֹ כִּי
רַב הוֹדוֹ, וְכִי כַבִּיר מָצְאָה יָדוֹ, בַּשָּׁלוֹם שׁוֹדֵד יְבוֹאֶנּוּ, וְעֵינָיו פָּקַח וְאֵינֶנּוּ,
בְּכָל עֵת הוּא מְזֻמָּן לְתַלְאוֹת, חוֹלְפוֹת וּבָאוֹת, וּבְכָל שָׁעוֹת, לְמָאֹרָעוֹת, בְּכָל
הָרְגָעִים, לִפְגָעִים, וּבְכָל הַיָּמִים, עָלָיו אֵימִים. אִם רֶגַע יַעֲמֹד בְּשַׁלְוָה, פֶּתַע
תְּבוֹאֵהוּ הֹוָה, אוֹ בְמִלְחָמָה יָבוֹא וְחֶרֶב תִּגְּפֵהוּ, אוֹ קֶשֶׁת נְחוּשָׁה תַּחְלְפֵהוּ, אוֹ
יַקִּיפוּהוּ יְגוֹנִים, אוֹ יִשְׁטְפוּהוּ מַיִם זְדוֹנִים, אוֹ יִמְצָאוּהוּ חֳלָיִים רָעִים וְנֶאֱמָנִים,
עַד יִהְיֶה לְמַשָּׂא עַל נַפְשׁוֹ, וְיִמְצָא מְרוֹרַת פְּתָנִים בְּדָבְשׁוֹ. וּבְעֵת כָּאֵבוֹ יִגְדַּל,
כְּבוֹדוֹ יִדַּל, וּנְעָרִים יִתְקַלְּסוּ בוֹ, וְתַעֲלוּלִים יִמְשְׁלוּ בוֹ, וְיִהְיֶה לָטֹרַח עַל יוֹצְאֵי
מֵעָיו, וְיִתְנַכְּרוּ לוֹ כָּל רֵעָיו. וּבְבוֹא עִתּוֹ יֵצֵא מִמְּצָרָיו לַחֲצַר מָוֶת, וּמִצֵּל חֲדָרָיו
לְצַלְמָוֶת, וְיִפְשֹׁט רִקְמָה וְתוֹלָע, וְיִלְבַּשׁ רִמָּה וְתוֹלָע, וְלֶעָפָר יִשְׁכַּב, וְיָשׁוּב אֶל
יְסוֹדוֹ אֲשֶׁר מִמֶּנּוּ חֻצָּב.

XXXVII(d)

Encumbered thus,[240] when, pray, shall man contrive
A time for penitence, to wash away
His heart's corrosion, his backslidings shrive?
Too crowded is his round, too short his day,[241]
And taskmasters haste urgent[242] here and there,
While Father Time doth wear
Sardonian smiles, and He that doth exact
Day-labour presseth, nor doth ever spare:
Wherefore remember, Lord, how man is racked
By these turmoils that come so thick and strong;
And if I have done wrong
Make me so live my latter end to sense
Correction's benefit, nor recompense
Measure for measure one whose sin denies
The metewand's scale, who joyless lived and joyless dies.[243]

וְאִישׁ אֲשֶׁר אֵלֶּה לוֹ מָתַי יִמְצָא עֵת תְּשׁוּבָה, לִרְחֹץ
חֶלְאַת מְשׁוּבָה, וְהַיּוֹם קָצֵר וְהַמְּלָאכָה מְרֻבָּה, וְהַנּוֹגְשִׂים אָצִים, וְהַלּוֹחֲצִים חָשִׁים
וְרָצִים, וְהַזְּמַן שׂוֹחֵק, וּבַעַל הַבַּיִת דּוֹחֵק. לָכֵן אֱלֹהַי זְכָר נָא אֵלֶּה הַתְּלָאוֹת,
אֲשֶׁר עַל אָדָם בָּאוֹת, וְאִם אֲנִי הֲרֵעוֹתִי, אַתָּה תֵיטִיב אַחֲרִיתִי, וְאַל תִּגְמֹל מִדָּה
בְמִדָּה, לְאִישׁ אֲשֶׁר עֲווֹנוֹתָיו בְּלִי מִדָּה, וּבְמוֹתוֹ יֵלֵךְ בְּלֹא חֶמְדָּה.

XXXVIII(a)

Lord, if my sin is great—too great to bear—[244]
How wilt Thou shield thine own yet greater name
From obloquy?[245] And if I may not dare
Hope for thy mercies, on whom have I claim
For pity, save on Thee? Nay, then, I say,
E'en though Thou shouldst me slay
Nathless my hope on Thee should still abide;[246]
And if my sin Thou searchest,[247] then away
From Thee I flee—to Thee, myself to hide
In thy shade from thy broiling wrath, and cling
Fast to thine apron-string

Of mercy, till Thou bidst thy mercy hold
Me firm, nor will I let Thee go, unless
Like Jacob's angel Thou dost deign to bless.[248]
Remember I am clay that Thou didst mould,[249]
And yet by all these toils I am oppressed
Subjected to thy test;
Nay, bring me not to book for every deed
Of wantonness,[250] nor on my work's fruit make me feed:
But be Thou slow to anger for my sake,
Nor haste my day of reckoning ere yet
Provision for my journey home I make;
Press not to have me out the land,[251] nor fret
To drive me forth with sin I sought to bake
Half-leavened in its kneading-trough, and set
Upon my shoulder; nay, when Thou must take
My sins to weigh them up, against them let
My cares be poised—here, rebel thoughts of ill
And evil deeds, there, troubles that ne'er leave me still.[252]

אֱלֹהַי אִם עֲווֹנִי מִנְּשֹׂא גָדוֹל, מַה תַּעֲשֶׂה לְשִׁמְךָ הַגָּדוֹל, וְאִם לֹא אוֹחִיל
לְרַחֲמֶיךָ, מִי יָחוּס עָלַי חוּץ מִמֶּךָּ, לָכֵן אִם תִּקְטְלֵנִי, לְךָ אֲיַחֵל וְאִם תְּבַקֵּשׁ
לַעֲווֹנִי, אֶבְרַח מִמְּךָ אֵלֶיךָ, וְאֶתְכַּסֶּה מֵחֲמָתְךָ בְּצִלֶּךָ, וּבְשׁוּלֵי רַחֲמֶיךָ אַחֲזִיק
עַד אִם רַחַמְתָּנִי, וְלֹא אֲשַׁלֵּחֲךָ כִּי אִם בֵּרַכְתָּנִי. זְכָר נָא כִּי כַחֹמֶר עֲשִׂיתָנִי, וּבְאֵלֶּה
הַתְּלָאוֹת נְסִיתָנִי, עַל כֵּן לֹא תִפְקֹד עָלַי כְּמַעֲלָלָי, וְאַל תַּאֲכִילֵנִי פְּרִי פְעָלָי,
וְהַאֲרֵךְ לִי אַפְּךָ וְאַל תַּקְרִיב יוֹמִי, עַד אָכִין צֵידָה לָשׁוּב אֶל מְקוֹמִי, וְאַל תַּחֲזַק
עָלַי לְמַהֵר לְשַׁלְּחֵנִי מִן הָאָרֶץ וּמִשְׁאֲרוֹת אֲשֶׁמַי צְרוּרוֹת עַל שִׁכְמִי. וּבְהַעֲלוֹתְךָ
בְּמִשְׁקָל עֲווֹנוֹתַי, שִׂים לְךָ בְּכַף שְׁנִיָּה תִּלְאוֹתַי, וּבְזָכְרְךָ רִשְׁעִי וּמִרְדִּי, זְכָר עָנְיִי
וּמְרוּדִי,

XXXVIII(b)

Lord, bear in mind, I pray, how long a while
Through No-man's-land my path Thou hast made wind
And unwind, and assayed me in exile
Like metal, in a crucible refined
Of my main dross. I know the reason why
My patience Thou didst try

Is for my good; thy faithfulness stands fast,
When Thou afflictest,[253] 'tis to amplify
That benefit Thou bringest at the last[254]
Through testing toils; let, then, thy mercies, Lord,
Be moved for me, and poured
Out plentiful: thy fury's entire might
On me alone consume not, nor requite
Me as my doings merit, but rebuff
The angel who, to venge, destroys: say him 'Enough!'[255]

וְשִׂים אֵלֶּה נֹכַח אֵלֶּה, וּזְכָר נָא אֱלֹהַי כִּי זָה כַּמֶּה לָאָרֶץ נוֹד צְנַפְתָּנִי,
וּבְכוֹר גָּלוּת בְּחַנְתָּנִי, וּמֵרֹב רִשְׁעִי צְרַפְתָּנִי, וְיָדַעְתִּי כִּי לְטוֹבָתִי נִסִּיתָנִי, וֶאֱמוּנָה
עִנִּיתָנִי, וּלְהֵיטִיב לִי בְּאַחֲרִיתִי בְּמִבְחַן הַתְּלָאוֹת הֲבֵאתָנִי, לָכֵן אֱלֹהַי יֶהֱמוּ עָלַי
רַחֲמֶיךָ, וְאַל תְּכַלֶּה עָלַי זַעְמֶךָ, וְאַל תִּגְמְלֵנִי כְּמַעֲבָדַי, וֶאֱמֹר לַמַּלְאָךְ הַמַּשְׁחִית
דָּי,

XXXVIII(c)

For is my quality of such degree
Of excellence, that Thou each fault must trace[256]
And post o'er me a watch?[257] Couldst Thou view me
As a hart-royal,[258] meet for Thee to chase?
Are not my days near passed, their most part done,
And those few still left, run
With festering sores of sin?[259] If, then, today
I stand before thee, by tomorrow's sun
Thine eye shall light on where I stood, but nay,
I am no more.[260] Must, then, I now expire,
And shall thy mighty fire
Consume me straight?[261] Lord, let thine eye rest kind[262]
On my few days still left, that straggle frail—
Pursue them not: that wretched crop my hail
Of turbulence hath spared, let it not find
The locust of my sin to strip its grain:[263]
For 'twas thy hand that formed me, and what gain

Thereof to Thee accrueth,[264] if the brood
Of worms take me, thy handiwork, to be their food?[265]

וּמַה מַּעֲלָתִי וְיִתְרוֹנִי, כִּי תְבַקֵּשׁ לַעֲווֹנִי, וְתָשִׂיםעָלַי מִשְׁמָר, וּתְצוּדֵנִי כְּתוֹא
מִכְמָר, הֲלֹא יָמַי חָלַף רָבָּם וְאֵינָם, וְהַנִּשְׁאָרִים בָּהֶם יִמַקּוּ בַּעֲווֹנָם, וְאִם הַיּוֹם
לְפָנֶיךָ הִגַּנִּי, מָחָר עֵינֶיךָ בִּי וְאֵינֶנִּי, וְעַתָּה לָמָּה אָמוּת, כִּי תֹאכְלֵנִי הָאֵשׁ הַגְּדוֹלָה
הַזֹּאת. אֱלֹהַי שִׂים עֵינֶיךָ עָלַי לְטוֹבָה לִשְׁאֵרִית יָמַי הַמְעַטִּים, וְאַל תִּרְדֹּף הַשָּׂרִידִים
וְהַפְּלֵטִים, וְהַפְּלֵטָה הַנִּשְׁאֶרֶת מִבְּרָד מְהוּמוֹתַי, אַל יַחְסְלֶנָה יֶלֶק אַשְׁמוֹתַי, כִּי יְצִיר
כַּפֶּיךָ אָנִי, וּמַה יִּסְכָּן לָךְ כִּי רָמָה תִקָּחֵנִי לְמַאֲכָל, יִגִּיעַ כַּפֶּיךָ כִּי תֹאכֵל.

XXXIX

Lord, may it be thy will that Thou to me
In mercy wilt return, and wilt effect
That I in perfect penitence to Thee
Return to stand before thy face:[266] direct
My suppliant heart to make his plea sincere,
And do Thou lend thine ear,[267]
Yea, to thy law ope wide my heart, and plant
The seed in all my thinking of thy fear:
Decrees for good enact o'er me, and grant
Decrees made for my hurt be nullified:
Place me not where my pride
Bids me test Thee, and tempted I might fall,
Nor where, contemning Thee, I should be seen
Myself contemned,[268] but do Thou be my screen
From ill encounters saving me, till all
Disasters are passed by, keep me concealed
With thy shade for my shield;[269]
Be with my musing, be Thou with my lips,
And guard my ways, to check from sin when my tongue
slips:[270]

Spare me a thought when Thou rememberest
Thy folk in thy good will, and wouldst renew

Thy temple: when thy chosen ones are bless'd
May I be witness,[271] privileged to view
Each dawn thy shrine, now desolate, its spilled
Rubble to cherish;[272] soon its wasted stones rebuild.

יְהִי רָצוֹן מִלְּפָנֶיךָ, יְיָ אֱלֹהַי לָשׁוּב עָלַי בְּרַחֲמֶיךָ, וְלַהֲשִׁיבֵנִי בִּתְשׁוּבָה שְׁלֵמָה
לְפָנֶיךָ, וְלַתְחַנְתִּי תָכִין לְבָךְ תַּקְשִׁיב אָזְנֶךָ, וְתִפְתַּח לִבִּי בְּתוֹרָתֶךָ, וְתִטַּע בְּרַעְיוֹנֵי
יִרְאָתֶךָ, וְתִגְזֹר עָלַי גְּזֵרוֹת טוֹבוֹת, וּתְבַטֵּל מֵעָלַי גְּזֵרוֹת רָעוֹת, וְאַל תְּבִיאֵנִי לִידֵי
נִסָּיוֹן, וְלֹא לִידֵי בִזָּיוֹן, וּמִכָּל פְּגָעִים רָעִים תַּצִּילֵנִי, וְעַד יַעֲבֹר הַוּוֹת בְּצִלְּךָ
תַּסְתִּירֵנִי, וְהָיָה עִם פִּי וְהֶגְיוֹנִי, וּשְׁמֹר דְּרָכַי מֵחֲטֹא בִלְשׁוֹנִי, וְזָכְרֵנִי בְּזִכְרוֹן עַמֶּךָ,
וּבְבִנְיַן אוּלַמֶּךָ, לִרְאוֹת בְּטוֹבַת בְּחִירֶיךָ, וְזַכֵּנִי לְשַׁחֵר דְּבִירְךָ הַשָּׁמֵם וְהֶחָרֵב וְלִרְצוֹת
אֲבָנָיו וַעֲפְרוֹתָיו, וְרִגְבֵי חָרְבוֹתָיו, וְתִבְנֶה שׁוֹמְמוֹתָיו.

XL(a)

Lord, well I know that they who supplicate
Thy grace, should send before what they have done
Of pious works to be their advocate,
And gifts of charity: but I have none:
My shaken folds show no good deed of mine,[273]
But bare as some stripped vine[274]
I own no righteousness, nor is my way
Demure, no loyalty to love divine,
No uprightness, nor e'en the mind to pray
Beseechingly; no faith nor innocence,
No virtue, naught of worship, no true penitence.

אֱלֹהַי יָדַעְתִּי כִּי הַמִּתְחַנְּנִים לְפָנֶיךָ יָלִיצוּ עֲלֵיהֶם מַעֲשִׂים טוֹבִים אֲשֶׁר הִקְדִּימוּ,
אוֹ צִדְקוֹתֵיהֶם אֲשֶׁר הֵרִימוּ, וַאֲנִי אֵין בִּי מַעֲשִׂים כִּי אֲנִי נָעוּר וָרֵק, כְּגֶפֶן בּוֹקֵק,
וְאֵין בִּי לֹא צֶדֶק וְלֹא כֹשֶׁר, לֹא חֶסֶד וְלֹא יֹשֶׁר, לֹא תְפִלָּה וְלֹא תְחִנָּה, לֹא תַמָּה
וְלֹא אֱמוּנָה, לֹא צֶדֶק וְלֹא מִדָּה טוֹבָה, לֹא עֲבוֹדָה וְלֹא תְשׁוּבָה.

XL(b)

So on thine own will I depend, O Lord,
Who art our fathers' God and ours, above
All worlds in sovereignty: may it accord
With thine intent to grant me, of thy love,
Compassion: let me always find Thee near,[275]
To be my scrutineer
Whose visitations from thy favour spring;
To make thy countenance shine on me clear[276]
And let me find thy grace: nor on me bring
Requital to my deeds proportionate,
To be held reprobate
Scorned as a churl:[277] take me not hence midway
In my days' course,[278] nor hide from me thy face;[279]
Purge me of sin, but cast me not from grace
Far from thy presence:[280] grant me life today
Midst glory, taking me hereafter crowned
With trailing clouds of glory,[281] when doth sound
The hour for Thee to lead me hence, and send
Me peaceful to the life of that world without end.

וּבְכֵן יְהִי רָצוֹן

מִלְּפָנֶיךָ יְיָ אֱלֹהֵינוּ וֵאלֹהֵי אֲבוֹתֵינוּ רִבּוֹן כָּל הָעוֹלָמִים לְרַחֵם עָלַי, וְהָיִיתָ קָרוֹב
אֵלַי, לְפָקְדֵנִי בִּפְקֻדַּת רְצוֹנֶךָ, וְלָשֵׂאת אֵלַי אוֹר פָּנֶיךָ, וּלְהַמְצִיאֵנִי חִנֶּךָ, וּכְפִי מַעֲשַׂי
אַל תִּגְמְלֵנִי, וְחֶרְפַּת נָבָל אַל תְּשִׂימֵנִי, וּבַחֲצִי יָמַי אַל תַּעֲלֵנִי, וְאַל תַּסְתֵּר פָּנֶיךָ
מִמֶּנִּי, וּמֵחַטָּאתִי טַהֲרֵנִי, וּמִלְּפָנֶיךָ אַל תַּשְׁלִיכֵנִי, וּבִכְבוֹד תְּחַיֵּנִי, וְאַחַר כָּבוֹד
תִּקָּחֵנִי, וּבְעֵת מִן הָעוֹלָם הַזֶּה תוֹצִיאֵנִי, לְחַיֵּי הָעוֹלָם הַבָּא בְּשָׁלוֹם תְּבִיאֵנִי,

XL(c)

And when thy summons cometh, raised on high[282]
Let me with saints for company recline,
Mustered midst martyrs, they that qualify
For everlasting life:[283] may thy face shine
On me, as worthy in that wondrous light
To find all my delight,[284]

Reviving me, from earth's depths once more raised[285]
To say 'Thy praises, Lord, will I recite
In thanks, for that thy wrath which sometime blazed
On me, is turned, and Thou dost comfort me.'[286]
Such love, O Lord, from Thee
Alone deriveth,[287] richly manifest
In all that bounty wherewith Thou hast bless'd[288]
Me heretofore and which Thou wilt display
In undiminished bounty till my dying day.

וְאֶל

עַל תִּקְרָאֵנִי וּבֵין הַחֲסִידִים תּוֹשִׁיבֵנִי, וְעִם הַמְּנוּיִים מֵחֵלֶד חֶלְקָם בַּחַיִּים תִּמְנֵנִי,
וְלָאוֹר בְּאוֹר פָּנֶיךָ תְּזַכֵּנִי, וְתָשׁוּב תְּחַיֵּנִי, וּמִתְּהֹומֹות הָאָרֶץ תָּשׁוּב תַּעֲלֵנִי, וְאֹמַר
אוֹדְךָ יְיָ כִּי אָנַפְתָּ בִּי יָשֹׁב אַפְּךָ וּתְנַחֲמֵנִי, וּלְךָ יְיָ חֶסֶד עַל כָּל הַטּוֹבָה אֲשֶׁר גְּמַלְתַּנִי,
וַאֲשֶׁר עַד יוֹם מוֹתִי תִגְמְלֵנִי.

XL(d)

And for all this am I in duty bound
To sing Thee hymns of gratitude and praise:
In all Thou didst create let there abound
Thy lauds;[281] let them that sanctify Thee, raise
Thrice-holy acclamation: let those seek
Who know Thee for unique
To tell mankind, and be thy glory told
By them that glorify Thee: when they speak
Who would extol Thee, be by them extolled,
And when thine exaltation they proclaim
Exalted by thy name:
Midst them that some style gods, not one is there
Could with Thee, Lord, or with thy works compare.[290]
My words, and my heart's musings, pleasing be
To Thee, my Lord and Rock: 'tis Thou redeemest me.[291]

וְעַל כָּל זֶה אֲנִי חַיָּב לְהוֹדוֹת לְהַלֵּל לְפָאֵר וּלְרוֹמֵם

אוֹתְךָ: תִּשְׁתַּבַּח בְּפִי בְרוּאֶיךָ, תִּתְקַדֵּשׁ בְּפִי מַקְדִּישֶׁיךָ, תִּתְיַחֵד בְּפִי מְיַחֲדֶיךָ, תִּתְפָּאֵר

בְּפִי מְפָאֲרֶיךָ, תִּתְרוֹמֵם בְּפִי מְרוֹמְמֶיךָ, תִּתְנַשֵּׂא בְּפִי מְנַשְּׂאֶיךָ, כִּי אֵין כָּמוֹךָ

בֵאלֹהִים אֲדֹנָי וְאֵין כְּמַעֲשֶׂיךָ. יִהְיוּ לְרָצוֹן אִמְרֵי פִי וְהֶגְיוֹן לִבִּי לְפָנֶיךָ יְיָ צוּרִי

וְגוֹאֲלִי.

EPILOGUE

In 1972, the assumed 950th anniversary of Ibn Gabirol's birth was celebrated by a conference, held in Malaga, at which I delivered a lecture. During the conference Reed Armstrong's statue of Ibn Gabirol was formally dedicated: it stands in a public garden opposite the site of the Roman theatre. At the ceremony I recited the following Hebrew poem, which I had composed while at Malaga; after my return to England I made an English sonnet of it. It is reprinted, together with the Spanish sonnet into which Alfonso Canales rendered the English, from the *Proceedings* of the Conference.[1]

לְאִישׁ נָשָׂא בְּכַנְפֵי שִׁיר וְעָמוּ   מְקוֹר חַיִּים אֲשֶׁר הֵאִיר לְעַמּוֹ
וְהוֹדִיעָם מְקוֹם כֵּס־יָהּ וְסִתְרוֹ   וְחָכְמָתוֹ אֲשֶׁר יָסַד הֲדוֹמוֹ
יְהִי זֵר וְתִפְאֶרֶת לְרֹאשׁוֹ   אֲשֶׁר בָּאנוּ וְחָקַרְנוּ מְקוֹמוֹ
בְּמָאלְקָה לְעוֹרֵר הֵד דְּבָרָיו   בְּמוֹלַדְתּוֹ גְּנִינוֹת קוֹל נְעִימוֹ
בְּנֵי עַמּוֹ וְגַם אַנְשֵׁי סְפָרָד   תְּנוּ שָׁלוֹם שְׂאוּ לָכֶם שְׁלוֹמוֹ
וְתָבוֹאנָה בְּנוֹת הַשִּׁיר רֵעָדָיו   נְהַלֵּל יָהּ וְאֵלֶּה לִשְׁלֹמֹה

'Twas thou that soared on winds of song, to find
  That Fount of Life whence for thy folk might shine
  Illumination from the mystic shrine
Which veils God's throne, that they might glimpse
                          His mind
Whose wisdom formed the Cosmos, and assigned
  Earth for his footstool: glory, then, be thine
  In garlands this our homage doth entwine
Who trace where once thy infant steps did wind

Here in thy birthplace, echoes to revive,
Thy honeyed song and reasoned argument,
Standing as Israel's sons next sons of Spain
To hail thee, and from thee peace to derive;
Come, Hebrew Muse, and all with one consent
Praise God, that yet a Solomon doth reign.

Recordemos al docto que, en alas remontado
    de la voz, alumbraba la Fuente de la Vida
    para su afín; le daba esa verdad tupida
de Dios, por la que el mundo le sirve como estrado.
Si en la Málaga suya hemos resucitado
    con pasos y con ecos tal voz de miel, unida
    quede a esa frente nuestra corona florecida.
Fundando una memoria de paz eterna, al lado
    del hijo de su raza, el español proclame
    su gloria, junto a todos los que la paz anhelan.
    Venga también la hebraica musa que resucitas
    con arte, Salomón; y todo el que se inflame
    de Dios, por quien tus versos se remontan y vuelan,
    igual que los del sabio rey de los israelitas.

APPENDIX

The Basis of Medieval Hebrew Metrics

QUANTITATIVE verse depends for its effect, insofar as form is concerned, on the tension between a metrical pattern of long and short syllables, the stress-position within the individual words, and the weight of each word (in regard to the sense) within its clause or the sentence. Widely used in the classical periods of Latin and Greek, the system was taken up in Arabic poetry, whence it was adapted to Hebrew from the tenth century onwards. Modification was necessary, not least because whereas Arabic word-formation (like that of Latin or Greek) frequently produces consecutive short syllables, Hebrew does not. That is because the vocalization integral to massoretic Hebrew grammar, as reflected in the traditional ('Tiberian') system of vowel-points, represents not the language of conversational speech but a formalized diction designed to secure maximum audibility, whatever the acoustic conditions, for the declamation of the Bible and its associated liturgy in the service of the synagogue.

Massoretic Hebrew grammar distinguishes between long vowels (e.g. *ā*, indicated by a *qamaṣ* and short *ă*, indicated by a *pathaḥ*). For purposes of medieval prosody, i.e. the scansion of metrical poems, this distinction is ignored, the full vowels being treated as 'long' and the vocal *shewa*—whether simple or compound, i.e. *ḥathaph pathaḥ*, etc.—being regarded as vowels and as being 'short'. The only exception is that the initial *u-* (= *and*) which in some circumstances replaces *we-* (with *shewa*), is not considered 'long' as would be a medial *u*, e.g. in *yaqum*, but 'short', like its equivalent *we-*.

This classification makes possible two approaches, of

165

which the first (a) is simple, merely utilizing the rhythm of a constant number of beats between pauses, in the manner of a drum marking the pace of the march. The other (b) is complex.

(a) ignores all the 'short' syllables as defined above. (Since it is used for liturgical poems intended to be sung, each 'long' syllable may carry more than one note.) For an example, see the poem '*shin'anim sha'ananim*' (pp. 101f.), the scheme of which is

$$-- - \mid --- \mid --- \mid ---$$

the last word of the fourth foot at the end of every stanza bearing the main rhyme throughout the poem, and the first two feet their own internal rhyme. In the following transcription the vocal *shewas*, whether simple or compound, are bracketed.

> shin'anim | sha'[a]nanim | [ke]niṣoṣim | yilhabu (l.1)
> [me]khon mishmar | hane['e]mar | [be]rosh ma[ḥa]noth |
> [ha]moneykha (l.11)

(b) utilizes various metrical patterns of long and short syllables, which in their modification from Arabic models have been made more rigid (one may compare Virgil's treatment of the Latin hexameter as handled by his predecessors, e.g. Lucretius). For example, whereas Arabic, like Latin or Greek, could treat the dactyl ($-\smile\smile$), the anapaest ($\smile\smile-$), and the spondee ($--$) as metrically having the same weight, Hebrew, for reasons already stated, can use only the iambus ($\smile-$), the spondee, and combinations of the two yielding e.g. $\smile---$. A licence permits some manipulation of the *shewa* in order either to produce a desiderated short vowel, or to eliminate a superfluous one. For the latter purpose they may be ignored, as in (a), where all *shewas* are metrically insignificant. Conversely, a silent *shewa* may be 'promoted' to the status of a vocal *shewa* and treated as constituting a short syllable. Thus, whereas the normal pronunciation, in verse as in prose, of *holekhim* would yield the vowel-pattern $-\breve{}-$, it may be reduced to (*hol[e]khim*), and *'aphqid*, which would normally be scanned $--$, may be read *aphᵊqid*, yielding $-\breve{}-$. (In the examples transliterated below, the vocal *shewa* and the silent *shewa* artificially vocalized are represented, as in the foregoing, by ə, and the vocal element in a compound *shewa* by a raised letter.)

The metrical schemes involve matched hemistichs, either (i) of identical pattern, or (ii) the pattern of the second being a slightly heavier variation of that of the first, in order to indicate what is normally the sense-pause. In the case of (ii), the first member of the first pair of hemistichs only will anticipate the metre of its fellow, in order clearly to introduce the 'major' scheme to the listener's ear. Thus the first four hemistichs of the lament over Yequthiel (p. 72) exhibit the following pattern:

$$--\breve{}-|--\breve{}-|--- \,||\, --\breve{}-|--\breve{}-|---$$
$$--\breve{}-|--\breve{}-|--\breve{}- \,||\, --\breve{}-|--\breve{}-|---$$

biymey yᵊqu|thiel 'asher | nigmaru || 'oth ki shᵊḥa |
qim laḥᵃloph | yuṣṣaru

simu lᵊba | b[ᵊ]khem tedᵊ‘u | ki hazᵊman || yakhin
lᵊ‘am | shiḥoth wᵊlo | noṣaru

In order to identify the scansion (and so also the metre) of any particular poem, it is consequently necessary to scrutinize its first two complete lines, and then to apply the scheme throughout. Thus, the well-known hymn beginning 'adon 'olam reveals in its first two lines that the metre is formed by the repetition of an iambus ($\breve{}-$) + a spondee ($--$) for each hemistich, thus:

$$\breve{}---|\breve{}--- \,||\, \breve{}---|\breve{}---$$

'adon 'olam | 'asher malakh || bᵊṭerem kol | yᵊṣir nibra

It thus follows that in the third line the first hemistich has to be scanned

wᵊ'aḥ[ᵃ]rey ki | khᵊloth hakkol,

the first word being syncopated by the omission of the second vocal *shewa*, and the second word, which would normally be pronounced *kikhloth* (−−), being given the value −˘− to fit the metrical pattern.

Above the Hebrew of each poem printed in the book there has been set an indication of its metrical pattern. Regarding the rigorousness with which the purity of rhyme is maintained, see p. 117.

NOTES

Biblical quotations are from the Authorized Version.
Full bibliographical information will be found in the Select Bibliography, pp. 189-191.

1: *The Historical Background*

1 This summary conflates two variant traditions, recorded by Isaac Abravanel at the end of his commentary on Kings, and by Solomon ibn Verga, *Shevet Yehudah*, ed. A. Shochat (Jerusalem, 1947), p. 33.

2 See the *General Estoria* of Alfonso X (the Wise), completed in 1284, ed. A. García Solalinde (Madrid, 1961), ii, 2, pp. 344f. The evidence regarding the earliest attested Jewish presence in Spain is surveyed by H. Beinart, 'Cuando llegaron los judíos a España?', *Estudios* 3 (Buenos Aires, 1962), pp. 1–32.

3 See pp. 98f.

4 For discussion as to the authenticity of the story see *Encyclopaedia Judaica* 6, 1446f., and more fully E. Ashtor, *The Jews of Moslem Spain*, 1, pp. 429f.

2: *Solomon ibn Gabirol*

1 Trans. Joshua Finkel, 'An Eleventh Century Source for the History of Jewish Scientists in Mohammedan Land (Ibn Sa'id)'. *Jewish Quarterly Review*. New Series 18 (1927–8), pp. 51–2.

2 Bargebuhr, *Salomo Ibn Gabirol*, p. 54.

3 See his poem *halo 'esdaq*, Jarden, *Shirey hol*, no. 38, pp. 65f.; H. Schirman, *Keneset*, 10 (1946–7), pp. 244–57, especially 250f.

4 Hebrew translation B.-Z. Halper, *Shirath yisra'el*, 1924, pp. 69f; relevant extract in Jarden, *Shirey hol*, p. 29, cf. A. S. Halkin's version reproduced by Jarden in *Shirey ha-qodesh*, 2, p. 709, which is on the whole followed here.

5 Regarding Moses ibn Ezra's unreliability in the matter of dates, and the prejudices revealed in this account, see Bargebuhr, *Salomo Ibn Gabirol*, p. 90, 140f.

6 The passages are all assembled by Jarden, *Shirey ha-qodesh*, 2, p. 717.

7 *Maqama* 18, ed. P. de Lagarde (Göttingen, 1883), p. 89.

8 See *Jewish Encyclopedia.*, 6, p. 91.

9 *Nihar geroni*. Jarden, *Shirey hol*, 111, pp. 227f., see ll.23–28. A story was alive in the seventeenth century to the effect that Ibn Gabirol was denounced for possession of a female *homunculus* of wood that he had constructed to perform menial chores for him, and that when he was challenged by the authorities he demonstrated how to disassemble it. (Reported in Samuel Ashkenazi's *Meṣareph la-ḥokhmah* (1629), part i. 9, on the *Taʿalumoth ḥokhmah* of Joseph Delmedigo of Crete (1591–1655). Bargebuhr, *Salomo Ibn Gabirol*, p. 62, is of the opinion that it was either an anatomical model or else a 'microcosm'.)

10 *Mah lakh yehidah, op. cit.*, no. 122, pp. 233f., ll.28f.

11 *Lekhah reʿi*, Jarden, *op. cit.*, no. 39, pp. 68f., ll.18f. See below, pp. 58f.

12 An abbreviation of his work was included by Abraham b. David in his *Sepher ha-qabbalah*, ed. A Neubauer, *Mediaeval Jewish Chronicles*, 1 (Oxford), p. 93, reproduced by Jarden, *Shirey ha-qodesh*, 2, p. 716.

13 *Sepher yuhasin*, ed. H. Filipowski (London and Edinburgh, 1857), pp. 217, 219.

14 Gedaliah ibn Yaḥya, died 1578: *Shalsheleth ha-qabbalah*, ed. Venice, 1587,f. 39v, reproduced by Jarden (see note 12 above), 2, p. 724.

15 Discussed by Bargebuhr, pp. 89–98, especially 95f.

16 *Ke-shoresh ʿeṣ*, ed. Jarden (see note 9 above), no. 95, l.24, p. 179.

17 *Shaʿar ha-ḥesheq*, (Halberstadt, 1862),f. 17v.

18 See M. Steinschneider, *Hebraeische Übersetzungen*, 522, p. 849f., also p. 543; *Bodleian Catalogue*, col. 2295; C. Brockelmann, *Geschichte der arabischen Literatur*, Supplement I (Leiden, 1937), p. 908; I. Davidson in I. Zangwill, *Selected Poems*, p. xxx, 133, no. 46.

19 ? Apollonius of Tyana (born a few years before the BCE–CE divide). Steinschneider, *op. cit.*, 520, pp. 845f.; if the identification is correct, there is an obvious anachronism.

20 See below, pp. 25, 29f.

21 The passages are assembled by Jarden, *Shirey ha-qodesh*, 2, pp. 712f.

22 Jarden, *Shirey hol*, pp. 375–83.

23 Jarden, *Shirey ha-qodesh*, 2, pp. 392–441.

24 Dr H. Ben-Shammai informs me that fragments of the Arabic original, some of them evincing a longer text, have been identified amongst manuscripts from the Cairo *Genizah* in the Cambridge University Library, T.-S. Ar. 43.36 (?20 folios), 73 (10ff.), 124 (2ff.), 128 (1f.), 197 (2ff.). He tells me that there are almost

certainly more fragments awaiting identification.

25 A. Cohen's translation, no. 100, p. 42.
26 *Op. cit.*, no. 196, p. 56.
27 *Op. cit.*, no. 553, p. 111.

3: *Ethics*

1 See R. T. Wallis, *Neoplatonism* (London, 1972); T. Whittaker, *The Neoplatonists*, 2nd ed. (Cambridge, 1918); Colette Sirat, *A History of Jewish Philosophy in the Middle Ages*, ch. 3.
2 See A. Altmann and S. M. Stern, *Isaac Israeli, a Neo-platonic Philosopher of the Early Tenth Century* (Oxford, 1958); C. Sirat, pp. 57f.
3 Edited, with an English translation, by Steven S. Wise, *The Improvement of the Moral Qualities*, etc, 1901: for the title, see p. 50. Arabic sectionf. 73a.
4 Wise, pp. 10, 12f., 13f., n. 4.
5 S. Rosenblatt, *The Book of Beliefs and Opinions* (New Haven, 1948), pp. 357f. Wise, pp. 3f., 15, 27.
6 Wise, p. 17, n. 3.
7 So P. K. Kokovtzov, 'The Date of the Life of Bahya ibn Paqoda', *Livre d'hommage ... à ... Samuel Poznanski* (Warsaw, 1927), pp. 13–21.
8 Wise, pp. 17, 27f., 29, 45.
9 *Ibid.*, p. 48.
10 *Ibid.*, pp. 32, 42.
11 *Ibid.*, p. 13.
12 *Ibid.*, pp. 17f., 35f.
13 *Ibid.*, p. 29. Arabic text printed by Wise from MS Oxford, Bodleian, Huntington 382 (Neubauer, *Catalogue*, no. 1422),f. 59b. In the following notes the *locus* will be given in brackets ( ), following the page reference to the English translation.
14 *Ibid.*, p. 32, n. 1, (61b).
15 *Ibid.*, p. 34, (62b), cf. Sa'adiah, ch. x, 1, Rosenblatt (see note 5 above), p. 358.
16 *Ibid.*, p. 35, (62b).
17 *Ibid.*, p. 35, (63a): Wise, n. 4, states that the source is 'Platonic'.
18 *Ibid.*, p. 36, (63a).
19 *Ibid.*, p. 37, (64b).
20 The text here refers to grace unto the *lowly* ('*aniyyim* or '*anawim*), but in view of what follows no word-play with '*eynayim*, *eyes*, need be assumed.
21 Wise (see note 13 above), pp. 37–8, (64b–65a).

22 *Ibid.*, p. 50, (72b).

23 *Ibid.*, pp. 42, 44f., (68b).

24 Arabic *'ala islaḥ al-aḥlaq*, cf. the title of the tract.

25 (See note 13 above), pp. 46f., (70bf).

26 *Ibid.*, pp. 48f., (72a).

27 *Ibid.*, p. 49, (72a).

28 *Ibid.*, p. 102, (104a).

29 *Ibid.*, pp. 18f., 27.

30 *Ibid.*, pp. 63f., (80a–81a).

31 The name being common, further identification is hazardous. One may however note that Abu Sahl al-Faḍl ibn Naubaḥt, the librarian of Harun al-rashid (ninth century) was author of an astrological work. Steinschneider, *Hebraeischen Übersetzungen*, p. 856; Brockelmann, *Geschichte der arabischen Litteratur*, Supplement I, 1937, p. 391.

32 (See note 13 above) , pp. 91f., (97a–98a).

4: *Metaphysics*

1 See note 15 below. For popular acclamation, cf. the echo in the *Jewish Encyclopedia*, 6, p. 527 (1904): 'Munk concluded that Avicebron or Avencebrol, who had for centuries been believed to be a Christian scholastic philosopher, was identical with the Jew Ibn Gabirol.'

2 As much of the Arabic as is known to survive was published by S. Pines, '*Sepher 'arugath ha-bosem, ha-qeṭa'im mi-tokh sepher meqor ḥayyim*', *Tarbiz*, 27, 1948, pp. 218–33. Abraham b. Azariah, the author of the work in which the fragments are embedded, lived in Bohemia in the thirteenth century. Steinschneider, *Hebraeischen Übersetzungen*, p. 380, lists four manuscripts of the Arabic known to him.

3 Steinschneider, *ibid.*

4 *ibid.*, pp. 370f.

5 Edited by S. Weil (Berlin, 1919); the relevant passages are assembled by Jarden, *Shirey ha-qodesh*, 2, pp. 715f., summarized in English by C. Sirat, *A History of Jewish Philosophy in the Middle Ages*, p. 81.

6 C. Sirat, *ibid.*

7 Edited by M. Bis(sel)liches (Pressburg, 1837).

8 Passages assembled by Jarden, pp. 719f.: see the citation from p. 122.

9 *Encyclopaedia Judaica*, 2, 551; C. Sirat, pp. 81, 343.

10 Aquinas refers to Avicebron in his *Summa Theologiae* I, q.50, a.2,

ed. P. Caramello (Turin, 1948), i, pp. 253–4 (English translation,
T. Gilbey, London & New York, no date, ix, pp. 11–13); q.66, a.2,
p. 323 (Gilbey, x, p. 35), q.115, a.1, p. 539 (Gilbey, xv, pp. 91, 93); *De
Anima*, q.vi, 17, ed. J. H. Robb (Toronto, 1968), p. 109.

11 Steinschneider, p. 484.

12 Reproduced by Jarden, p. 722.

13 f. 167b. Jarden, p. 723.

14 *Siphethey yeshenim*, f. 47v, *mem*, no. 301; similarly the Christian
bibliographers of rabbinic literature. Bartolocci (Rome, 1693), iv,
p. 371, no. 1705, J. C. Wolf (Hamburg and Leipzig, 1715), i.
p. 1044, no. 5.

15 *Mélanges de philosophie juive et arabe*, pp. 3–148: reprinted by J.
Blaustein as an appendix to his own Hebrew version of the Latin,
1950/51. The first notice of the identification was announced by
Munk in *Der Orient* (Literaturblatt) (Leipzig, 1846), no. 46 (12
November), pp. 721f. Wolf (see note 14 above) had stated that the
work existed in Hebrew in manuscript form: had he himself seen
it, or is it his inference from the circumstance that it had never been
printed? Similarly G. B. de' Rossi, *Dizionario ... degli autori ebrei*
(Parma, 1802), i, p. 124.

16 This summary depends on that given by J. Schlanger, *La
philosophie de Salomon ibn Gabirol*, pp. 20–30.

17 Letter to Samuel ibn Tibbon, printed in popular nineteenth-
century editions of Maimonides' *Letters* in Hebrew translation, see
e.g. ed. H. Zilberschatz (Warsaw, no date), f. 11a. English
translation, Leon D. Stitskin, *Letters of Maimonides Translated* (New
York, 1982 ed.), p. 135. The edition by M. Bar-Joseph (Tel Aviv,
1970), *'Iggeroth ha-rambam*, pp. 126f., omits the disparaging
reference to Isaac Israeli's practice of medicine.

18 I. Husik, *History of Mediaeval Jewish Philosophy* (Philadelphia,
1916), p. 79.

5: *Social Poetry*

1 See most recently Y. T. Assis, 'Sexual Behaviour in Mediaeval
Hispano-Jewish Society', in *Jewish History: Essays in Honour of
Chimen Abramsky*, eds. A. Rapoport-Albert and S. J. Zipperstein
(London, 1988), pp. 50f.

2 Jarden, *Shirey ḥol*, i, pp. *he-zayin* (Hebrew pagination, pp. 5–7).

3 *Op. cit.*, i, pp. 19f., no. 8.

4 Horace, *Odes*, i, 2.

5 Jarden, for reasons that are not apparent, prints *le*[ ]*kh*; metrical
space and sense alike dictate the reading *lebaddakh*, thee alone.

6 The reference is to 'Abba 'Arekha, known as Rab, 'the Master', of Sura, and Mar Samuel of Nehardea in third-century Babylonia, the leading rabbinic authorities of their time.

7 The reference is to the Mishnah, *Sukkah* v, 1f., which details the ceremony of water-libation on the feast of Tabernacles and asserts that 'one who never witnessed its joy could not, throughout his life, have had experience of real joy'.

8 Jarden (see note 2 above), pp. 68f., no. 89. The translation is by Nicholas de Lange. See the German translation, and commentary, by Bargebuhr, *Salomo Ibn Gabirol*, pp. 485f., also his book *The Alhambra*, particularly pp. 114f.

9 The fountain's original basin was removed, but is identified by Bargebuhr (*The Alhambra*, p. 123) with that now set in the floor of the Abencerages hall (see plate 7, p. 419, and reconstruction, plate 9, p. 421).

10 De Lange finds this obscure, and offers the following alternative rendering (assuming *saroth* for *sharoth*):

> We are princesses, we have necklets fair,
>
> Which capture every heart, they are so rare.

11 R. A. Nicholson, *A Literary History of the Arabs*, 1907, pp. 125, 206, 417, cites examples from al-A'sha (late sixth century) to ibn Quzman (Spain, died 1160). More fully, A. Spitaler's note in Bargebuhr, *Salomo Ibn Gabirol*, pp. 280f.

12 Jarden (see note 2 above), p. 354, no. 196. Bargebuhr (n. 11), pp. 277f.

13 I have translated Edward Fitzgerald's *Rubba'yat* into Hebrew quatrains in the style of Ibn Gabirol (*Gilguley merubba'im*, Jerusalem 1982: see pp. 38, 67). Fitzgerald substituted the *winding-sheet* of vine-leaves for a *bier* of vine-wood in the Persian original.

14 Horace, *Odes*, iv, 12, 28.

15 Jarden (see note 2 above), pp. 217f., no. 104; Bargebuhr, *Salomo Ibn Gabirol*, pp. 174f.

16 Hebrew *qoheleth*, the heading which gives the title to Ecclesiastes, the author of which tradition understands to be Solomon.

17 On, son of Peleth, was Korah's fellow-rebel against Moses: Numbers 16.1.

18 Genesis 19.11.

19 See pp. 20f. For the sources, and problems which they involve, see E. Ashtor, *The Jews of Moslem Spain*, 2, pp. 257, 348f., n. 199.

20 Judges 5.6.

21 Jarden (see note 2 above), pp. 290f., no. 156.

22 Cf. the lament over the death of Rabina. Talmud, *Mo'ed Qaton* 25b.

23 Cf. Amos 9.1, I Kings 7.41. In the latter passage *gulloth, bowls*, refers to the capitals of pillars. But it is possible that Ibn Gabirol visualized the 'bowls' as cusps: the cusped arch was introduced to Spain from the east by the Arabs, its supreme manifestation being in the mosque (now the cathedral) of Cordoba.

24 The brilliance of the play on words should be savoured; *naḥal* means a wadi (not a permanently flowing river, the Hebrew for which is *nahar*), and the poetic form (as in Psalm 124.4) *náḥalah* is here substituted as being homonymous with *naḥaláḥ = inheritance*.

25 The allusion is to the 'Ten killed by the [Roman] empire' ('*asarah harugey malkhuth*), i.e. Rabbi Aqiba, etc., associated in legend with a single incident although they were in fact not all contemporaries.

26 i.e. 1040; see p. 65.

27 II Kings 14.7 records that King Amaziah, having captured a rock in his war against Edom, gave it the name of [mount] Yoqte'el. According to II Chronicles 25.12, he hurled ten thousand captives from it to their death. It is suggested that Ibn Gabirol may well have visualized it as something like Gibraltar, in view both of its sheer rock-face and its having been named after Ṭariq, the successful Arab invader of Spain (*jebel al-ṭariq*).

28 The Hebrew doubles the verb *ḥ-l-ph*, first in the sense of *go by*, and then meaning *pass into desuetude*.

29 Daniel 11.34.

30 This word, now commonly used (with unwitting blasphemy) with reference to Hitler's near-extermination of European Jewry, is here used in its correct sense.

31 Jarden (see note 2 above), p. 331, no. 173; Bargebuhr (see note 11 above), pp. 176f., 224f.

32 Cf. Job 11.12; as there, the poem expresses the simile by use of the '*waw* of equation' (*waw adæquationis*), see *Gesenius' Hebrew Grammar*, ed. E. Kautzsch and A. E. Cowley, p. 499, § 161a.

33 Cf. Micah 7.6; Mishnah, *Soṭah* ix, 15 (towards end).

6: *Liturgical Poetry*

1 Jarden, *Shirey ha-qodesh*, 2 vols., 1971–73.

2 These '*azharoth* are printed in Sephardic prayer-books for *Shabu'oth* (the Feast of Weeks), for recitation prior to the afternoon service on the two days of the festival.

3 Jarden (see note 1 above), 2, pp. 337f., nos. 106, 107.

4 *ibid.*, pp. 338f., no. 108. The full text and translation will be found in R. Loewe, *The Rylands Haggadah* (London, 1988), ff. 39bf., pp. 41f. and 43.

5 Genesis 27.28.

6 I Kings 18.7 and 13. Tradition identifies Obadiah, the contemporary of Ahab and Elijah, with the (much later) minor prophet of the same name.

7 Deuteronomy 32.2.

8 Jarden (see note 1 above), 2, p. 468, no. 144.

9 Song of Songs, 2.9.

10 *ibid.*, 5.6; 8.14.

11 *ibid.*, 1.13.

12 *ibid.*, 5.9.

13 *ibid.*5.10f., 16.

14 Jarden (see note 1 above), 2, p. 334, no. 103.

15 Isaiah 11.1.

16 Song of Songs 2.11.

17 Genesis 27.29.

18 Psalms 102.7 (6).

19 Daniel 12.6–7.

20 *ibid.*, 12.4.

21 Jarden (see note 1 above), 2, p. 323, no. 95.

22 The literal meaning of *reshuth* is *permission*. The leader of the group at worship, who was not normally a salaried official and might himself be capable of composing liturgical poetry, is deemed in poems so styled to be asking the congregation to give him permission to proceed to recite the statutory prayer that follows, and to concentrate upon it closely.

23 Jarden (see note 1 above), 1, p. 20, no. 12.

24 *Berakhoth* 10a.

25 *yeḥidah* (= *unique*) is a synonym of *nephesh*, soul, Psalms 22.21 (20).

26 i.e. the rational soul, which is the prerogative of man (and the angels); see pp. 31f.

27 Cf. Ecclesiastes 12.5.

28 Cf. Psalms 103.1; 150.6.

29 Jarden (see note 1 above), 1, pp. 213–15, no. 62.

30 Ecclesiastes 3.19.

31 Job 13.12.

32 Leviticus 26.28.

33 Mishnah, *'Aboth* 3.1.

34 Jonah 4.10.

35 Proverbs 28.21.

36 Psalms 49.11 (10).

37 Isaiah 55.7.

38 Zephaniah 2.1; Isaiah 53.6.

39 Lamentations 3.41.

40 Hosea 12.2 (1), Isaiah 53.6.
41 II Chronicles 20.12.
42 See pp. 31f.
43 See Eliezer Ben-Yehudah, *Millon ha-lashon ha-'ibrith*, 12 (Jerusalem, 1946), p. 6032, n. 2.
44 Aristotle, *Nichomachean Ethics* 1098b 33 (A VIII 6 9).
45 Jarden (see note 1 above), 1, pp. 289–91, no. 87.
46 Ecclesiastes 5.14 (15).
47 Cf. Proverbs 27.8.
48 Proverbs 17.1, cf. Mishnah, *'Aboth* (6), 4.
49 *shikheḥi*, *forget*, seems to me the more probable reading; Jarden prints *shikhebi*, *lie down*, referring to Isaiah 50.11, where *ma'aṣebah* = [*place of*] *pain*.
50 Deuteronomy 33.27.
51 Proverbs 12.2, cf. Mishnah, *'Aboth* 2, 4.
52 Ḥagigah 12b.
53 I Kings 8.27.
54 Jarden (see note 1 above), 2, pp. 325–7, no. 98.
55 Psalms 102, 27 (26).
56 *ibid.*, 104.1.
57 *ibid.*, 96.4.
58 Nehemiah 9.5.
59 Psalms 139.14.
60 Genesis 26.26.
61 Ezekiel 1.5.
62 Genesis 41.19.
63 *Dictionary of National Biography*, 24, p. 289 (J. A. Fuller Maitland and J. Barclay Squire).
64 In an article (in Hebrew) in the volume (*Golah 'aḥar galuth*), edited by A. Mirsky, in honour of Professor Ḥayyim Beinart of the Hebrew University, Jerusalem, 1988, pp. 114–33.
65 The description has been translated from Aḥmed ibn Muḥammad al-Maqqari (died 1632), ed. M. 'Abd-al-ḥamid, Cairo, 1949, 1, pp. 363–4, ed. R. Dozy etc., i, 1, pp. 250–1. Although this is a very late source, it is obviously dependent upon an eye-witness account.
66 Jarden (see note 1 above), 1, pp. 89–92, no. 28.
67 Psalms 68.18 (17).
68 Cf. Genesis 3.24.
69 Ezekiel 1.7.
70 Isaiah 6.3.
71 Psalms 29.1.

72 Ezekiel 1.5f.

73 Isaiah 33.7, Ezekiel 1.4.

74 Daniel 12.1.

75 Psalms 68.18 (17).

76 Ezekiel 3.12 is exegetically construed as indicating the angels' ignorance of the exact location of the Deity. Cf. Talmud, *Hagigah* 13b, and the *qedushah* ('holy, holy, holy') in the additional service for sabbaths and festivals according to the Sephardic rite: 'his ministers ask, "where is the place of his glory . . . ?"'

77 On the loan-word *pargod* see my article (see note 64 above), pp. 116f.

78 Numbers 10.14.

79 Talmud, *Pesahim* 118a (foot); II Kings 2.11.

80 In *Pirqey de-rabbi 'eli'ezer* 4, presumably Ibn Gabirol's source, the commander of the third angelic division is called Uriel instead of Nuriel.

81 Job 26.11.

82 See note 76.

83 Exodus 3.14.

84 Cf. the *Royal Crown*, p. 131, and above, p. 95.

85 In the Talmud (*Hagigah* 13b) this is the function of the angel named Sandalphon, but in the apocryphal book of Tobit 12.15, a similar function is assigned to Raphael.

86 Cf. Isaiah 40.31.

87 *ibid.*, 46.3; in Jarden's text this line and the next appear in inverted order.

88 Ezekiel 1.7.

89 *Bazaq* in Ezekiel 1.14, occurs there only in the Bible and is generally considered by modern scholars to be an error for *baraq*, *lightning*. But the Talmud (*Hagigah* 13b) explains it in accordance with the rendering here offered (see Rashi *in loc.*).

90 Isaiah 6.3.

91 I. Davidson, *Thesaurus of Mediaeval Hebrew Poetry* 3 (Philadelphia, 1924), p. 65, no. 1428.

92 Jarden, *Shirey hol*, 1, pp. 227f., no. 111.

93 The only imperfect rhyme is *she-samta* (l. 1). No convincing emendation suggests itself to me.

94 *Odes* i, 1, ll. 29f.

95 Proverbs 3.14.

96 Psalms 40.3 (2), 119.168. See also 18.37 (36), 110.3.

97 Cf. *ibid.*, 69.4 (3).

98 Cf. Isaiah 1.18, Ezekiel 27.18.

99 Cf. Psalms 38.11 (10).

100 *ibid.*, 119.114.
101 *ibid.*, 18.3 (2); 144.2.
102 *ibid.*, 40.18 (17).

7: *The Royal Crown*

1 J. Schlanger, *La philosophie de Salomon ibn Gabirol*, pp. 37–42.
2 *ibid.*, p. 41, 'on s'aperçoit facilement que pour Ibn Gabirol bien que dans les deux cas il s'agisse du même Dieu, ils ne concernent pas la même totalité divine'.
3 Esther 2.17.
4 *Ḥagigah* 12b; see the poem on pp. 95f
5 R. Loewe, 'Ibn Gabirol's Treatment of Sources in the *Kether Malkuth*', *Studies in Jewish Religious and Intellectual History Presented to Alexander Altmann*, eds. S. Stein and R. Loewe (1979), pp. 183–94.
6 Joseph L. Blau, 'On the supposedly Aristotelian Character of Gabirol's *Keter Malkut*', *Salo Wittmayer Baron Jubilee Volume*, ed. S. Lieberman (Jerusalem, 1974), i, pp. 219–28.
7 391b, Loeb translation (D. J. Furley), (London-Harvard, 1955), p. 347, cf. 400b, p. 403.
8 The translator was 'Isa ibn Ibrahim al-nafisi, a physician at the court of Sayf ad-Daulah (944–67): see F. E. Peters, *Aristoteles Arabus*, The Oriental Translations and Commentaries on the Aristotelian Corpus (Leiden, 1968), pp. 61f. Brockelmann, *Geschichte der Arabischem Literatur*, 1, p. 226 (206) lists a translation of Aristotle, *de cælo et mundo*, 'after Al-biṭriq' (ibn Ya (Yuḥanna) Al-biṭriq), i.e. around 815; *Supplement* 1, p. 364 .
9 W. L. Lorimer, *American Journal of Philology* (1932), 53, p. 159, note 6.
10 Loewe (see note 5 above), pp. 185f.
11 For Ptolemy's figures see Bernard R. Goldstein, 'The Arabic Version of Ptolemy's Planetary Hypotheses', *Transactions of the American Philosophical Society*, New Series, 57, iv, 1967.
12 See Goldstein's remarks communicated to R. Loewe (see note 5 above), p. 188.
13 *Centos* XXXIV, XXXV(a)–(c), and part of XXXVI, *Jewish Quarterly Review*, Old Series, 7, 1895, pp. 461–4.
14 *Centos* I–IV, VI–IX, XXIX, XXXI–XXXIV, XXXVIII(a)–(b), XXXIX–XL, *ibid.*, 8, 1896, pp. 71–3, 239–44.
15 'Abraham ibn Ezra, Peter Abelard, and John Donne', *Tel Aviv Review*, 1, 1988, pp. 190–211, see p. 193.
16 Mishnah, *Sanhedrin* vi. 1.

17 Esther 2.17.

18 I Chronicles 29.11.

19 Talmud, 'Erubin 22a (Rabbi Joshua b. Levi), cf. Mishnah, 'Aboth ii, 16.

20 Exodus 2.2.

21 Psalms 39.2.

22 Ecclesiastes 4.10.

23 ibid., 7.24.

24 Psalms 144.4.

25 Genesis 3.22.

26 Alluding to the literature of early Jewish mysticism (heykhaloth, 'palaces'), devotees of which were called yoredey merkabah ('charioteers'), because of the prominence in their nexus of ideas of the chariot-throne vision in Ezekiel 1.

27 Nehemiah 9.5.

28 Deuteronomy 3.24.

29 Talmud, Yoma 69b.

30 Genesis 6.4.

31 ibid., 22. 14.

32 Numbers 23.13.

33 Deuteronomy 10.17.

34 Pesiqta Rabbathi 8, on Zephaniah 1, 12, ed. M. Friedmannf. 30a, W. G. Braude's English translation, p. 153.

35 Esther 5.1.

36 Ecclesiastes 3.20.

37 Psalms 36.10 (9). For Ibn Gabirol's use of this as a title for his philosophical treatise, see p. 40.

38 See p. 30.

39 Proverbs 8.30; there is here a play on words between 'amon = craftsman and 'amun = nurtured [child].

40 For ḥepheṣ (= object [of delight]) in the sense of prime matter, I. Davidson in a note to Zangwill's Selected Poems of Solomon Ibn Gabirol (p. 177, l. 96) cites evidence from Isaac Arama and Jacob ibn Yiṣḥaqi.

41 Pseudo-Empedocles (preserved in an Arabic translation) held that particles continually flying off the surface of bodies encounter others, proceeding from the eye. Spanish translation by M. Asin Palacios, Abenmasarra y su escuela, (1914). English translation (The Mystical Philosophy of Ibn Masarra and his Followers) by E. H. Douglas and H. W. Yoder (Leiden, 1978), cf. pp. 53f.

42 Isaiah 40.12.

43 Exodus 26.4: the system of lacing together the fabric of the mobile Tent of Meeting used by Israel for cultic purposes in the wilderness

NOTES

is metaphorically applied to the series of emanations which, in the
Meqor ḥayyim, link universal spiritual matter to the individual
natural matter experienced in the phenomenal world. See p. 48.

44 Various notions were current as to the supposed arrangement of
the elements earth and water. The one here presented corresponds
with that detailed in the *Epistles of the Brethren of Purity* (see p. 113),
4, part i, ed. Beirut, i, p. 163, 'half of the earth ... is exposed, like an
egg [partly] submerged'.

45 Ecclesiastes 1.6.

46 Cf. *Meqor ḥayyim* i, 16, Schlanger's translation, p. 52. See p. 45.

47 Genesis 2.10.

48 For the astronomical quantities cited here and in the following
centos, see the tables on pp. 115–116.

49 'Deep or slight' (*peshuṭim, 'amuqqim*, literally *simple* and *deep*) hints
at the variation of lunations mentioned in the Talmud, *Rosh
ha-shanah* 25a.

50 Ibn Gabirol repeatedly stresses the subordination of astrological
influences to the divine will (*raṣon*); cf. *cento* XXI (the Zodiac),
pp. 134f. The will is likewise a key concept in the thought of the
Brethren of Purity, who in the present connection stress the part
played by the universal soul.

51 Psalms 145.12.

52 *Yareaḥ*, the common biblical word for the moon (as used here), is
masculine; the rarer *lebanah*, which became normal in post-biblical
Hebrew and occurs below (*cento* XVII), is feminine. *Shemesh*, the
word for the sun used here, is in the Bible of common gender, and
the rarer *ḥammah*, which effectively displaced *shemesh* in post-
biblical Hebrew and which occurs in *cento* XV, is feminine. The
poet's characterization of the two luminaries as male or female
seems to vacillate until the climax (*cento* XVII), where marital
imagery used with the utmost delicacy clearly assigns the male role
to the sun. In translating, I have consequently treated the sun as
male and the moon as female throughout.

53 Genesis 1.14.

54 That the moon's light is reflected from the sun was already known
in antiquity; Aristotle (*Physics* i, 628) describes it as 'bastard'.

55 The Dragon (*teli*: not *quiver*, but a homonym derived from
Assyrian *attala*, *eclipse*, cf. Syriac *'athliya*, the mythological serpent
that swallows the heavenly bodies, causing their eclipse) is an
astronomical term applied to the line between the two points
where the orbit of a heavenly body intersects the sun's apparent
orbit in the celestial sphere.

56 I Kings 8.60.

57 II Samuel 1.10.
58 Ecclesiastes 5.7 (8).
59 Midrash *Genesis Rabbah*, vi, 1. ed. Wilnaf. 18b.
60 Isaiah 41.20.
61 I Kings 15.13.
62 Psalms 144.14.
63 Talmud *Sabbath* 156a.
64 Proverbs 1.4.
65 Isaiah 61.10.
66 See note 63.
67 Deuteronomy 33.14.
68 Psalms 75.8 (7).
69 Proverbs 8.2.
70 Esther 2.14.
71 Job 38.31.
72 Psalms 92.15 (14).
73 Job 26.14.
74 Genesis 24.10.
75 Leviticus 13.23.
76 Exodus 25.37.
77 See note 52.
78 Psalms 19.6 (5).
79 Nahum 2.4 (3).
80 See note 63.
81 Psalms 32.4.
82 Isaiah 59.7.
83 *ibid.*, 1.21.
84 See note 63.
85 Psalms 46.10 (9).
86 *ibid.*, 9.9.
87 Isaiah 28.21.
88 Exodus 28.8.
89 Isaiah 40.26.
90 Numbers 4.49.
91 Ezekiel 1.10.
92 Numbers 27.20.
93 Leviticus 21.23.
94 Cf. Jeremiah 51.30.
95 Genesis 21.20.
96 Deuteronomy 9.29.
97 Jonah 2.1 (1.17).
98 Genesis 25.16.
99 The diurnal sphere is called in Arabic *al-muḥiṭ* (encompassing). The

Brethren of Purity equated this ninth sphere with the divine throne of the Qur'an.

100 Talmud *Sanhedrin* 91b.

101 Isaiah 40.17.

102 The tenth sphere is Ibn Gabirol's own postulation, in addition to the conventional nine: see p. 115.

103 Leviticus 27.32.

104 Habakkuk 3.4.

105 Song of Songs 3. 9–10.

106 Genesis 4.7, cf. Song of Songs 7.11; for Ibn Gabirol's use here of *teshuqah* in the sense of Arabic *shawq* = yearning, see R. Loewe, note 5 above, pp. 184–5.

107 Genesis 3.24.

108 Ezekiel 1.12.

109 With this description of the angels, their origin, divisions etc., cf. the poem '*Shin'anim sha'ananim*', pp. 99f.; *Pirqey de-rabbi Eliezer*, ch. 4.

110 Psalms 45.2 (1).

111 Palestinian Talmud, *Rosh ha-shanah* ii, 4 (Rabbi Simeon b. Yoḥai).

112 Psalms 68.5 (4).

113 Lamentations 2.19.

114 Psalms 65.7 (6).

115 The angels' prayer here echoes that of Israel in the 'thanksgiving' (*hoda'ah, modim*) section of the '*amidah* (eighteen benedictions) recited thrice daily.

116 Psalms 100.3.

117 Cf. Isaiah 43.10.

118 Cf. Job 23.2.

119 The throne of Glory corresponds to prime universal matter in the *Meqor ḥayyim*, here indicated by *yesod* = foundation.

120 Exodus 34.3.

121 Deuteronomy 3. 14.

122 Talmud, *Sabbath* 152b (Rabbi Eliezer).

123 I Samuel 25.29.

124 Isaiah 40.31.

125 Genesis 9.19.

126 Exodus 38.8, cf. Talmud, *Yebamoth* 49b.

127 Exodus 34.23–24.

128 II Samuel 9.13.

129 Genesis 49.20.

130 Cf. Deuteronomy 12.9.

131 Numbers 13.27.

132 See Talmud, *Ḥagigah* 12b, where the stored forces of nature are

located in the sixth of the seven heavens (*Makhon*).

133 Isaiah 59.20.

134 Ezekiel 38.22.

135 Proverbs 22.14.

136 Zechariah 14.6.

137 Job 24.19.

138 Habakkuk 1.12.

139 Cf. Isaiah 51.1.

140 The apparent inconsistency between this passage and *cento* XXIX regarding the source whence the soul is created may be resolved: see R. Loewe (see note 5 above), pp. 189f.

141 Cf. Genesis 2.15.

142 Exodus 19.18.

143 Ibn Gabirol uses the adjective *ḥakhamah* = wise in poetry as the equivalent of *maskeleth* = applying the intelligence, to describe the *rational* soul (cf. pp. 31f., and the poem, pp. 87f.). The term goes back, through the Arabic *nāṭiqa*, to the Greek *noētikē* (Aristotle, *de Anima* 429a, 28).

144 Ecclesiastes 7.26.

145 Proverbs 31.25.

146 Isaiah 54.8.

147 *ibid.*, 49.21; cf. Leviticus 13.46.

148 *ibid.*, 12.4.

149 Psalms 16.11.

150 Cf. Genesis 2.7, as paraphrased in the first of the morning prayers (*'elohai neshamah ...*).

151 Cf. Numbers 11.17.

152 Exodus 25.11.

153 Psalms 116.16.

154 II Samuel 7.27.

155 Cf. Job 11.6.

156 I Samuel 29.4: the verse, which is here truncated at *rashe'* = *heads of*, in its biblical context continues *ha-'anashim ha-hem* = *'these men'*, but the poet intends that 'heads [of chapters]' be understood.

157 Cf. *centos* II, IV, V, IX, VIII.

158 Genesis 2.7.

159 Psalms 144.4.

160 *ibid.*, 78.39.

161 *ibid.*, 140.4 (3).

162 Jeremiah 17.9.

163 Ezekiel 44.9.

164 Psalms 36.4 (3).

165 Isaiah 6.5.

166 Proverbs 28.18.
167 *ibid.*, 19.2
168 Deuteronomy 31.27.
169 Cf. Mishnah, *'Aboth* iii, 1.
170 Cf. Esther 4.16.
171 Ezekiel 22.24.
172. Numbers 11.4.
173 Cf. Psalms 65.8 (7).
174 I Kings 8.34.
175 The statutory alphabetic form of confession, repeatedly recited during the services of the Day of Atonement, is here elaborated, 'we' being replaced by 'I'.
176 Cf. Nehemiah 9.33.
177 Sa'adiah considers that the divine act by which man was created is itself an act of beneficence (iii, beginning, S. Rosenblatt's translation (p. 172, n. 5), p. 137 cf. i, end, p. 86).
178 Cf. Genesis 2.7.
179 Cf. Numbers 11.12.
180 Cf. Psalms 22.10 (9).
181 Cf. Hosea 11.3.
182 Cf. Proverbs 1.2.
183 Cf. Isaiah 26.20; 51.16.
184 Cf. Talmud, *Megillah* 13b (Resh Laqish).
185 *Niddah* 31a (Rabbi Eleazar, on the beneficiaries of unperceived miracles).
186 Cf. Psalms 58.7 (6).
187 Deuteronomy 28.59. There are echoes in this passage of the latter part of the prayer (*we-'ilu phinu* ...) recited on sabbaths and festivals expressing the sense of obligation to render thanks for God's continuing beneficence.
188 *ibid.*, 8.5.
189 Psalms 74.18.
190 Leviticus 13.23.
191 *ibid.*, 11.33.
192 Genesis 32.11 (10).
193 Cf. Zechariah 3.1.
194 Job 9.18.
195 Cf. *ibid.*, 41.5 (13).
196 Cf. Jonah 1.13.
197 Cf. Psalms 33.10.
198 Cf. *ibid.*, 89.35 (34).
199 Cf.*ibid.*, 120.7.
200 Cf. *ibid*, 110.1.

201 I Kings 2.5.
202 Cf. Genesis 32.9 (8). The 'crossing of the Jabbok' (v. 23 (22)) has become a conventional Jewish metaphor for the hour of death.
203 II Samuel 18.3.
204 Numbers 22.6.
205 Psalms 102.25 (24).
206 Cf. Job 1.21.
207 II Samuel 14.32.
208 Jeremiah 10.24.
209 Proverbs 21.6.
210 Job 28.25.
211 Isaiah 53.4.
212 *ibid.*, 41.2.
213 Ecclesiastes 3.15.
214 Cf. Exodus 16.20.
215 Cf. Psalms 1.4.
216 Proverbs 28.21.
217 Cf. Numbers 30.3 (2).
218 Cf. Psalms 147.13.
219 Cf. Jeremiah 9.20 (21).
220 Cf. Judges 16.9.
221 Jarden reads here *yig'eh* = *waxes proud*: Zangwill's text (see p. 81, note 40), p. 116, reads *ba'* = *comes*, which is Davidson's conjecture from the reading *nibba'* = *prophecies* in a manuscript of a *mahzor* dated 1415 in the Jewish Theological Seminary of New York. That conjecture has been followed in the translation.
222 Cf. Judges 13.25.
223 Cf. Song of Songs 4.8.
224 Ezekiel 1.13.
225 Cf. Job 31.25.
226 *ibid.*, 15.21.
227 *ibid.*, 27.19.
228 *ibid.*, 20.25.
229 Cf. Isaiah 47.11.
230 Job 20.24.
231 Cf. Psalms 124.4–5.
232 Deuteronomy 28.59.
233 Cf. Job 7.20.
234 *ibid.*, 20.14.
235 Cf. Isaiah 17.4.
236 Cf. II Kings 2.23.
237 Cf. Isaiah 3.4.
238 Cf. Ezekiel 26.16.

239 Cf. Job 7.21; Genesis 3.19; Isaiah 51.1.

240 Genesis 38.25.

241 Mishnah, *'Aboth* ii, 15.

242 Exodus 5.13.

243 Cf. II Chronicles 21.20.

244 Cf. Genesis 4.13.

245 Joshua 7.9.

246 Cf. Job 13.15.

247 *ibid.*, 10.6.

248 Genesis 32.27 (26).

249 Job 10.9.

250 Cf. Jeremiah 21.14.

251 Cf. Exodus 12.33–34.

252 Lamentations 3.19; (I Kings 20.29: see beginning of next *cento*).

253 Cf. Psalms 119.75.

254 Cf. Deuteronomy 8.16.

255 Cf. II Samuel 24.16.

256 Job 10.6.

257 *ibid.*, 7.12.

258 Isaiah 51.20.

259 Cf. Leviticus 26.39.

260 Cf. Proverbs 23.5.

261 Cf. Deuteronomy 5.22 (25).

262 Cf. Jeremiah 24.6.

263 Cf. Exodus 10.5, Deuteronomy 28.38.

264 Job 35.3.

265 Psalms 128.2.

266 Cf. the prayer for repentance in the daily *'amidah* (eighteen benedictions).

267 Cf. Psalms 10.17: the sense requires *libbi, my* heart (modified from the biblical text's *libbam*, their heart). *Libbi* is printed by Zangwill Davidson with no variants cited (pp. 120, 244), rather than *libbekha, thy* heart, as read by Jarden.

268 From the prayer (Talmud, *Berakhoth* 60b) incorporated into the daily morning prayers.

269 Cf. Psalms 57.2 (1).

270 Cf. *ibid.*, 39.2 (1).

271 *ibid.*, 106.4–5.

272 Cf. *ibid.*, 102.15 (14).

273 Nehemiah 5.13.

274 Hosea 10.1.

275 Genesis 45.10.

276 Cf. Psalms 4.7 (6).

277   *ibid.*, 39.9 (8).
278   Cf. *ibid.*, 102.25 (24).
279   *ibid.*, 27.9.
280   *ibid.*, 51.4 (2), 13 (11).
281   *ibid.*, 73.24.
282   Cf. Hosea 11.7.
283   Psalms 17.14. There are clearly present here echoes of the quotation of this verse in Talmud, *Berakhoth* 61b, where the angels' remonstrance with God at the martyrdom of Rabbi Aqiba is described. See R. Loewe, 'The Bible in Medieval Hebrew Poetry', *Interpreting the Hebrew Bible: Essays in honour of E. I. J. Rosenthal*, ed. J. Emerton and S. C. Reif (Cambridge, 1982), pp. 139f.
284   Cf. Job 33.30.
285   Psalms 71.20.
286   Isaiah 12.1.
287   Psalms 62.13 (12).
288   Cf. I Samuel 24.17.
289   There are echoes here of the prayer which on sabbath and festival mornings concludes the psalmody (*be-phi yesharim tithromam ...*).
290   Psalms 86.8.
291   *ibid.*, 19.15 (14).

Epilogue

1   *Seis conferencias en torno a Ibn Gabirol* (Malaga, 1973), pp. 56–7.

BIBLIOGRAPHY

The literature concerning Solomon ibn Gabirol is very extensive. A full
list is set out chronologically in Jarden, *Shirey ha-qodesh*, 2, pp. 722–90
(down to 1972/3) and supplemented in his *Shirey ḥol*, 1, pp. 403–6 (to
1974); and similarly by Bargebuhr, *Salomo Ibn Gabirol* (1976), pp.
749–57. Bibliographies are also included in Schlanger, *La philosophie de
Salomon Ibn Gabirol* (1968), pp. 317–21, and in the *Encyclopaedia Judaica*
(1971) s.v. Gabirol, 7, 245–6. The following list has consequently been
restricted to indispensable works noted by the aforementioned scholars
and a few items that have been published subsequently. Any serious
address to the philosophy and poetry of Ibn Gabirol ought to begin with
study of the original texts with the assistance of the works of Schlanger,
Jarden, and Bargebuhr.

Original Works

(i) Philosophy (prose)

The Improvement of Moral Qualities (Tiqqun middoth ha-nepesh)

Wise, Stephen S., *The Improvement of The Moral Qualities by Solomon
    ibn Gabirol*, from an unique Arabic Manuscript, together with a
    translation . . ., Columbia University Oriental Series 1, New York,
    1901. The Hebrew translation by Judah ibn Tibbon has been
    frequently printed.

Bar-On, Noaḥ, *Ribbi shelomoh ben gabirol, sepher tiqqun middoth
    ha-nephesh*, Tel Aviv (?), 1951 (new Hebrew version. Reprinted,
    together with ibn Tibbon's translation, in *'Oṣar ha-maḥashabah shel
    ha-yahduth*).

The Choice of Pearls (Miḥḥar ha-peninim)

Ascher, B. H., *Ethical Sentences* . . . The Hebrew text . . . English
    translation, London, 1859. The Hebrew translation is Judah ibn
    Tibbon's.

Cohen, A., *Solomon Ibn Gabirol's Choice of Pearls*, Library of Jewish
    Classics IV, New York, 1925.

Haberman, Abraham Me'ir, *Sepher mibḥar ha-peninim*, Jerusalem, 1947.

The Fountain of Life (Fons Vitæ, Meqor ḥayyim)

Baümker, Clemens, *Avencebrolis (Ibn Gabirol) Fons Vitæ ex arabico in*

189

latinum translatus ab Johanne Hispano et Dominico Gundissalino ...
Beiträge zur Geschichte der Philosophie des Mittelalters, Münster,
1892–95.

Munk, Salomon, 'Extraits hébraiques', *Mélanges de philosophie juive et arabe*, Paris, 1857–59 (reprinted 1927, 1955). (Selections translated into Hebrew by Shem ṭob Falaquera.)

Blaustein, Jacob, *Sepher meqor ḥayyim le-ribbi shelomoh ben-gabirol*, Jerusalem, 1926 (new Hebrew version, complete, including the Falaquera selections).

Pines, Shelomoh, '*Sepher ʿarugath ha-bosem, ha-qeṭaʿim mi-tokh sepher meqor ḥayyim*', *Tarbiẓ* 27, 1958, pp. 218–33. (Fragments of the Arabic original.)

Schlanger, Jacques, *Salomon Ibn Gabirol, Livre de la Source de Vie (Fons Vitæ)*, Traduction, introduction et notes, Paris 1970.

Wedeck, Harry Ezekiel, *The Fountain of Life, Fons Vitæ, by Solomon Ibn Gabirol, 'Avicebron'*. Translated from the Latin [Part III only], London, 1963.

(ii) Poetry

Jarden, Dov, *Shirey ha-qodesh le-ribbi shelomoh 'ibn gabirol ʿim perush*, 2 volumes, Jerusalem, 1971–3 (see following item).
Shirey ha-ḥol le-ribbi shelomoh 'ibn gabirol ʿim perush, 2 volumes, Jerusalem, 1975–6. (Note that the chronological bibliography quoted in this book from *Shirey ha-qodesh*, 11, pp. 709–90 is in the second edition transferred to *Shirey ha-ḥol* 11, pp. 615–707.)

Brody, Ḥayyim, Shirman, Ḥayyim, and Ben-David, Israel, *Shelomoh 'ibn gabirol, shirey ha-ḥol*, Jerusalem, 1975.

Zangwill, Israel, *Selected Religious Poems of Solomon Ibn Gabirol* translated into English verse from a ... text edited by Israel Davidson, Schiff Library of Jewish Classics, Philadelphia, 1923.

Lewis, Bernard, *Solomon Ibn Gabirol, The Kingly Crown*, newly translated with an Introduction and Notes, Tiptree, Essex, 1961.

De Lange, Nicholas, 'Solomon Ibn Gabirol: Four Poems' [translated], *The Tel Aviv Review*, 1, 1988, pp. 59–66.

Some Recent Studies of Ibn Gabirol

Schlanger, Jacques, *La Philosophie de Salomon Ibn Gabirol[;] Étude d'un néoplatonisme*. Études sur le judaisme médiéval 3, Leiden, 1968.

Bargebuhr, Frederick P., *Salomo Ibn Gabirol, Ostwestliches Dichtertum*, Wiesbaden, 1976.

Cano, M. J., *Selomoh Ibn Gabirol, Poemas I. Seculares. I*, Granada, 1987.

Loewe, Raphael, 'Ibn Gabirol's Treatment of Sources in the *Kether*

Malkhuth', *Studies in Jewish Religious and Intellectual History Presented to Alexander Altmann*, edited by S. Stein and R. Loewe, Alabama, 1979, pp. 183–94.
The Rylands Haggadah, London, 1988.
'*Shin'anim sha'ananim' le-ribbi shelomoh 'ibn gabirol'*, *Golah 'ahar galuth, sepher ha-Yobhel li-Khebod Professor Hayyim Beinart*, edited by Aharon Mirsky *et al.*, Jerusalem 5749/1988, pp. 114–33.

Background (Jewish and General)

Steinschneider, Moritz, *Die hebraeischen Übersetzungen des Mittelalters und die Juden als Dolmetscher*, Berlin, 1893 (reprinted Graz, 1956).

Baron, Salo Wittmayer, *A Social and Religious History of the Jews*, 2nd edition, vols. 7 and 8, Philadelphia, 1958.

Brockelmann, Carl, *Geschichte der arabischen Litteratur*, Supplement, vols. 1–3, Leiden, 1937–42; 2nd ed., embodying supplementary matter, 2 volumes 1943–9.

Bargebuhr, Frederick P., *The Alhambra. A Cycle of Studies on the Eleventh Century in Moorish Spain*, Berlin, 1968.

O'Callaghan, Joseph F., *A History of Medieval Spain*, Ithaca and London, 1975.

Ashtor, Eliahu, *The Jews of Moslem Spain*, 3 volumes, Philadelphia, 1973–84.

Asín Palacios, Miguel, *The Mystical Philosophy of Ibn Masarra and his Followers*, translated by Elmer H. Douglas and Howard W. Yoder, Leiden, 1978.

Sirat, Colette, *A History of Jewish Philosophy in the Middle Ages*, Cambridge and Paris, 1985.

INDEX